amazon

amazon

Managing Extraordinary Success in 5-D Value

Benjamin Wall

NEW YORK

LONDON • NASHVILLE • MELBOURNE • VANCOUVER

amazon

Managing Extraordinary Success in 5-D Value

Published in New York, New York, by Morgan James Publishing. Morgan James is a trademark of Morgan James, LLC. www.MorganJamesPublishing.com

ISBN 9781642794380 paperback
ISBN 9781642794397 eBook
Library of Congress Control Number: 2019930801

Cover Design by:
Megan Dillon
megan@creativeninjadesigns.com

Interior Design by:
Chris Treccani
www.3dogcreative.net

Morgan James is a proud partner of Habitat for Humanity Peninsula and Greater Williamsburg. Partners in building since 2006.

Get involved today! Visit
MorganJamesPublishing.com/giving-back

To the many who said no, and the few who said yes

Contents

Acknowledgements

The development of the ideas presented in this book began twenty years ago, when I began thinking about immaterial value and how it might be useful as an approach in my work as a consultant.

Since then, dozens and dozens of people have seen and responded to the ideas as they have matured, from which the ideas and myself have greatly benefited. The people who gave particularly fruitful feedback or helpful support are, in roughly chronological order: Bruce Mathers, Raymund Scheffrahn, Rosemary Wyatt, Heather Marshall-Heyman, Mats Heyman, Mirko Hilsheimer, Birgit Schlaitz Tillack, Roger Bayly, Roger Neininger, Sibylle Kammer-Keller, Roger Meier, Rainer Stutz, Andreas Boller, Günther Müller-Stewens, Willi Diez, Toni Tomasone, Peter Affolter, Rudi Budruss, Marina Budruss, Robert Gisler, Dirk Stieger, Goran Tasic, Vincent Pomi, Michele Soavi, Philipp Meus, Mark Gianelli, Laurent Uldry, Alexandra Strauss, Tomer Lanis, Johannes Post, Jonathan Clay, Laura Castoldi, René Exenberger, Christian Alig, Andrea Wieland, Alexander Zimmermann and Flavio Battaini.

This book would not be a reality without the infectious engagement and highly professional competence of the people at Morgan James Publishing. Terry Whalin and Bonnie Rauch guided me through the steps needed to move from manuscript to published book. Jim Howard and David Hancock contributed to the book becoming a complete and consistent whole. Aubrey Kincaid took on, courageously without qualms, the mountainous task to bring the language and formatting of the manuscript into conformity with contemporary publishing standards. Standing behind these people are many more with noteworthy contributions.

My heartfelt thanks to all of you, named and unnamed.

Introduction

A mazon has achieved success on a scale scarcely approached by any other firm. This book examines the reasons for the success of Amazon in terms of its value management. The managerial framework of 5-D Value presented in this book rests on the notion of dimensions of value, which shape the content of firms' transactions, structure market competition, and steer internal operations. 5-D Value will be applied in-depth to the Amazon organization to explain Amazon's outstanding development and to examine prospects for the firm's future. As part of the latter, 5-D Value will be applied at a high level to Whole Foods Market, acquired by Amazon in summer 2017, because the healthy foods supermarket chain will be a key part of Amazon's future. Thus, the book presents a complete view of Amazon's success in managing value, in the past, present, and future.

In this Introduction, Amazon as an organization and its role in US retail will be introduced. The successes and the major criticisms of the firm will be touched on. Then the managerial framework of 5-D Value will be introduced, showing the role that dimensions of value play in the internal and external success factors for a firm. Finally, the structure of the book will be outlined.

Amazon and the US online retail market

The first online retailers of books in the US, e.g. books.com, were in operation in 1994 when Amazon was founded. Thus, Amazon entered an already existing market, although tiny and in its infancy. Very soon the industry matured and by 1997 Amazon was locked in a fierce contest with the leading chain of bookstores, Barnes & Noble, for leadership in online book sales. In 1998 Amazon began to extend the categories of products it sold beyond books and began selling music CDs. At the beginning of 1999, Amazon selected toys and electronics as the new product categories to develop. In 2000, Amazon signed a deal with Toys'R'Us to sell their toys on the website, then in early 2001, also signed deals with the book chain Borders, AOL, and the electronics retailer Circuit City. This extension mirrored the general development of the online retail market to other product categories where online sales began to take hold.

In the course of the first decade of this century, virtually all retailers opened up webshops; the bulk of producers of consumer goods did the same. In this way online shopping has become a fixed and stable element of shopping in the US. As an absolute share of retail sales, its sales volume remains modest. However, online sales are growing more rapidly than offline sales, and in certain product categories, e.g. books and electronic goods, online sales dominate offine sales. Thus, interest today centers on its growth rate, which should lead tomorrow to a large share, and at some point the majority, of retail sales in the US.

The growing importance of online retail in the US can be illustrated with a few figures from Figure 0-1. Total retail sales have been growing recently at a modest rate between 2 percent and 5 percent, whereas total online sales have throughout the decade to date grown at a yearly rate around 15 percent. Excluding items not normally bought online, including fuel and automobiles, as well as sales in restaurants and bars, e-commerce sales represented 13.0 percent of total retail sales in 2017, higher than the 11.7 percent in 2016 and 10.5 percent in 2015. The growth in the volume of online sales in 2017 represented 49 percent of all retail sales growth in 2017, higher than the 42 percent in 2016. Growth in total retail sales is increasingly due to rising online sales.

Year	Total Retail Sales					
	All Items			w/o Fuel, Autos, Restaurants		
	Annual	Growth		Annual	Growth	
		Volume	Rate		Volume	Rate
2015	$4,708	$70	1.5%	$3,247	$120	3.8%
2016	$4,846	$138	2.9%	$3,375	$128	3.9%
2017	$5,076	$230	4.7%	$3,496	$121	3.6%

Year	Total Online Sales			Total Online Sales / Total Retail Sales w/o Fuel etc.	
	Annual	Growth		Annual	Share in Volume of Growth
		Volume	Rate		
2015	$341	$43	14.6%	10.5%	36%
2016	$395	$53	15.8%	11.7%	42%
2017	$454	$59	15.0%	13.0%	49%

Sources: Zaroban 2016, Zaroban 2017, Zaroban 2018

Figure 0-1: USA Retail Sales (in billions)

The growing importance of online retail can also be illustrated by its negative impact on traditional, "brick and mortar" offline retailing. In 2017 there were several major bankruptcies in the US retail market, including the children's clothing retailer Gymboree, shoe discounter Payless ShoeSource, the specialist in teenager clothing rue21, and Toys 'R' Us. Their business difficulties are attributed to the severe competition from online selling. Other offline retailers have closed thousands of stores and laid off tens of thousands of workers in a cost-cutting exercise which is seen as necessary due to the competition from online selling.

The phenomenon Amazon

Amazon has gone from being an unheard-of start-up in the early 1990's to a household name in this century. Its website is the place where millions of shoppers around the world begin their shopping procedure, even if they do not intend to buy there—it is simply the best spot to inform oneself as a shopper. And the majority of those beginning their search at Amazon end up making their purchase there. Amazon dominates its "home territory" of online sales in the US. Its annual growth in volume of sales, both on own account and in total, i.e. including the sales from third-party sellers, has increased in every year since 2015 (see Figure 0-2). The firm's growth rate in total sales including third parties during these years has been remarkably high, just over 30 percent annually. Amazon's total online sales as a share of all online sales in the US has risen rapidly from one-third in 2015 to nearly half in 2018. Although its share of total retail sales is well below 10 percent and thus modest in the entire market, Amazon's growth in sales accounts for a substantial portion of the growth in retail sales: in 2018 its sales growth accounted for close to 90 percent of growth in online sales and 35 percent of growth in total retail sales. The data in Figure 0-2 will be updated annually and made available on www.dimensions-of-value.com.

Year	Amazon Online Sales						
	Own Account			Total Incl. Third Parties			
	Annual	Growth		Annual	Growth		
		Volume	Rate			Volume	Rate
2015	$79	$9	11%	$112			
2016	$85	$6	7%	$149		$37	33%
2017	$91	$6	7%	$197		$48	32%
2018*				$258		$61	31%

Year	Amazon Total Online Sales			Growth in Amazon Total Online Sales	
	as Share of Total Online Sales	as Share of Total Retail Sales w/o Fuel etc.	as Share of Total Retail Sales	as Share of Growth Volume in Total Online Sales	as Share of Growth Volume in Total Retail Sales w/o Fuel etc.
2015	33%	3%	2%		
2016	38%	4%	3%	70%	30%
2017	44%	6%	4%	81%	40%
2018*	49%	7%	5%	88%	35%

* Forecast

Sources: Zaroban 2017; Zaroban 2018; Thomas & Reagan 2018, and extrapolations

Figure 0-2: Amazon Online Retail Sales (in billions)

Capturing this large share of growth in retail sales presents Amazon as the driving force in the market, based on its strengths in the Prime membership program, the firm's ability to attract a substantial share of the business transacted via mobile smartphones, and sales via third-party sellers. Amazon had 65 million Prime members in 2016, more than double the number two years earlier, which leaped to 100 million members globally in 2017. Eighty percent of Prime members are reported to shop on amazon.com at least once

In 1999 the firm overreacted in building toys inventory for the Christmas season, buying from rival retailers, and then had to write off $39 million in unsold toys afterwards. In 2000 Amazon lost around $1 billion. In the five-year span of 1995-2000 Amazon borrowed $2 billion and lost $1.74 billion of it. Shortly after this run of failures, in early 2001, 1,300 employees were fired, which amounted to 15 percent of the workforce.

Along with downfalls in business, Amazon has engaged in practices which have not always been received with favor by its surrounding communities. In the activity which many people still regard as the signature business area of the firm—i.e. book sales—it has been the subject of criticism. In 1998 reporters discovered that Amazon charged publishers $10,000 to feature books under headings such as "New and Notable". This was standard practice in bookstores, but Amazon was supposed to be more customer-centric than any other firm. As of 1999 Amazon posted notices when placement of a book had been paid for by the publisher. Journalists found something to report again in 2012/13 when reporters from the New York Times revealed that Amazon was desperately deleting thousands of book reviews which it suspected were manipulated or unfounded. Manipulated reviews could be biased either in a positive direction (written by relatives of the author) or negative (written by a rival author). Unfounded reviews included the case of Harriet Klausner, a sixty-year-old retired librarian. For ten years she had written an average of seven reviews daily, for a total of 250,000. More than 99.9 percent of the reviews had four or five stars. In response, Amazon claimed that it had improved its system which recognized and removed inappropriate book reviews. Finally, the practice of recommending the highest-selling books to readers while discounting them to increase their attractiveness has led to concern about the status of so-called "mid-list" books. Such serious works in the hands of knowledgeable publishers and bookstore employees can be conveyed to a public unaware of such treasures, growing to become reasonable sellers in their own right and building a broad-based and diversified fundament of authors to enrich the literary landscape. Yet Amazon's pricing and recommendations policy contributes to a rising disjoint in book sales: a few titles with massive sales and a massive number of books with few sales, and little in-between. It has been argued that the accumulated effect of Amazon's pricing policy, its massive volume, and its metric-based recommendations system is, in fact, to diminish real choice for the consumer. Indeed, already in 2009 the American Booksellers Association warned, "If left unchecked ... predatory pricing policies will devastate not only the book industry, but our collective ability to maintain a society where the widest range of ideas are always made available to the public."

Amazon has also earned negative publicity in its wider business operations. In this decade Amazon has faced controversies over its not having to pay sales tax, tussles with producers when it sells under minimum advertised price, and its efforts to promote e-books even at a loss, or wanting to introduce a feature on Kindle that books were read out loud but authors were not getting paid for audio rights. And when Amazon wanted to open fulfillment centers in Paris and Hamburg, it met with stiff resistance from local residents, politicians and even the police. They feared traffic congestion and neighborhood disturbance.

Finally, the work environment at Amazon has at times appeared in a harsh light, with indications of a highly-pressured and impersonal atmosphere. Already in the 1990's there was considerable tension between the early believers who first joined the firm, ready to give themselves to any task, and the older, more experienced managers hired later from outside whose knowledge was sought to consolidate Amazon's market position. The perception of something like a two-tier caste system has continued into this century, where employees with seniority regard themselves as a bit like royalty and feel more secure in their jobs. Work at Amazon has been described as taking place in an "adversarial atmosphere with almost constant friction ... Many managers refer to Amazon's 'gladiator culture'." The researcher into Amazon continues: "Many Amazon employees live in perpetual fear. Good performance reviews are rare. Employees spend their days anticipating their termination. There are few perks or unexpected performance bonuses." A thoroughly researched piece of investigative journalism in the New York Times, appearing in 2015, highlighted the considerable strains experienced by many employees. One reported, "Nearly every person I worked with, I saw cry at their desk." A woman was pressured to quickly return to work and raise her metrics following the stillborn death of her child. These and other remarks and stories painted a bleak picture of work practices grinding people down to the bone. The New York Times article alleges a "punishing corporate environment: long hours, disparaging bosses, high stress, and no time or space to recover." For another journalist it was not surprising to learn that Amazon was reported to have one of the lowest rates of retention of employees in the US.

Amazon as a firm would not be moved by many of these points, indeed would even agree with most of them from its own point of view. The manner in which Amazon does business, forming the lens with which Amazon would regard these apparent criticisms, is examined at length in this book. Thus, how Amazon would respond to the above arguments is only touched on here. The American Customer Satisfaction Index showed in 2018 that customers ranked Amazon the number one firm for the eighth year in a row; a comparable index in the UK reported the same result for the fifth time in a row. How the firm does business cannot be all that bad. Furthermore, the failures around the turn of the century simply are part of being an innovative firm; any firm taking risks is sure to lose some of them, but as long as the winners outshine the losers, there is no essential problem. Indeed, failures— as long as there are not too many—are typically beneficial in that firms can learn from them and be more successful in the future. Regarding practices in book sales, Amazon would almost certainly point out that hardly any other firm or organization has done as much as it has to maintain, indeed revive, the prominent status of books, an age-old industry, in our high-tech society. The reaction of localities to the prospect of an Amazon fulfillment center is rarely negative; indeed, localities generally compete with one another to attract the jobs and local development associated with a fulfillment center or other Amazon facilities. The huge interest during 2017 and 2018 from over one hundred municipalities in the US to win the location of Amazon's second and third headquarter sites underlines the overweening attraction of Amazon as a local employer. And as for the work environment, Amazon sets not only a high bar for performance, but also for responsibility and learning on the job. In other words, tens of thousands of Amazon employees have blossomed in the demanding environment because they were given challenging tasks from which they could benefit enormously. They have experienced a quantum leap in their career. Virtually all of the people that Kantor and Streitfeld spoke to acknowledged that working at Amazon was an experience unlike that at any other firm, which many openly admit to miss. And in 2018 Amazon was rated number one in LinkedIn's Top Companies List, which ranks the most sought-after places to work in the US.

Thus, Amazon assumes a prominent, if not to say at times controversial, position in both the business world and the general public. In this book the practices of the firm will be assessed, not as good or bad, but rather neutrally investigated to understand the nature of the value it contributes to society, and how it has been able to generate so much value in a comparatively short space of time.

Dimensions of Value

Firms offer value to all counterparties in their transactions on markets, typically:

- Customers in markets for goods and services;
- Personnel in the labor market;
- Business partners in markets for distribution and supplies; and
- Investors in the capital market.

Firms offer value to their counterparties—"parties" for short—in five dimensions, four of which are typical and well-established in business, while the fifth is just emerging. In the Degree dimension, the firm boosts the party to a relative degree, i.e. higher status, such that the party can "own" a higher position in the "pecking order" within a society, market, or organization. Degree value represents the goal/"end" of attaining a higher standard of living or "standard of working"—material and immaterial rewards, authority, functional excellence, etc.—as recognized by others in the party's environment. In Dexterity, the firm provides all-around benefits for the party to know how to function in the context of a society, market, or organization. Dexterity value gives parties the means to make their way through their environment, delivering standardized solutions which can be applied in many different contexts and repeatedly over time. In the Deed dimension, the firm empowers the party to do specific activities which optimize the circumstances of the moment, exactly fitting to the ever-changing situation of the party. Deed value gives parties the means to pursue changing objectives in the form of a "platform" which can be adjusted to the circumstances. In Delight, the firm realizes a personal vision for the party to feel that she or he is (becoming) what it wants to be in a variety of contexts, often in association with others. The realization of this end often takes place in association with others, e.g. consumers with family and friends, personnel with work colleagues, and investors within the investment community. Lastly, in the newly emerging Deep-Connect dimension, the relation to the firm integrates the essence of the party with the essence of multiple contexts to give meaning to the life of that party. The multiple contexts include the design, production, marketing, and consumption of the products and services, the societal setting of the parties, the business setting of the economy, and the environmental setting of humankind.

Firms offer primary value in the dimension, or "D", in which the firm's offer is most compelling and will attract the most interest from parties. Secondary value is offered in the D in which the firm exhibits further competitive advantages and additionally attracts interest from parties. Basic value is offered in a D where the firm's offer merely meets the minimum expectations of parties. No party chooses to transact with a firm due to basic value, but if at least basic value is not offered in each dimension, the party will not consider a transaction with the firm at all.

Five Markets Value Factors

Competition between firms in the customer market will be understood in this book in terms of the volume of value a firm is able to generate for customers by winning their business: in other words, the turnover of the firm. Five factors determine the amount of value created by a firm in a market:

1. **Number of primary and secondary D's:** The higher the number of primary and secondary D's, the greater the chances of appealing to a larger volume of parties;

2. **Weight of party preferences:** Offering strong value in a D or D's in which the party preferences are weightiest improves the chances of a larger volume of parties;

3. **Fewer direct rivals in the same strong D or D's:** The fewer the number of rivals appealing to parties with the same preferences, the greater the "market share" of the firm within this group of parties, and hence the larger the volume of parties;

4. **Others' resources raise own appeal:** The firm raises the appeal of its own offers via the effective use of others' resources, e.g. from rivals (replicating their innovations in its own offers) and from suppliers (benefiting from their product quality); and

5. **Multiple distribution channels:** Operating different channels, principally online and offline, enables the firm to address a wider range of ways that a given party segment wants to shop as well as a wider range of party segments with different preferences.

Online retailers are active in multiple markets for different types of parties—customers, personnel, business partners, and investors—and therefore compete for the volume of value, such as sales turnover, number of employees, volume of supplies, and the amount of capital, in multiple markets. Competition in these multiple markets takes place in terms of the five factors listed above. They are termed "Markets Value Factors" to underscore that they apply to the competition for the volume of value generated in the multiple markets of the firm.

Managing the Value Exchange => Managerial Do Well's

Firms offer value to parties in transactions in return for which the parties input different kinds of value to the firms. Customers input revenues and something of themselves, e.g. knowledge or enthusiasm; personnel input their time and capabilities; business partners input supplies or access to distribution channels; and investors input capital and sometimes their business sense. The value inputs from the parties constitute the material and immaterial means for the firm's operations, forming the wherewithal for the firm to generate value. Thus, there is a cycle of value exchange between the firm and its parties: the value inputs are utilized to generate value offers, the value offers call forth further value inputs, leading to yet more value offers, and so on.

This value exchange occurs in different ways specific to the different value dimensions. Managing the value exchange such that the value inputs are aligned to generate value in a given D is here treated as a Managerial Do-Well (MDW). MDW's are the internal managerial capabilities which enable the firm to meet the Markets Value Factors. The MDW of aligning inputs and offers is needed for the firm to achieve the first Markets Value Factor (MVF) defined above, i.e. the number of strong D's. For each of the MVF's identified above there is a corresponding MDW for a firm to score high on the MVF (see Figure 0-3), as follows:

1. To encourage parties to place a high weight on the firm's strong D's (MVF 2), the firm manages the external demand interfaces to attract parties to the appeal of the D's (MDW 2);
2. To face fewer direct rivals in the same strong D's (MVF 3), the firm manages the internal supply interfaces so as to generate a D value which is more appealing than that of the rivals, which ultimately drives them out of the market and prevents entry (MDW 3);
3. To utilize others' resources in its own relations to parties (MVF 4), the firm operates with a business model which can take advantage of others' resources in its own relations with parties (MDW 4); and

4. To manage multiple channels (MVF 5), the firm practices a steering logic for its activities which enables it to manage value in different channels (MDW 5).

The five Markets Value Factors are matched with the corresponding five Managerial Do-Well's in Figure 0-3[1].

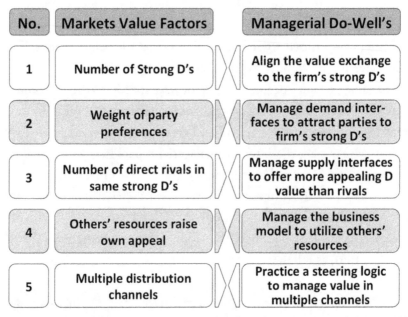

Figure 0-3: Five Markets Value Factors and Five Linked Managerial Do-Well's

Structure of this Book

In Part I of this book, the five dimensions of value will be applied to customer value offers in the US online retail market. Chapter 1 presents the value offers of the largest players on the market, where it will be shown that

---

1   The dimensions of value framework has also been applied to the automobile markets in the USA and Europe; see Benjamin Wall, *Tesla, the Big Three and Toyota: Leaders in Managing 5-D Value in the American Auto Industry* (printed by CreateSpace, 2016) and Benjamin Wall, *BMW, Daimler, Fiat, PSA, Renault and Volkswagen: Leaders in Managing 5-D Value in the European Auto Industry* (printed by CreateSpace, 2017).

Amazon offers primary value in three dimensions (Degree, Dexterity, and Deed) and Whole Foods Market in two (Degree and Dexterity). In Chapter 2 the market competition between Amazon and its rivals, and the way in which the firm dominates the industry, will be examined in terms of the five Markets Value Factors.

In Part II, the five Managerial Do-Well's will be applied to Amazon, one chapter for each MDW, to show how Amazon manages primary value in Degree, Dexterity, and Deed. The five MDWs will be applied to the whole of Amazon, i.e. also examining its business activities outside of the online retail market, such as AWS, e-books and films, yet without including Whole Foods Market. Part II also includes brief analyses of the success factors for Amazon on the labor, business partner, and capital markets. Thus, Part II will examine how Amazon has managed to be so successful in the numerous markets in which it is active. The final chapter in Part II examines the inherent weaknesses—in the sense of limits to success—of Amazon's Managerial Do-Well's.

In Part III, the future of Amazon will be evaluated including some speculative analysis. Chapter 9 considers the benefits Amazon can be expected to gain from the acquisition of Whole Foods Market in the context of two expected developments in the ongoing present of retail: the rise of online retail for services as well as omnichannel retail. It will be suggested that Amazon could make the most out of both the acquisition of Whole Foods Market as well as the two expected developments in the retail market if it would introduce Delight value into its organization at the secondary level. The final chapter considers the long-term future of Amazon in the context of a speculative development in the retail market, where retail becomes a force in driving/reacting to societal transformation. The speculation takes trends which have begun in retail and in the business world and extends them further, in which the retail market is disrupted and society is transformed towards a more collective determination of the world. In this context, a prospective long-term future for Amazon is outlined, in which the firm continues to be on the forefront of developments in the retail market and business generally. To remain cutting-edge it is speculated that Amazon will integrate the newly emerging Deep-Connect dimension of value into its organization at the primary level.

The information presented in this book is drawn entirely from published sources for three reasons. First, it confirms that the information selected is in fact important to the management of the firms reviewed: another author thought them significant enough to publish them. Second, the information has gone through a publishing process and therefore is reasonably reliable. Third, all the information used is transparently available to all, without confidential or anonymous sources, e.g. from interviews.

Including all the documentary material in this volume would have weighed it down considerably. The countless facts would have diverted the reader from the principles of market competition and value management as illustrated by Amazon in the online retail industry, the analytical-conceptual focus of this book. Therefore, information is presented at a medium level of detail to explain and illuminate the parameters of the study.

PART I

Value Offers and Markets Value Factors in US Online Retail

Chapter 1

Value Offers in US Online Retail

In this chapter, value offers in US online retail for customers will be examined. In a first step, a primary value offer in each of the five D's as found in the US online retail market will be presented. This serves to build familiarity with the nature of each dimension specifically as it is exhibited in the online retail industry. Then the value configuration—the combination of primary and secondary value which makes up the entire value offer of a firm—of the leading online retail firms will be discussed. The chapter will be rounded out by looking at the value configuration of Whole Foods Market, which is active in the online retail market but, more importantly, has been purchased by Amazon and thus is a relevant topic.

Primary Value Offer to Customers in each D in US Online Retail

In this section, the primary value offer from five rivals to Amazon are presented to provide an initial overview of the online retail market in the US in order to set Amazon in the context of its market. This topic will then be pursued in greater depth in the following chapter with the Markets Value Factors.

In examining the value offers from the firms in each D, the focus is on the firms as they present themselves at their best (the extent to which the firms have diverged from their value promises in individual offers or during specific time periods is not systematically treated in this book). Furthermore,

3

shopping customers will be understood as the consumers in households and not other businesses buying from these retailers, e.g. the case at Costco. That is, the focus in this chapter, indeed in this book, is on the B2C market and not the B2B market.

An overview of the value offers of the five firms, one for each D, follows.

Apple offers value in Degree: The products and the customer experience on the website boost the customer to a relative degree, i.e. higher status as a consumer in society, such that the customer can "own" a higher position in the "pecking order" within the society.

Apple has offered Degree value to customers with the elevated living standard of their products, which have provided status, elegance, and a luxurious image. The elevated status of Apple products has also been based on the advanced technology to be found in and around its products. On the website, the shopper is presented with the look and feel of refinement: the stylish "San Francisco" font plus background colors of black, white, or gray, which gracefully set off the photos in bright colors. The many photos showing the product in the possession of a person help the shopper assess how other people will perceive the shopper if he or she were to possess the Apple product.

Costco offers value in Dexterity: Costco provides all-around, one-size-fits-all benefits on its website and in its products, from which the customer can know how to function as a shopper in the environment of online retail.

At Costco, the all-around benefits of Dexterity have constituted the primary value offer. Alongside national brands at reduced prices, for nearly twenty years Costco has been building the range of products covered by its private label brand, Kirkland Signature. These are Costco's signature products that offer, according to the website, the perfect combination of quality and price. They are continuously improved so that they remain a benchmark for the features which have been tested as tried and true on the market. The website is strong in offering widely accepted online retail features, for example, customer product reviews to underline the reliability of shopping at Costco, extended warranty plans to mark the durability of the products, and free technical support for electronics products to provide a high level of customer service. Indeed, the customer service section of the site is the most developed, presenting more topics than any other section. This demonstrates Costco's intention to offer assurance to customers regarding the terms and conditions of shopping at Costco. By building tried-and-true features from the market into its website, offering the choice of national brands, and providing its own label products, Costco assures its customers that they are not missing out on worthy innovations: one can not go wrong shopping at Costco.

QVC offers primary value in Deed: The QVC website empowers the customer to do specific activities while shopping which optimize the circumstances of the moment, individually fitting to the ever-changing "shopping mission" of the customer.

QVC is for the active shopper who gains Deed value from the activities of searching for and finding bargains. QVC offers a set of continually updated promotions for the active shopper to seek out what best suits at the moment: as described on the website, "a curated, ever-changing collection of name brands and unique finds." The shopper can go to the QVC site every day and find new and different bargains to actively consider. The QVC website is a platform of shopping opportunities, and the customer exercises his or her individual leeway in utilizing the platform.

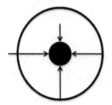

Macy's offers value in Delight: Shopping at Macy's enables the customer to realize the personal vision to feel that she or he is (becoming) who they want to be in a variety of lifestyle contexts, often with the feeling of a community.

Macy's chain of stores embodies an integrated whole which resonates as a convincing and encompassing vision in Delight for the customer. As stated by the firm itself, "Macy's embraces customers and provides an experience that transcends ordinary shopping." Macy's website conveys the same sense of magic in Delight value. In October 2017, the home page opened to a photo of three laughing women, intriguingly dressed, with interlocked arms, obviously having a grand time together. They looked straight into the eyes of the visitor to the website, inviting him or her to join in the fun. The range of skin and hair color amongst the women suggested that anyone and everyone would be welcome to become part of the group, or more so, part of the jovial community. In the online shop, the products are grouped into categories and presented in ways which speak to the lifestyle of the customer, including a link to lifestyle stories related to the clothes. The Delight value of shopping on the Macy's site is bound to the personal tastes and preferences of the individual in relation to the specific nature of clothes as a functional and lifestyle product. The customer has a vision of what he or she seeks in clothes and/or the customer is willing to take on the vision developed by Macy's of what the clothes should be.

Patagonia offers primary value in Deep-Connect: The relation to the firm integrates the essence of the customer with the essence of multiple contexts to give meaning to the life of the customer. The multiple contexts include the relation to the clothes, the business setting of the firm and the economy, the daily life of the customer, how the clothes are sourced and produced, the social setting of the customer, and the environmental setting of humankind.

The high-quality assortment of clothes and accessories for outdoor sporting activities offered by Patagonia generate Deep-Connect value for customers in multiple contexts. First, the materials are chosen and processed and the functional design of the clothes is made to closely match how people experience themselves in the specific circumstances and requirements of a given outdoor activity. The customer perceives how the materials and design are suited to the activity, and thus perceives himself or herself as being more deeply entrenched in the activity. The customer feels a greater depth in himself or herself, giving more meaning for the customer in undertaking the outdoor activity.

Second, the durability and longevity of the clothes has the consequence that the article comes to represent the personal history of the wearer. The website refers to "stories we wear" in that people's own experiences are pressed into the rips, stains, and improvised repairs of their clothes. Indeed, the website suggests that the articles gain value with time as a result: "better than new." The website underlines these kind of connections by showing videos and photos of the articles in use, supplemented with personal stories from people who wear Patagonia clothes.

Third, Patagonia clothes are superb pieces of modern design, as well as the embodiment of the latest technology. The customer feels connected to the future, becoming a connoisseur of the modern. And buying from Patagonia is a statement that America can still be the home of ground-breaking industrial technology and the manufacture of prized goods. The customer becomes a sponsor of modern technology as found in American manufacturing.

Fourth, Patagonia has become well-known for its stance on the environment. Wearing clothes from Patagonia can project messages about the environment with which the wearer identifies. This can lead to interactions with others on this topic, making for profound experiences during the day. The Deep-Connect value when wearing the clothes is a deeper meaning in daily life.

Fifth, the raw materials and the production processes of both Patagonia and its suppliers are conducted so as to reduce the harmful impact on the environment. Furthermore, Patagonia actively promotes worker rights and sound working conditions at its suppliers. Both of these efforts are unusual in the clothing industry. The informed Patagonia customer experiences new meaning in consuming clothes and feels much freer to wear the clothes he or she wants due to the Deep-Connect value in the context of Patagonia's responsible operations.

Sixth, Patagonia is actively engaged in societal transformation with initiatives to improve the environment and make businesses more responsible. By doing business with Patagonia—i.e. buying its products—the customer gains Deep-Connect value in transforming the conditions under which business is conducted. The Patagonia customer is connected to a new paradigm of business practice which transforms the economy, society, and the environment.

Value Configurations in Leading US Online Retail Offers to Customers

Following the examples above of primary value in each of the D's as found in the US online retail market, in this section, the value configurations of six leading firms are examined. Figure 1-1 shows their US online sales and their value configuration of primary and secondary D's.

Firm	Sales $ billion				Degree	Dexterity	Deed	Delight
	2014	2015	2016	2017				
Amazon	70	79	85	91	**Amazon**	Amazon	Amazon	
Apple	21	24	17	20	**Apple**	Apple	Apple	Apple
Walmart	12	14	14	15	**Walmart**	Walmart	Walmart	Walmart
Macy's	5	5	5	5		Macy's		**Macy's**
Costco	3	4	4	5		**Costco**	Costco	
QVC	5	5	4	4	QVC		**QVC**	

* **Primary D in bold type**; Secondary D in normal type
** Sales where firm is seller of record, i.e. without third-party sales
Sources: www.nrf.com; Zaczkiewicz 2017; www.retail-index.emarketer.com

Figure 1-1: Value Configuration* of Leading US Online Retailers**

The six firms listed in Figure 1-1 exhibit a wide mix of value configurations. Amazon offers primary value in three dimensions: Degree, Dexterity, and Deed. Apple and Walmart each offer primary value in one dimension—Degree for both—and secondary value in the other three dimensions. The remaining three firms offer primary and secondary value each in one dimension only. The value configurations of these six firms are presented in turn.

Amazon offers primary value in Degree, Dexterity, and Deed, and basic value in Delight

The primary Degree offer to shopping customers by Amazon is an elevated living standard: on the one hand due to the customer service which is like "room service" at the beck and call of the customer and, on the other hand, due to the low prices—for both the goods themselves as well as the shipping costs—which enables the customer to enjoy more consumer products.

The core offer to customers in terms of "room service" has become the low shipping costs. Purchases over $35 in value and shoppers who are members of Amazon Prime incur no shipping costs. The Prime subscription started at $79 per year, rose to $99 in 2014 and then to $119 in 2018. The Prime offer includes a kind of "free shipping" of thousands of movies and TV series in the form of unlimited streaming and other benefits. Prime Free Same-Day and Prime Free One-Day delivery are available in more than 8,000 cities and towns in the US. Prime Now offers same-day delivery on selected items in more than fifty cities worldwide. In addition, in certain cities, Amazon has introduced Sunday deliveries as well as Amazon Fresh, a same-day or early morning delivery service for fresh food, prepared foods, and speciality items suitable for entertaining. Further to the "room service," the information on the website about the timing of the availability of items, plus the choice of different speeds for delivery, represent a much higher level of service to customers than is normal in postal distribution.

The "room service" is intended to impact the psychology, and thus behavior, of online shoppers: it is the home delivery which sets online shopping apart from going to the store. Research shows that shipping costs are the number one reason for shopping cart abandonment; however, when shipping is free, there is no reason to stop. Regarding the timing, the overall approach has been to promise a conservative shipping time and then hopefully deliver sooner in order to create a positive surprise rather than disappointment. And Amazon has reduced shipping time to same-day delivery in selected cities. In sum, the "room service" aims to heighten loyalty from customers who can determine the shipping terms best suited to them, including the possibility for many shoppers of the "instant" gratification from receiving their order two days, one day, or even several hours after buying. An even faster delivery service will be discussed later on in the book.

Regarding the low purchase prices for consumer products, a 2011 study by Wells Fargo found that Amazon was up to 19 percent cheaper than Walmart stores on a basket of goods—or 9 percent cheaper when the shipping costs for Amazon are included in the calculation. The Amazon prices did not include sales tax. Pricing at Amazon benefits from automatic programs that compare prices at rivals and adjust prices to keep to Amazon's pledge to offer the lowest price anywhere. In general, Amazon is widely regarded as offering the lowest prices, or at least being among the lowest prices, for the items it stocks.

Amazon offers primary Dexterity value to shopping customers in terms of their consumer experience in two ways: first, by trying to "guarantee" that customers will be satisfied with their consumption experience, and, second, by offering market leading terms and conditions.

A major vehicle for customers to fully inform themselves about a product, and thus be "guaranteed" the consumption experience they expect from the product, is the customer reviews. Sixty-two percent of shoppers read consumer-written product reviews online, 80 percent say their purchase decisions have been directly influenced by reviews, and 70 percent of shoppers share product reviews with their friends, family, or colleagues. Study after study shows that customers trust each other more than they trust marketers. It has been estimated that 55 percent of people visit Amazon prior to purchasing anything on the internet, specifically because of the product reviews. This is true even if they don't end up purchasing from Amazon. With the help of a new, machine-learning algorithm, Amazon selects those reviews which are most helpful to customers and displays them more prominently. Specifically with regard to books, Amazon directs readers of e-books to the passages most appreciated by other readers and provides a social media platform for interaction amongst readers. In addition to customer reviews, Amazon presents lengthy and robust product descriptions. It has been shown that 67 percent of consumers who have visited an online store with the intent to purchase have left if there was not enough information about the product for the customer to feel comfortable enough to buy online. Amazon draws from multiple sources to give the customer the best possible product information.

In this way, the offline experience of actually consuming a product becomes quasi-guaranteed; with so much information provided, the customer should not be unpleasantly surprised when it comes to actually consuming the product.

Second, the terms and conditions are designed to be very generous, and in many instances, Amazon bends over backwards to please the customer when replacing damaged items—even when there is no fault of their own, or e.g. video playback quality has been sub-standard. Furthermore, when customers pre-order an item from Amazon, the firm guarantees the lowest price offered by it between the order time and the end of the release date. As discussed later in the book, in managing customer service personnel in the call centers as well as suppliers and sellers whose products are on their website, Amazon insists on settling open issues in favor of the customer.

Amazon offers primary Deed value to shopping customers in the form of optimizing their shopping mission in an online ecosystem, principally when shopping on the Amazon site, but including shopping on other sites, as well as internet devices such as the smart speaker Echo to ease the mechanics of shopping. In recent years, the online experience has been enlarged beyond shopping to include the consumption of books and streaming services. The huge product range, the many features on the website or in smart devices to support shopping, the payment convenience on Amazon.com and other sites, the noteworthy richness when fulfilling the shopping experience online, plus the streaming services, cumulate to a striking value offer.

On the Amazon site, a huge range of products is available, offered both from Amazon and from third-party sellers who use the site as an additional distribution channel. Shopping customers benefit in that they need only go to the Amazon site in their search process, confident that virtually anything they would want can be found on the site. In 2010, Amazon offered about fourteen times the number of products that Walmart does (e.g. Amazon had 2,016 types of digital camcorders compared to ninety-six at Walmart).

The shopping functionalities on the website raise the convenience and efficiency of shopping, while also improving the shopping experience: search procedures, hyperlinks, 1-Click payment, "Look Inside the Book," "Search Inside the Book," a wish list, and "save the shopping cart" all make shopping at Amazon easier and more fruitful, even more enjoyable, than what is possible in a store. Furthermore, the personalization features of the site support a shopping experience online on a mass scale which is much more targeted to the individual interests of shopper than is possible in a store. For example, Amazon's home page is never the same for an individual visitor and is different between visitors. Sections like "New for you," "More items to consider," and "Recommendations for you" constantly track what has been viewed and adjust the items appearing in the lists accordingly. Plus, Amazon shows customers what other customers purchased in addition to what the original customer is buying, making customers aware of accessories and alternative products that others have purchased. Furthermore, shoppers can integrate charity donations into the online experience or use their Amazon account as the basis for making payments on other websites. Amazon has made shopping on its site easier for families. Amazon Coins are intended primarily for children who, with the permission of their parents, shop on Amazon. Kindle Free-Time Unlimited offers children from three to eight years old unlimited access to books, games, videos, apps, TV series, and films. The parents can define a profile for each child to determine what the child can consume, including time limits. As of 2013, the Amazon Appstore served customers in almost 200 countries, with over 200,000 apps and games. The online interface has been extended to include the streaming services as well as the games and other apps. Indeed, the e-book reader, originally launched as Kindle and now also named Fire, functions in effect as an online interface. Books can be purchased via the device and functionalities support the reading of books.

The range of shopping missions which are optimized has become so wide, and the associated experience has become so rich, that Amazon refers to its "ecosystem of products and services." For example, the smart speaker Echo functions as an offline extension of online shopping. In real time, the Echo collects the spoken shopping orders of the customer and then submits them online at the customer's wish.

Lastly, Amazon offers basic value in the Delight dimension. The huge range of products enables shopping customers to choose those products which come closest to their personal preferences. In this way, they can live out their personal vision of themselves as a consumer, able to find those products which best fulfill their personal vision of who they are as a consumer.

Apple offers primary value in Degree and secondary value in Dexterity, Deed, and Delight

Apple customers gain primary Degree value from the functional excellence and the master craftsmanship of Apple products. On the website, the elegant background colors and font provide the dignified setting for the classy photos of people who are elevated by the Apple product in their hand.

Apple secondarily offers Dexterity all-around benefits on its website and in its products. The website presents readily absorbable product information as well as a high level of customer support in both information and services regarding maintenance and repair. Apple products score well on generic features such as battery life.

Apple secondarily offers Deed value in its products, marked by the intuitive ease of handling and a huge range of apps and functions supporting the daily activities of the customer. On the website, navigation is very clear and Apple Pay is a payment feature which can be used to easily pay for purchases on the Apple website, in thousands of shops, in many apps, and for any online purchases using the Safari browser.

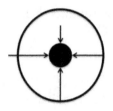

Apple secondarily offers Delight value in the connectivity of its products to the many aspects of the customer's whole person. On the website, the animation and variety of the photos, short videos, and information give the feeling of an active, enjoyable, and fulfilling lifestyle for Apple customers

Walmart offers primary value in Degree and secondary value in Dexterity, Deed, and Delight

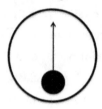

Walmart customers gain primary Degree value from a higher living standard via the Every Day Low Price for all products, including leading brands. In addition to this systematically consistent offer, the website prominently displays: "rollbacks," an ongoing commitment to reduce prices even more whenever possible; special buys, a greater quantity of product for the same price; and clearance items, marked down to clean out inventory.

Walmart offers secondary value in Dexterity with its private label brand, providing its customers the beacon of assuredness that the goods they consume represent the market benchmark. The website offers high quality customer service and support regarding orders (problems, tracking, or cancelling) and products (refunds, returns, replacements, and damaged or defective items).

Walmart offers secondary value in Deed via its optimized individual shopping experience. The website presents a large range of goods and services, providing the convenience of one-stop shopping for numerous shopping needs. Many features make shopping easier, including a reorder list and multiple payment options. The customer can optimize the shopping process to his or her own situation by taking advantage of items available online only, the discounts on pickup items, or same-day pickup of fresh groceries ordered online, where Walmart loads the customer's car.

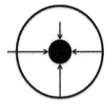

Walmart offers secondary value in Delight by its dedication to serve all American consumers, even the poorest customers in isolated and declining regions. On the website, customers can choose amongst an affordable, wide-ranging product assortment including many leading national brands. They can thereby come closer to the lifestyle they want to lead and who they really want to be as consumers.

Macy's offers primary value in Delight and secondary value in Dexterity

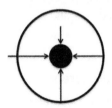

Macy's offers primarily Delight value to customers in addressing, and stimulating them to explore, the diversity of their personal tastes in pursuing their lifestyle to the fullest. The website communicates a feeling of belonging to a community, where the shopper can personally engage with the people on the site and thus also with the clothes.

Macy's offers secondarily Dexterity value in assuring satisfaction. The website is very encouraging with regard to customer feedback, urging the customer to share his or her "knowledge" of what they experienced in a store, online, or when paying with a credit card. Different lines of communication are presented in order that the customer can feel as comfortable as possible giving feedback. Customer support is also extensively present on the site, with many help topics offered.

Costco offers primary value in Dexterity and secondary value in Deed

Costco offers primary value in Dexterity with its products and customer service. Its private label brand constitutes its signature products that offer the perfect combination of quality and price to remain a benchmark in the dynamic market. The website offers all-around use value.

Costco offers secondary value in Deed in the "doing" of shopping: tracking and handling orders, delivery options, an app for coupons, etc. The ease of one-stop shopping is offered by the very wide range of products and services on the website. Costco also offers Deed value on its site outside of the shopping experience itself, in that it offers what it describes as a very popular cookbook series with more than 2,400 cross-indexed recipes.

QVC offers primary value in Deed and secondary value in Degree

QVC offers primary value in Deed to the active shopper searching for bargains. The webset presents a set of continually updated promotions for the active shopper to seek out what best suits at the moment, including a limited number of items at a reduced price for twenty-four hours only, new items appearing for the first time, the hot sellers of the day, and one specially reduced item for the day.

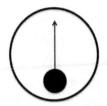 QVC offers secondary value in Degree in that selected national brands and products are offered at very reduced prices. Customers are thus enabled to benefit from a higher living standard.

Primary, Secondary, and Basic Value in Degree

Before proceeding further, it is worthwhile to first clarify the level of value in Degree offered by the six largest online retailers. In Figure 1-1, three firms offer primary value, one secondary value, and two basic value. What is the basis for categorizing the firms in this way?

First, the firms offering primary value in Degree may be considered. At one extreme is Apple, whose up-market offer of Degree value in an elegant design and functional excellence positions customers at the upper end of the "totem pole." At the other extreme is Walmart, whose down-market offer of Degree value enables customers to afford national brands, shifting themselves upward from an initial position lower down the totem pole. The Degree value from Amazon is somewhere in between the other two. Amazon offers low prices analogous to Walmart's down-market value, coupled with delivery and logistical services—the "room service" effect—which are functionally excellent and at the high end of the market, analogous to Apple's up-market value.

Second, the distinction between primary and secondary versus basic value in Degree on the online retail market may be considered. All of the retailers in Figure 1-1 utilize lower prices in one form or another and communicate this prominently. In this way, they all enable their customers to attain a higher standard of living: being able to afford more and higher quality goods sold by the retailer, as well as having more money leftover to purchase other consumer goods and services. Why is it that, in particular, Amazon and Walmart, and to a significantly lesser extent QVC, enjoy a competitive advantage in this regard?

Lower prices due to economies of scale, loss leaders, discounts, rebates, special price promotions, and so forth represent what is simply expected of a large online retailer. The reduced prices offered by Macy's and Costco are an example of what in this book is termed basic value. Basic value in a D represents the situation where a firm's value offer in that dimension simply meets generalized market expectations. In the context of its trendy and up-market product assortment, Macy's offers prices which are generally lower than what would be expected from a smaller retailer—supplemented by special offers to stimulate added interest—but this kind of pricing policy is simply what is expected from a large online retailer. Costco offers even lower prices than Macy's, but again the low price level is simply what is expected from this kind of firm. Costco is a membership warehouse with a relatively limited product assortment that, to a significant degree, operates as a kind of wholesaler for small businesses. Reduced prices are simply the expectation in such a shopping environment. QVC offers a secondary value in Degree—that is, exhibits a competitive advantage in this regard—in that it applies prices to a selection of leading brands that are very much below market level. This pricing policy represents the offer of a higher standard of living related to a restricted product range. The customer can benefit from the quality in consumption which the selected brand names offer, yet at prices which are substantially below market level. Thus, the QVC offer in Degree can selectively raise the level of consumption of customers. However, it is only Walmart and Amazon that consistently and systematically make lower prices—including lower shipping costs—the essence of product design and supply chain management throughout their entire product range and operations. Amongst the US online retailers, Walmart and Amazon uniquely position a comprehensively higher standard of living due to reduced customer expenditures at the core of their value offer.

The Value Configuration to Customers at Whole Foods Market

Whole Foods Market (WFM) offers a combination of primary value in Degree and Dexterity to position the customer in the exclusive fruits of modernity: the customer is placed in the position to benefit from what the modern world knows about healthy eating and about community building inside and outside the store. WFM constantly positions its offer above that of other retailers.

WFM offers Degree value by selecting the highest quality food for healthy eating as well as working up the perishables into ready-made dishes: a kind of "room service." The title page of the 2014 Annual Report proudly announces the exclusivity of WFM: "The highest standards weren't available, so we created them." Later in the same Report, it is declared, "We hold the idea of 'food' to a higher standard, banning hundreds of ingredients commonly found in other stores." Thus, WFM offers food with market-leading Dexterity standards.

Another differentiating and elevating aspect of the offer to customers is the uplifting experience of being in the store. The product range and displays raise the customer into a select world of first-class nourishment, as in Degree. What's more, WFM cultivates in the stores a new kind of "all-around environment," as in Dexterity. That is, people are accustomed to their positions at home or at work. WFM believes that its stores play a "unique role as a third place, besides the home and office, where people can gather, interact and learn while at the same time discovering the many joys of eating and sharing food." The WFM store positions the customer in an environment bearing all the accouterments of what is now regarded as modern in the society: environmentally-friendly infrastructure, community structures inside and outside the store, interaction between customers and personnel, healthy food produced in a manner which is in harmony with Nature, and a kind of "infotainment" (information mixed with entertainment) regarding healthy eating. This combination of Degree and Dexterity value is state-of-the-art in food retailing.

In addition to the up-market aspect of the Degree offer, WFM also offers the down-market aspect of Degree value: high-quality products at affordable prices. Already in 1997, WFM launched the 365 Everyday Value® line. These products adhered to the strict quality standards of the firm at competitive prices, making it easier for more people to eat better. Recently, WFM began offering weekly deep discount promotions, which were supported with an enhanced ad campaign highlighting the quality differences to the rivals. More systematically, in fiscal year 2016, WFM opened three stores in a new value store format, 365 by Whole Foods Market. This new format complements the Whole Foods Market brand, enabling the firm to address the value-quality proposition through a convenient, smaller footprint and curated product selection. The format is designed around affordability and convenience and supported by enhanced digital experiences, thereby broadening the firm's reach to new customers and new markets.

Taking Stock

The landscape within which value competition takes place in the US online retail market has been presented in this chapter. The following chapter will show how rivalry plays out in the market by applying the five Markets Value Factors. That is, Chapter 1 has presented the raw material with which the analysis in Chapter 2 can be performed.

| Chapter 2 |

Markets Value Factors in US Online Retail

In this chapter, five Markets Value Factors (MVFs) will be applied to the current state of the US online retail market. Success will be understood in terms of the volume of value a firm is able to generate for customers by winning their business, i.e. the turnover of the firm.

Five factors, formalized as Markets Value Factors (MVF's), will be applied to the US online retail market to explain the relative levels of success of the six firms. For example, it may be noted in Figure 1-1 in the previous chapter that Amazon has a volume of sales over five times larger than the nearest rival, Apple. Apple and Walmart follow Amazon at a substantial distance, yet are themselves three times larger in terms of sales volume than each of the next three rivals. Thus, there is a significant spread of success within the US online retail market to be explained. The application of the five MVFs will provide this explanation.

Markets Value Factors

The five Markets Value Factors (MVFs) introduced in the Introduction set out the range of factors under which competition takes place in a market with regard to the value offers of the firms. Each MVF has a structural perspective (rivalry between the firms at a point in time) and a dynamic perspective (changes in the rivalry of the firms over time). Collectively, the five MVFs go a long way in explaining the volume of value generated by a

21

firm. They show what a firm needs to achieve in order to be more successful on the markets, i.e. what the firm needs to aim for in its positioning on its markets. How they achieve their success, and how they can attain their aims for market positioning, is the topic of the Managerial Do Well's in Part II.

Markets Value Factor 1: Number of Primary and Secondary D's

The examination of the competitive conditions in the US online retail market begins by applying the first Markets Value Factor: the number of primary or secondary D's in a firm's total value offer. The reasoning behind MVF 1 is that firms enjoy competitive advantages over rivals in dimensions where they have a strong offer, i.e. primary or secondary value. In evaluating these competitive advantages, customers will favor those offers which demonstrate strength in the D's which they themselves prefer. The greater the number of strong D's a firm can offer, the higher its chances of meeting the weightiest preferences of a greater number of customers. In addition, customers will count the number of D's in which a retailer offers something special and compare this to the spread of their own preferences across the dimensions. In this regard as well, the same conclusion can be drawn about the success arising from the number of strong D's in a firm's offer. In sum, the greater the number of strong D's a firm can offer, the greater the range of customer preferences the firm can meet, and thus the higher the chances of gaining favor from a greater number of customers. Figure 2-1 illustrates MVF 1: the breadth of strong D's which the firm can internally generate and offer in addressing customer preferences.

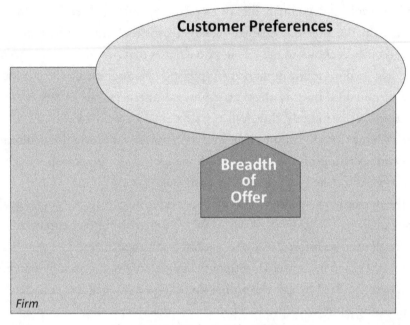

Figure 2-1: Markets Value Factor 1

Markets Value Factor 1 has a structural as well as a dynamic perspective. Structurally, a firm's score on this MVF is determined by the number of D's in which it offers primary or secondary value over the time period as a whole. Dynamically, a firm can add or lose a strong D over time, temporarily or permanently.

Markets Value Factor	Market Structure	Market Dynamic
1	Number of firm's primary or secondary D's	Number of primary or secondary D's at each firm	Firms gaining or losing a strong D

As seen in the columns of Figure 1-1, in the structural perspective of MVF 1, Amazon offers three primary D's, while the others offer only one. Apple and Walmart offer secondary value in three dimensions, and the other three retailers demonstrate one secondary D. The structural perspective of MVF 1 is aligned to the relative sales volume of the six firms. Amazon is well ahead of Apple and Walmart due to its primary value in three D's, which as discussed in the previous chapter makes it overwhelmingly the systematic online retailer of choice in the US. It is no wonder that Amazon is in a category of its own in the American market. Apple and Walmart display strong value offers in four D's, putting them at a great advantage to the others. Indeed, their turnover is roughly threefold higher than Costco, Macy's, and QVC. These three are roughly at the same level of turnover, reflecting their common value configuration of one primary and one secondary dimension, which in fact is typical for the bulk of firms in business.

The dynamic perspective of MVF 1 provides insight into changes in the success of firms. Amazon itself began its history with fundamentally a one-size-fits-all offer to inform customers about books which could be purchased online rather than in a store. This strength in Dexterity was soon supplemented by strength in Deed, where the online shopping experience was enhanced by an increasing number of product categories plus the personalization and the channeling of individualized offers to specific customers. Afterwards, Amazon improved supplier relations and logistics in the supply chain in order to be able to systematically offer low prices and fast, cheap delivery. In this build-up of primary value in three D's, Amazon advanced to become the dominant player in online retail. In fact, Amazon is probably regarded as the most dynamic player in retail in general, both online and offline. Amazon's market capitalization, which places Amazon ahead of Walmart, at least suggests that this is the prevailing view held by the capital market.

The history of Amazon also demonstrates the loss of a strong D. In the last years of the twentieth century, customers made their first steps into the exciting and high-tech world of online retail when shopping at Amazon. They fulfilled their personal vision of themselves as modern, sophisticated, and even a bit adventurous shoppers. Thus, simply the new nature of the service operated by Amazon, and its alignment to the rise of the internet and related developments which gripped and fascinated society at the time, enabled Amazon to offer secondary value in Delight to shoppers. However, time went by, and online retail became commonplace, while Amazon undertook few initiatives to retain the Delight aspects of its offer. Thus, by the second decade of the twenty-first century, the value offer in Delight had slipped down from the secondary to the basic level.

A more dramatic example of the loss of a strong D in the US retail market is the case of Kmart, now part of Sears Holdings. In the 1960's–1980's, Kmart was the largest so-called "big box" retailer in the US—where "big box" refers to a supermarket chain offering much more than simply food in stores with vast floorspace. The firm offered primary value in Deed in the form of special and ever-changing promotions for the active shopper; multiple retail formats to fit to the different situations of customers when shopping—one day quickly for a few targeted items, the next day more leisurely to cover the week's needs and maybe discover some new products in the store; and a product assortment in each store tailored to the specific kinds of shopping missions which the local population undertook. Secondary value in Degree was offered in reduced prices for national brands sold exclusively in Kmart, the most popular being the Martha Stewart line of household goods. Beginning in the 1990's, the agility and flexibility of the Deed value offer faded away and Kmart focused on the Degree offer only. It positioned itself on the market as offering the best in products and customer service, resting on its status as market leader at the beginning of the decade. However, by the end of the decade, its view of what constituted up-market products was no longer in line with the times, having been blinded by its self-confidence in being the best. Furthermore, the pricing policy lacked clarity, fluctuating between special promotions or reduced prices, but not really being convincing in either. The management continued a misguided strategy built simply on the premise of being at the top of the market. The narrowed base of value offered in only one D weakened its business performance and led to bankruptcy in 2002. In 2003, Kmart emerged from Chapter 11 proceedings, and in 2004 merged with Sears to form Sears Holdings. Since then, the merged firm has been able to stay in business, but has not been able to regain its leading position. In 2016, online sales at Sears Holdings totaled just over $2 billion, ranking it as number twelve in the US for online retail.

Concluding, the structural perspective of MVF 1 corresponds roughly to the rank ordering of the six largest online retailers in the US in 2016. The dynamic perspective of MVF 1 shows that additions or reductions in the number of strong D's in the value offering will lead to a boost or decline in the level of success of the involved firm.

However, simply the number of dimensions with primary and secondary value does not fully explain why Amazon is so far ahead of its rivals. To explain this, the other four Markets Value Factors need to be examined, turning now to MVF 2.

Markets Value Factor 2: Weight of Customer Preferences

The second MVF is the distribution of the customer preferences across the different value dimensions. The customers in the online retail market have chosen the offer of a given firm based on a correspondence between the benefits of the strong D's and their own demands, i.e. they have shopped on a site because they placed the greatest weight on the site's offers in the primary and secondary value dimensions. Firms that offer strong value in the dimensions favored by the greatest number of customers will have greater sales. The spread of the strong value offered by the six firms across the four value dimensions in Figure 1-1 suggests that there is correspondingly a spread of customers with preferences in each of the D's. That is, the relative sales volumes of the six firms can be roughly allocated to the different D's, taking approximate account of the greater and lesser pull of the primary and secondary value offers. This allocation shows the underlying preferences—or what are sometimes termed as "revealed" preferences—of the customers.

Figure 2-2 presents the circumstances influencing MVF 2. In the lower half of the Figure, each firm addresses customer preferences via marketing messages—shopping features, communication, point-of-sale design, etc.— in its strong D's, trying to convince customers to raise the weight of their preferences for the D's in which the firm is strong. The upper half of the Figure shows that customers live within a societal setting, where societal trends also influence the weight of customer preferences for each D. The diagonal leading up and to the right shows that firms address multiple segments of customers, e.g. demographic, regional, or socio-psychological, where each segment is in a different societal setting, and thus influenced by different trends in different ways. The middle of the Figure shows that firms "win" customer preferences to their strong D's via convincing marketing messages as well as societal trends favoring one or more of their strong D's. Firms "lose" customers when their marketing messages are not convincing and/or societal trends move against their strong D's. These changes play out in multiple market segments and the associated societal settings.

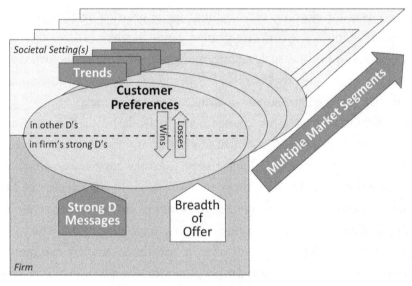

Figure 2-2: Markets Value Factor 2

From the structural perspective, the six online retail firms compete with one another in terms of the "market share" of their strong D's: the proportion of customers whose preferences are strongest for the dimensions in which the firm offers primary and secondary value. The firm with strong D's in the dimensions most favored by the customers will tend to sell more. The success of any given firm depends in part on the size of the customer segments which place the greatest weight on the D's in which the firm offers primary or secondary value. Turning this logic around, the strong D's of the firms with the greatest sales volume are presumably the dimensions which represent the weightiest preferences of the customers in total.

From the dynamic perspective, customer preferences are not fixed for all time. The weights which customers have assigned to different D's, consciously or unconsciously, can change over time for many reasons. For example, as a customer gains more and more experience in online retail, he or she may feel less of a need to be supported in shopping on the site, with a corresponding reduction in the weight of the Deed dimension. Or a customer may set the greatest weight on Dexterity for the household necessities (e.g. products for cleaning and washing) while prioritizing Delight for the occasional whimsical luxuries (e.g. new candleholders). Depending upon which shopping mission such a customer is pursuing, he or she will display varying preferences on the market. Furthermore, trends and developments in the customer's environment—political, economic, social, technological, environmental, or legal—can change his or her relative preferences for the different D's. For example, in times of uncertainty, focusing on the certain value of sober Dexterity would make sense for some customers, who then in more freer times would allow themselves to switch to the frivolity of Deed promotions and bargains. Finally, the priorities of customers can respond to an outstanding advance in the value offer in a given dimension; when a firm can make great strides in the value offer in one dimension, this can motivate customers who previously favored other dimensions to adjust their preferences to the new balance of offers on the market. For example, QVC is innovative in offering several different kinds of special bargains and promotions for the active shopper, representing a leap in Deed value. It is reasonable to assume that these innovations drew a number of customers to this dimension for the first time. Summing up, customer preferences can dynamically shift and take on different weights over time. Firms whose strengths are in value dimensions where party preferences are growing will become more successful.

MVF 2 thus takes account of the level of competition in the market between the dimensions of value: which D's bestow more market share to the firms with a strong offer in that dimension.

Markets Value Factor	Market Structure	Market Dynamic
2 Weight of customer preferences in firm's strong D's	Distribution of customer preferences in the different D's	Shifts in customer preferences between D's

In the structural perspective of MVF 2, examining the relative sales volume of the firms in Figure 1-1 and their strong D's gives an indication of which D's are weightiest in customer preferences. The order in Figure 1-1 suggests that Degree is by far the D which is most preferred by US online retail customers. The top three firms offer primary value in this D, while the sixth largest firm offers secondary value. The second and third weightiest D's appear to be Dexterity and Deed, where both show five firms offering strong value in the dimension. The least weighty D is Delight, with strong value offers from only three firms. Primary value in Delight is offered only by Macy's, whose sales volume is well below that of the top three online retailers.

Thus, Amazon offers primary value in the three most important D's.

Turning to the dynamic perspective on MVF 2, it was suggested above in the discussion of MVF 1 that Amazon built up a primary value offer first in Dexterity, then Deed, and finally Degree. This development in Amazon's capabilities may well parallel the development in customer preferences, roughly sketched here. In the early days of online retail, customers were principally interested in the one-size-fits-all Dexterity value of being able to learn about a book online, order it, and then receive it without going to a store. As time went on, customers became more sophisticated and the website became more complex. Thus, customers developed a heightened interest in the Deed value of an enhanced online shopping experience. At the same time, customers may well have placed increasing weight on the Delight value of being a modern and sophisticated shopper, taking part in the exciting new wave of the internet and all it could offer to society. Once customers could readily find, inform themselves about, and purchase products online, their interest turned to the Degree value of systematically reduced prices and delivery at high speed with a low or zero shipping fee. As online retail lost the allure of being new and diferent but settled down to the everyday, the preference for Delight value may also have diminished. Thus, it may be suggested that the developments in customer preferences drove Amazon to develop in parallel its own capabilities in value offers.

Concluding, MVF 2 links the distribution of customer preferences in the four dimensions to the D's in which a firm has strong offers. In this sense, MVF 2 investigates the competition between the dimensions of value, i.e. the competition between the sets of firms with primary or secondary value in each D. The winning firms in this competition are determined by some mix of luck, foresight, and ability out of the past: luck in having chosen to offer strong value in a D which turns out to have a weighty preference; foresight to have deliberately chosen to offer strong value in a D which had been correctly forecasted to carry weighty preferences; and/or ability to convince customers to shift their preferences to the firm's strong D's. Amazon had all three.

Markets Value Factor 3: Number of Direct Rivals with Same Strong D's

In the US online retail market, the five leading firms after Amazon offer primary value in one of the four conventional dimensions of value: one with primary value in up-market Degree, one with primary value in down-market Degree, and one each in Dexterity, Deed, and Delight. The observation that one firm in each of the "five" dimensions—counting up-market and down-market Degree as separate dimensions for the moment—has taken on a leading position in the market suggests one of two alternative possibilities. The first possibility is that the firm had the luck that no other firm hit on the same D in its primary value offers to customers. Thus, the firm could grow and prosper in a quasi-monopoly position as the only firm in the industry from which parties with a priority in that D could gain primary value. The second possibility is that the firm successfully beat the competition within the same dimension to emerge as the winner in the battle for the customer preferences most heavily weighted in that D. Under the latter circumstances, the winning firm made a value offer in the D which was more appealing than those from the firms who ended up further down in sales volume. In any case, it may be concluded that there is a heightened level of rivalry between firms with a strong offer in the same D. The level of rivalry between firms exhibiting the same strong D is more intense than that taking place between firms with different strong D's, and results in winners who rise up in sales volume and losers who fall down in sales, or never rise far up in the first place. Rivalry of this dramatic kind takes place principally within a D, not between them.

While MVF 2 measures the competition between D's, MVF 3 estimates the competition within a D. MVF 3 thus takes account of the level of rivalry between different firms with strong offers in the same D. Thus, MVF 3 determines how firms with strength in the same D share out amongst themselves the total volume of customer preferences for a given D—the latter as determined by MVF 2.

Dynamically, the number of firms in a market with strong value offers in the same D can change over time due to entry and exit, as shown in the lower right of Figure 2-3. Structurally, the greater the number of firms with strong value offers in the same D, the higher the level of rivalry and the lower the individual market shares amongst those firms. The outcome of this rivalry is decided by the appeal of a given firm's value offers (generated within the firm, as shown in Figure 2-3) relative to the appeal of the rivals' offers coming from the market (again as shown in Figure 2-3). Thus, MVF 3 determines how firms with strength in the same D share out amongst themselves the total volume of customer preferences for a given D—the latter as determined by MVF 2.

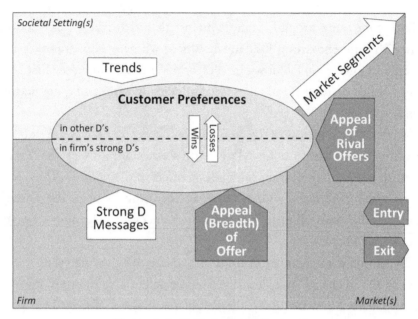

Figure 2-3: Markets Value Factor 3

Considering the dynamic perspective of entry conditions, entry into the D of a market will be more difficult the greater the number of existing firms with strong value offers in that D. A firm can enter a market under four conditions of entry, ranging from the most to the least promising conditions for the entering firm:

a. where there is no existing *strong* offer—primary or secondary value—in the entering firm's primary D;

b. where there is no existing *primary* offer in the entering firm's primary D;

c. where there is no existing *combination of strong offers in two D's* in the entering firm's own combination of primary and secondary value;

d. where there *is an existing* combination of strong offers that match the firm's own strong offer.

The dynamic perspectives of MVF 1 and MVF 2 are also relevant in understanding what were promising or less promising circumstances for a firm to enter the market. When an incumbent firm loses a strong D, as in MVF 1, or the weights of customer preferences shift towards the entering firm's strong dimensions, as in MVF 2, the entry conditions are more favorable and the business opportunities are greater. In the other direction, when an incumbent firm gains a strong D or customer preferences shift away from an entering firm's strong dimensions, the entry conditions are less favorable and the business opportunities are smaller.

The number of firms with strong offers in a given D is also dynamically influenced by the exit conditions. Where there are high exit barriers, e.g. a retailer strong in offline business who persists in online retail via a kind of internal cross-subsidy, firms which are not competitive in online retail will nevertheless remain in the market. Although not entirely successful, they will nevertheless absorb a share of the customer demand in the D's in which their offers are strong. The level of rivalry in those dimensions is thus higher, and all firms with strong value offers in those D's, both the competitive ones and the non-competitive ones, will be less successful.

Structurally, the level of rivalry between firms with strong value in the same D will be determined by the number of firms and the relative appeal of their offers. The value offer which is most appealing will gain market share at the expense of the others. Indeed, it is possible that the secondary offer of a firm in a given dimension is more appealing to customers than the primary offer of another firm. The more equal the appeal of the offers, the higher the level of rivalry between the firms, and the more stable their market shares. Where there are divergences in relative appeal, market shares will shift to the firm with the more appealing offer. The firm with falling relative appeal may be driven out of the market. The dynamic perspective tracks changes in the number of strong offers in each D due to entry and exit of firms.

	Markets Value Factor	Market Structure	Market Dynamic
3	Number of firm's direct rivals in same strong D's	Distribution of strong D's at firms as well as relative appeal in the D's	Entry and exit conditions

As noted above, the five leading online retailers after Amazon do not offer primary value in the same D. Thus, none of them compete directly with one another. They have risen up within their dimension and beat back the direct rivals with primary value in their same D who have smaller sales volumes. Rather, the five all compete directly with Amazon. It will be shown in the following paragraphs that Amazon offers a more attractive relative appeal in Degree, Dexterity, and Deed than its respective rival with primary value in the same D. Only in Delight is Amazon less appealing than any rival. The value offers of the six leading firms in US online retail were presented in the previous chapter; in this chapter, they will be briefly reviewed in order to draw the comparision in the offers.

Amazon offers shopping customers primary value in Degree via a systematically higher living standard in two ways. First, the delivery service is like "room service" at the beck and call of the customer. Amazon offers a much higher level of service to customers than is normal in postal distribution, with a choice of different delivery speeds. In addition, Amazon Prime is an annual membership program with unlimited free shipping on tens of millions of items. In certain cities, the service Prime Now offers delivery within two hours, or even within one hour for a modest fee. The elevated living standard comes as well from the systematically low prices—for both the goods themselves as well as the shipping costs—which enables the customer to enjoy more consumer products. A 2011 study by Wells Fargo found that Amazon was substantially cheaper than Walmart. Automatic programs compare prices at rivals and adjust Amazon's prices to keep to its pledge to offer the lowest price anywhere, which enables the customer to enjoy more consumer products.

Briefly considering the leading rivals with primary value in Degree, with regard to "room service," Apple and Walmart offer high-quality, reliable delivery services. However, they do not come close to the relative appeal of the Amazon offer regarding the range of delivery times and the low—or zero—shipping costs. Turning to the down-market Degree offer of price levels, the Wells Fargo study confirms Amazon's claim to offer the lowest prices anywhere. Regarding the up-market Degree offer, Apple wins out against Amazon in terms of its own products: Apple products cannot be purchased on the Amazon website.

Otherwise, Amazon offers a huge range of up-market products beyond simply Apple products, whereas Apple sells only its own products.

Thus, with the single exception of Apple products, Amazon demonstrates a much greater appeal in its Degree offer relative to that of its rivals in that D, Apple and Walmart.

Amazon offers primary value in Dexterity to shopping customers in terms of their after-sales customer experience in two principal ways. First, Amazon wants to ensure that customers will not be disappointed by the product they have purchased. The many and varied customer reviews, as well as the lengthy and robust product descriptions, provide a great deal of information, such that the customer should not be unpleasantly surprised when it comes to actually consuming the product. Thus, Amazon aims to "guarantee" the quality of customers' consumption experience with the products they have purchased. Second, the terms and conditions from Amazon are very generous; Amazon does not hesitate to decide to the benefit of the customer regarding damaged or defect goods. In addition, automated systems search for situations where Amazon has provided a customer service that isn't up to its own standards, e.g. an interrupted streaming broadcast, and then proactively refunds the customers. Finally, when customers pre-order an item from Amazon, the firm guarantees to charge the lowest price between the time of the order and the date on which the order is filled.

The leading rival with primary value in Dexterity, Costco, offers a high level of product information and customer support, as well as attractive business terms and conditions. Nevertheless, the firm does not offer nearly the same level of detail in product descriptions nor in the depth and range of customer reviews. Customer support may well be comparable to that of Amazon, but it is widely acknowledged that Amazon leads the market in the generosity of its terms and conditions.

Thus, Amazon demonstrates a much greater appeal in its Dexterity offer relative to Costco.

Amazon offers primary value in Deed to shopping customers in the form of the convenience and richness of the online experience. Shopping on the Amazon website is enhanced by the huge product range, the many personalized features, the payment convenience on Amazon.com which also can be used on other sites, and the powerful search engine. Customers can "do" their shopping mission efficiently and effectively. The personalized online experience extends to e-mails pointing out bargains and items of interest fitting the individual profile of the customer. Furthermore, Amazon Coins enable children to shop on the site, over 200,000 apps to support daily activities are available, and charity donations can be integrated into the online experience.

Comparing Amazon's Deed value offer to that of QVC, the latter offers a considerably smaller product range, and the features and functionality on the website are simply typical for an online shop. However, for a customer entirely intent on discovering a bargain in order to enjoy the thrill of the hunt, the set of special offers on QVC—the Big Deal, New items, Trending items and Today's Special Value®—are likely to be more appealing than what Amazon offers. For this very particular shopping mission in Deed, QVC is more appealing relative to Amazon. For all other aspects of Deed value, Amazon is clearly ahead.

Thus, with the exception of one special kind of shopping mission, Amazon demonstrates a much greater appeal in its Deed offer relative to that of its rival in that D, QVC.

Lastly, Amazon offers basic value in the Delight dimension. The huge range of products enables shopping customers to choose those products which come closest to their personal preferences. In this way, they can live out their personal vision of themselves as a consumer, able to find and afford those products which best fulfill their personal vision of who they are as a consumer. Amazon exhibits a lower level of appeal in its Delight offer relative to that of the primary value of Macy's, as well as the secondary value of Apple and Walmart, which are described above.

The entry and exit conditions have been heavily influenced by the rise of the internet in general and online retail specifically in the past twenty years. During this time period, virtually every offline retailer in the US has felt compelled to enter online retail, while a number of firms specializing purely in online retail have also entered.

It has been suggested above that as the US online retail market developed in its first years, whenever customer preferences for a given D became weighty,

Amazon was more or less at the same time positioned to offer primary value in Dexterity, Deed, and then Degree or secondary value in Delight. Thus, any firm entering the online retail market encountered Amazon already in a strong position in any D that was relevant. In addition, of course, there were quickly numerous other firms in the market, in particular Macy's, Apple, and Walmart with their strong offers in Delight. Thus, for all intents and purposes, any firm entering the online retail market after Amazon did so under condition d) above, i.e. any new entrant faced competition from at least one rival with strong value offers in its own strong D's. Given this level of rivalry within its own D from established firms, it was very difficult for any new entrant to rapidly gain a substantial level of sales. Newcomers can of course grow rapidly when they begin from a small volume of sales, but this growth soon levels out to roughly match that of the online market as a whole.

The overwhelming relative appeal of Amazon may be measured by means of the "Death by Amazon" index. The stock market research firm Bespoke Investment Group created an index of the major retail names it thought would be must hurt by Amazon. Those companies—there are now fifty-four of them—include Barnes & Noble, Costco, Best Buy, GameStop, Macy's, Nordstrom, Sears, Target, CVS, Caremark and Rite Aid, and Walmart. As of July 2017, the index was down more than 20 percent over the course of the year. This represented a loss in market capitalization of $70 billion. In contrast, Amazon's market capitalization gained $120 billion in the first half of 2017.

Regarding exit conditions, almost all online retailers currently have fairly high exit barriers, explained as follows. All but a handful of the top fifty online retailers in the US in 2016 were also offline retailers. For such retailers it is very important to maintain a presence in both the online and the offline markets. There are numerous synergies in multi-channel retailing which an offline retailer cannot afford to eliminate. For example, the online and offline channels feed sales volume to each other and the greater turnover resulting from sales in both channels enables the retailer to negotiate improved terms and conditions with suppliers. Furthermore, image, reputation, and prestige are enhanced by operations in both channels. Finally, a retailer would suffer a great loss of face if it pulled out of the online market. Thus, a predominantly offline retailer would be willing to carry significant losses in its online operations rather than exit the online market. The synergies between online and offline channels will be further discussed with regard to MVF 5 later. Nevertheless, exit of this kind has taken place. The electronic goods retailer Circuit City filed for bankruptcy in 2009, followed by the book retailer Borders in 2011; both operated predominantly stores, but also an online shop. Online sales have been particularly disruptive in the product categories of electronic goods and books. The exit barriers for firms specialized in online retail are lower; a sub-par business performance would not satisfy the owners/investors and the business would be closed down. On the whole, the relatively high exit barriers have served to keep a large number of firms in the market and thus raise the level of rivalry in the US online retail market.

MVF 3 has provided more insight into the relative standing of the six firms. In particular, additional reasons for the overwhelming dominance of Amazon have been presented. Furthermore, an explanation has been presented for the value configuration of the other five retailers: how market rivalry within a D has led to the situation that each of the five leading firms offers primary value in its "own" D, where the Degree dimension is split into up- and down-market variants.

Nevertheless, the market shares of the six firms are not entirely explained by the analysis in MVF's 1-3. MVF 4 will shed more light on the market developments.

Markets Value Factor 4: Utilizing Others' Resources

MVF 4 continues in the vein of MVF 3 in addressing the volume of sales a firm can attract away from rivals on the market. In MVF 4, the firm gains sales volume by utilizing others' resources in a variety of ways, which fall into the structural or dynamic perspectives.

Structurally, an online retailer can utilize resources from reviewers and business partners. The many aspects of how an online retailer can benefit from reviewers and business partners are discussed in detail in the following chapter and simply summarized here. The key role of customer reviews in generating sales was discussed above in regard to Amazon's relative appeal in its Dexterity value offer. The same points about the importance of customer reviews apply, in fact, to any online retailer with customer reviews. Customer reviews originate from people in the societal setting of the firm, as shown in the upper, left-hand corner of Figure 2-4. In managing customer reviewers, online retailers build a relationship which takes account of their societal setting.

A second source of turnover for online retailers is utilizing the resources of its business partners. Different kinds of business partners can generate different kinds of turnover for a firm. First, third-party sellers can offer their goods on the website of a given retailer, or alternatively advertise them. With regard to third-party sellers, it seems at first glance that when an online retailer allows other retailers to sell or advertise on its site, it would be losing, and not gaining, business. However, in online retailing the logic is that the given retailer on the one hand earns fees from the sales or advertising of the third parties—often on products that the online retailer itself does not offer anyway—and on the other hand gains higher traffic volume on its own site due to the pull of the widened product range (the third-party sellers supplement the offer of the retailer itself). When shoppers are attracted to the site because of the widened product range from the third-party sellers, they may well end up buying a product from the online retailer while they are on the site. In addition, the online retailer can gain market knowledge from observing and analyzing how the third-party sellers conduct themselves to be successful. Second, a given online retailer can win customers when other websites point their visitors to the website of the given firm. The other websites provide a link to the online retailer, typically to a specific product. Third, developers can build into their apps a link to the online website so that app users are directed to where they can purchase specific products. The online retailer rewards the developer with a commission on sales coming from the app. In addition, developers can offer their apps on the website of the retailer, attracting traffic to the site from interested visitors and generating a commission on sales.

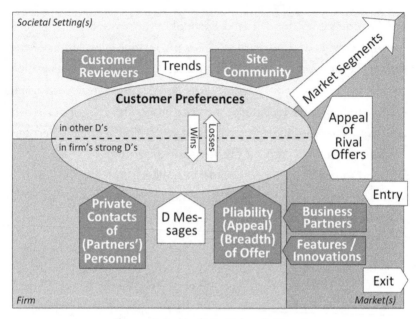

Figure 2-4: Markets Value Factor 4

Business partners are located in the market; to be precise, business partners have a position in the online retail market and in their own market. In managing relations to business partners, online retailers build relationships which take account of the market positioning of the partners. Furthermore, the extent to which the online retailers' offer is what will be here termed "pliable" determines the extent to which it can utilize the resources from business partners. The better and the more the online retailer can integrate and enhance the resources of the business partners into their own offers, the more successful they will be. The pliability to utilize resources from business partners improves the appeal and the breadth of the online retailer's own offer. These considerations are shown in the lower right-hand corner of Figure 2-4.

Another source of utilizing resources from parties is personnel. Employees working at the firm's sites—both offices and distribution facilities—maintain private relations with a circle of relatives, friends, colleagues, and acquaintances. The people in this circle of private relations can be more inclined to shop on a firm's site when they know someone who works for the firm. The source of utilized resources is the firm (its personnel) and thus shown in the lower left-hand corner of Figure 2-4. Furthermore, employees at the business partners also have a circle of private relations with a similar impact. Finally, people who live near a online retailer's site—office building or warehouse—can feel a sense of community with the firm from its local activities or simply as a local employer. This sense of shared community can lead such people to become customers of the online retailer, as shown in the upper right-hand corner of Figure 2-4.

On the whole, the greater the number of individual parties with relations to an online retailer, the greater the number of people with a predisposition in favor of the firm. The extent to which a firm is embedded in the society/economy—reviewers, business partners, sites, and the associated communities—affects both the number of people with a favorable predisposition to the firm as well as the volume of resources available for the firm to utilize. The extent of a firm's embeddedness influences its sales volume and constitutes the structural perspective of MVF 4.

Dynamically, online retailers can over time draw on the resources of rivals in that they copy or adapt into their own offers the successful features of their rivals. Firms track the features of rivals' offers, and when a feature or an innovation from a rival proves to be successful, firms can—with a certain delay—adopt the feature or innovation into their own offer. When the innovation is in a D in which the retailer is strong, adopting the innovation should be relatively straightforward. When the innovation is in a D in which the retailer offers only basic value, the organizational effort to incorporate the innovation into the retailer's own offer may be greater. In addition, it may well be the case that a "watered down" version of the innovation is offered, because the retailer does not have the proper resources to fully realize the innovation. In any case, the result of taking on innovations from rivals also raises the pliability of online retailers' offers, as shown in the lower right-hand corner of Figure 2-4.

Utilizing the features or innovations from rivals raises the range of features in the retailer's own offer. Value is offered in a variety of D's, in some of which the retailer may only offer basic value. Firms step beyond the confines of their own strong D's to offer features with value in other D's. As noted in the previous chapter, the spread of a given feature throughout the market can lower its level of value from primary to secondary and ultimately to basic value. In the dynamic perspective of MVF 4, features in firms' value offers continually develop over time. The features in the value offers change and grow, in particular with regard to the distinction between primary, secondary, and basic value. Competition therefore takes place between websites which can display individual features offering value in potentially any D.

	Markets Value Factor	Market Structure	Market Dynamic
4	Utilizing others' resources	Level of embeddedness: network of reviewers, business partners and people / communities	Adopting features and innovations from rivals

Considering first the structural perspective of MVF 4 in the US online retail market, Amazon is by far better embedded than the rivals. Amazon lists the top 10,000 reviewers on its website, an indication that there are even more. Roughly one-third of Amazon's sales turnover comes from third-party sellers. In 2014, Amazon operated 109 fulfillment centers around the world, such that by the end of 2017, there were close to one hundred in the US alone. Amazon forecasted 280,000 total employees in the US by mid-2018, the bulk of whom will be working in the fulfillment centers which are prominently located in communities spread around the country. None of Amazon's rivals come close to such a mass of parties linked to the firm who see their interests coupled with those of Amazon.

Turning to the dynamic perspective, at the risk of an over-simplification, the bulk of innovative features amongst US online retailers were originally established in the market by Amazon. Details of such features are presented above in the discussion of Amazon's relative appeal with respect to MVF 3. In addition, Part II will present further aspects of Amazon's innovations in the market. Amazon was not the original inventor for all of these features—it also scans the market for innovations or, in some cases, for inspirations which it then further improves—but it was almost always Amazon that made the innovation a success. What's more, by patenting many innovations,

Amazon has made it impossible, or at least more difficult, for rivals to copy its innovations. Perhaps the most prominent example is 1-Click Shopping. No other online retailer in the US is legally able to complete a purchase on its site with one click; there must be at least a second step. Thus, from the dynamic perspective of MVF 4, Amazon has largely been setting the agenda for the market, and the others have been catching up.

Concluding, Amazon's huge lead over its rivals with respect to MVF 4 is a further part of the explanation of its market dominance. The analysis of market success will be completed by considering MVF 5 in the next section.

Markets Value Factor 5: Managing multiple channels

In MVF 4, firms widen and deepen the segments of customers they address while still keeping within the confines of online retailing. In MVF 5, online retailers address additional segments of customers and/or additional shopping missions of customers by making value offers in other distribution channels, principally offline in stores. They address customer segments who do not want to shop online and shopping missions for which offline is better suited, the latter for three interrelated reasons. First, customers want to see, touch, and smell the product and/or converse live with a store employee. Second, shopping offline may fit to their situation on a given day, e.g. they are in the vicinity of the store and have time to go in. Third, certain product categories lend themselves better to offline shopping due to the nature and logistics of the product, e.g. fresh food involves requirements for packing and transport which, for the vast majority of customers, are best met in stores. A third distribution channel is televised home shopping, where Liberty Interactive Corporation, operating the QVC website, is the leading US retailer. Again, a given shopping mission may best be fulfilled in the television channel.

In the offline or television channels, firms compete on the basis of MVFs 1-4, just as in the online channel. In MVF 5, the elements making up MVFs 1-4 are designed and steered for each channel, and the firm can manage more than one channel, as illustrated in Figure 2-5. In principle, each channel could have its own value configuration and value offers, and each channel can gain sales on the basis of its own scores on MVFs 1-4 relative to rivals. However, in practice, the value configuration and the value offers of each of the leading retailers online, offline, and, in the case of QVC, on television are essentially the same. Thus, this section will not review MVFs 1-4 for the offline and television channels, because it would be redundant with the presentation above of the online value offers from the leading retailers. Rather, this section will present a high-level discussion of the benefits on the market which retailers can obtain from operating in two channels.

It is to be noted that the channels within the retail market are more complex than simply online, offline, and television. In the online market, sales can be transacted on a website or more recently via an app. In addition, direct marketing by means of e-mails is an important supplement to both. In the offline market, retailers operate a wide range of store formats with regard to size, breadth, and depth of product assortment, location, and so forth. Home televised shopping can be operated in various formats regarding the broadcast times as well as duration and structure of the individual presentations of products. Alternative channels are phone order and catalogues. Finally, Apple also sells some of its products offline via third parties such as third-party cellular network carriers, wholesalers, retailers, and value-added resellers. Nevertheless, for the purposes of this section, the discussion will simply consider online, offline, and television channels.

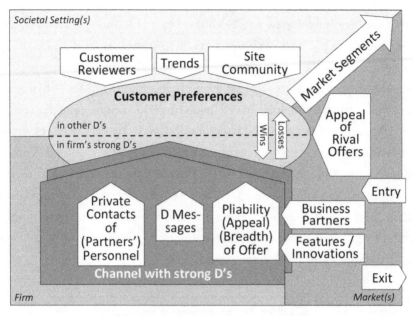

Figure 2-5: Markets Value Factor 5

Structurally, MVF 5 considers the number of channels which a retailer operates and the share of sales volume gained from each channel by the firm. None of the leading retailers operate more than two channels. Dynamically, firms have built their second channel at different points in time in their history and under different conditions, which impacts their ability to take full advantage of the synergies between the two channels.

	Markets Value Factor	Market Structure	Market Dynamic
5	Multiple distribution channels	Number of channels and their relative sales volume	Timing and conditions of operating the second channel

Figure 2-6 presents data on online sales relative to other channels for the six leading online retailers in the US in 2016 and 2017. For Amazon, until recently, nearly 100 percent of its revenues came from online sales, a value which fell below 70 percent in 2017. Amazon has diversified its sources of income, as touched on in the introduction to the firm in the Introduction and further discussed in Part II. The share of its revenues from offline sales in 2016 was negligible, grew to $1.3 billion in 2017, and will certainly grow in the future. Apple and Walmart have a relatively modest share of sales from online channels. Apple always had a marked offline presence amongst retailers, business partners, and its own chain amounting to 498 stores in twenty-two countries in July 2017. In 2016-2017, online sales represented under 10 percent of Apple's total revenues. Walmart, by far the largest retailer in the world regarding turnover and number of employees, gained 3 percent of its revenues online in 2016 and 2017. Roughly one-fifth of Macy's revenue stems from online sales; as a share of revenue, amongst traditional store retailers, Macy's has the most successful online shop. Costco gains only 4 percent of its revenue online. QVC is clearly quite dependent on online sales, which make up about half of its revenue.

	Online Sales ($ billion)		Online Sales as Share of Total Revenue	
Firm	2016	2017	2016	2017
Amazon	85	91	70%	63%
Apple	17	20	8%	9%
Walmart	14	15	3%	3%
Macy's	5	5	18%	21%
Costco	4	5	4%	4%
QVC	4	4	47%	50%

Figure 2-6: Online Sales in 2016 and 2017
Source: Zaczkiewicz 2017; www.retail-index.emarketer.com

The structural benefits of operating in more than one channel were presented above as widening and deepening first the range of customers and second the range of their shopping missions which a retailer can address. This overarching benefit can be broken down into five seperate benefits, in which the structural score on MVF 5 for each of the leading online retailers can be roughly evaluated. The online/offline benefits to Amazon of acquiring Whole Foods Market will be examined in Part III and are not discussed below. Information for the following discussion is drawn from the retailers' websites.

First, as noted above, there are three reasons why shoppers can use different distribution channels. To gain as much as possible of their consumer spending and to keep their loyalty, retailers need to offer a full product range in both on- and offline channels to cover as many shopping missions as possible. Walmart scores by far the highest, with a dense network of stores—90 percent of American residents live within ten miles of a Walmart store—and a very wide product range in its online shop. Apple has a fairly dense network of offline points of sales. Then come Macy's with stores in big cities and Costco with stores in transit points, followed by QVC, where television shopping fulfills a specific range of shopping missions. Amazon scores the worst in this regard, given that its offline presence was negligible until the acquisition of Whole Foods Market, and, even then, the store chain covers only a restricted product range of certain kinds of food as well as health and beauty products. Amazon's physical presence was minimally increased in 2017 by arranging for its customers to be able to return items purchased online to Kohl's stores in two cities.

Second, operations in both channels enables a retailer to combine the channels in interesting ways. An online shop is a convenient source of detailed information about store products which can be consulted by the customer at home or even in the store. One study shows that 34 percent of US shoppers have used a mobile device to research products while in a store; another study reveals that 71 percent of US shoppers who use smartphones for research in-store say that it has become an important part of the experience. Many store customers register themselves with the store such that they can be informed via e-mail or SMS messaging about store promotions and other events; registration can take place online or offline. And a positive shopping experience online or offline raises customer loyalty to the firm. These generalized benefits are probably most applicable to Apple, Walmart, Macy's, and Costco with their extensive operations both online and offline. In addition to these generalized benefits, the retailers combine their distribution channels in specific ways. Walmart offers discounts online for items which will be picked up in a store, fresh groceries can be ordered online and collected from a store on the same day, and, in both cases, store employees will even load the car. Apple offers the option for customers who have bought products online to receive technical support, including repairs, at one of their own stores or from an authorized distributor. Walmart, Apple, and Costco offer the option to return items purchased online to one of their stores. Macy's offers its stores as pick-up locations and, in an interesting twist, uses its online channel to market two sets of services in its stores. First, group tours of Macy's stores are sold online, where the tours include programs customized to provide insights on fashion, beauty, home style, and cooking. Second, Shopping Packages for specific stores, where shoppers are offered a special shopping experience including amenities and discounts, can be purchased online. Thus, in terms of combining channels, Walmart again appears to score the highest, followed by Macy's, and then Apple and Costco. QVC and Amazon—without Whole Foods Market—have had little to offer in this regard.

Third, knowledge about retailing operations gained in one channel can be deployed in the other channel in innovative ways, stimulating new kinds of offers in the retailing industry. For example, Macy's customers who are registered on the app can make use of the Mobile Checkout to avoid having to go to a cashier when in the store, paying as if they were online. Using the app, they can scan their purchase items throughout the store and then pay via credit card when leaving the store. Another innovation at Macy's is to use the online features of Virtual Reality and augmented reality to assist customers in the store when they are choosing furniture; the customers can test how different pieces of furniture fit together in their own rooms.

Fourth, for shoppers who welcome the recommendations from "their" online retailer, they would want the retailer to also have data about their offline shopping behavior so that the retailer has a complete picture of their preferences, from which even more customized tips can be derived. All leading retailers are making considerable efforts in this direction, but to date none can be sure to capture all online and offline purchases which a specific customer makes.

Fifth, operating in two channels raises the image of a retailer. As with the previous benefit, it is difficult to quantify the score of individual retailers in this regard.

Structurally, then, Walmart appears to score best in MVF 5, followed by Macy's, and then Apple. Costco enjoys certain market benefits from combining online and offline. Presumably, QVC gains certain market benefits from its channels in online and television shopping, which will not be investigated here. Acquiring Whole Foods Market is the most significant step for Amazon to catch up to the others; more on this in Chapter 9.

Dynamically, Amazon began selling online in 1994. The other retailers listed above began online sales in the course of the later 1990's, with varying levels of managerial attention as well as resources, and thus correspondingly with various levels of success. Starting in the beginning of the twenty-first century, they have all realized that the online channel is key to their overall success. Online sales have grown faster than offline sales in the twenty-first century, representing an important source of growth, as discussed in the Introduction. Customer requirements in this business area have accordingly risen at a rapid rate, raising the challenges in continually being successful online.

Perhaps the best demonstration of the importance of operating in multiple channels comes from three "failure" stories. In 2000, Amazon signed a deal with Toys R Us to sell their toys on its website, then in early 2001 added the book chain Borders and the electronics retailer Circuit City. These retailers have filed for bankruptcy one after another: Circuit City in 2009, Borders in 2011, and Toys R Us in 2017.

In the original agreement, Toys R Us was the exclusive supplier of toys to Amazon. Amazon complained that Toys R Us was not supplying sufficient stock and thus began to sell toys from other suppliers as well. Toys R Us sued in 2004 and won the right to terminate the contract. It set up its own website in 2006. Borders dissolved the working relationship with Amazon in 2008. Analysts have argued that these three firms faced difficulties because they began to build their own knowledge of the online channel later than their rivals. As written about Toys R Us, the firm "had missed out on the journey other retailers were taking, in figuring out the world of e-commerce and building up its own, innovative presence online." Presumably, the same can be said about Circuit City and Borders.

The principal conclusion from MVF 5 is that Amazon has suffered by operating almost exclusively in one channel. It can be assumed that Amazon came to the same conclusion in deciding to build up its offline activities. Indeed, it could even be suggested that Amazon's growth in online sales has been hampered by the lack of a significant offline presence. The other retailers supplemented their original channel—for QVC television, for the other four offline—with an online channel at an early enough point in time, and have devoted sufficient resources to online sales, to have avoided bankruptcy and, indeed, to be one of the leading online retailers today.

Taking Stock

The MVFs 1-5 have been applied to build up a high-level and comprehensive overview of competition in the US online retail market. In MVFs 1-4, Amazon scored far ahead of its rivals, cumulatively explaining its overweening dominance in the market. In MVF 5, Amazon in fact scored the worst of the top six online retailers, moderating its otherwise crushing lead over the other retailers. Starting in 2016, Amazon began to take steps to catch up with the others, and then in 2017 took a large step by acquiring Whole Foods Market.

This chapter ends the external view of Amazon on the market. In Part II, Amazon is examined from the inside with regard to its five Managerial Do-Well's.

PART II

Managerial Do Well's at Amazon

Chapter 3

MDW 1: Aligning the Value Exchange

Markets Value Factor 1	Managerial Do-Well 1
Number of strong D's	Align the value exchange to the firm's strong D's

This chapter examines the first Managerial Do-Well, which Amazon manages in order to achieve a high score on MVF 1. In MVF 1, firms offer primary or secondary value in as many dimensions as possible. In order to offer strong value in a given D, firms must align the value inputs from parties to the requirements of the given D. This alignment forms a value cycle: the inputs generate the offers, which elicit the inputs, which in turn generate the offers, and so on.

Cycle of Value Exchange with Shopping Customers

Amazon's value offers to shopping customers were presented in Chapter 1 and are summarized here. The shopping customer inputs, which complete the value exchange, are presented here for the first time. The value exchange can be set in four contexts, as summarized in the table below, corresponding to the contexts of the Markets Value Factors.

Party Type	Value Flow	Primary Degree	Primary Dexterity	Primary Deed	*Basic Delight*
Shopping customers	Area	Societal setting: Offline	Online Retail Market: After-Sale Customer Experience	Shopping Customer Activities: Online	*Consumer Being: Personal Vision*
	Offer	Elevated living standard	All-rounder benefits	Optimized shopping mission	*Realize personal vision*
	Input	Organizational assets	Shared market knowledge	Triggered value	*Enthusiasm*

Beginning in the leftmost column of the table above, shopping customers live in a societal setting as consumers. In this offline world of daily life, their accumulated consumption is their standard of living. As presented in Chapter 1, Amazon offers primary value in Degree via a systematically higher living standard in two ways: first, from the customer service in the supply chain which is like "room service" and, second, from the low prices which enable the customer to enjoy more consumer products. Placing the Degree value offer in the context of the societal setting identifies further aspects of the Amazon offer: shopping customers regard their status relative to their fellows as being modern and sophisticated in that they shop with the leading exponent of new technology in retail, indeed one of the leading exponents of new technology in business. In addition, they also may regard themselves as being elevated in society because they maintain a relation to one of the mightiest organizations in the US business world.

Shopping customers input primary Degree value in two forms of organizational assets which boost the status of Amazon in the offline world of consumption. First, shopping customers input the huge volume of revenue which "finances" Amazon's low prices, enabling the firm to generate operational cash flow despite the small margins. For example, Prime customers spent as much as 150 percent more after becoming Prime subscribers. Customers have responded to the offer of lower shipping costs with the input of significantly higher revenues. Second, shopping customers have collectively input the status of market leader to Amazon due to the dominant market share. The larger impact of Prime may well be that Prime subscribers stop buying elsewhere. Prime customers simply assume that Amazon's prices are competitive. With

Prime, shipping costs become irrelevant. Thus, there is little reason to shop elsewhere. This second input from shopping customers enables Amazon to prevent business going to its rivals, leading to the overwhelming market share. The mass of finance and dominant market share input by shopping customers enables Amazon to be a technology and business leader in the US. The cycle of value exchange is completed in that by enjoying this raised status due to the inputs from the shopping customers, Amazon in turn can offer the Degree value of higher living standards, modernity, and importance.

Moving to the second column in the table above, shopping customers are participants in the online retail market. As discussed in Chapter 1, Amazon offers shopping customers primary value in Dexterity in two major forms of all-around benefits. First, it offers a very high level of product information such that shopping customers are exceedingly well-informed about the product, ruling out nasty surprises when consuming the product. Amazon "guarantees" customers a satisfactory consumption experience with the products they have purchased. Second, Amazon offers very generous terms and conditions regarding the price which is ultimately charged, rebates for damaged goods, returns, compensation for delays in shipment, and so forth. Placing the Dexterity offer in the context of the online retail market shows that, actually, the value is gained after the sale: the customer experience of the product sold by Amazon and Amazon's treatment of the customer regarding payment and shipping. The after-sales customer experience is "very fair," representing a market-leading benchmark in online retail.

In the Dexterity dimension, Amazon shopping customers input primary value to the firm in the form of shared knowledge regarding their behaviors and preferences. That is, by making purchases and otherwise responding to Amazon's many products, features, and functionalities, shopping customers enable Amazon to build up better knowledge of the market. Customers "input" their data. As a specific example, Amazon asks, "Was this review helpful to you?" as a way to gain input from customers. This input to build Amazon's market knowledge in turn enables the firm to continue to offer leading quality in the after-sales customer experience, thereby completing the cycle of value exchange.

Turning to the third column in the table above, shopping customers engage in their shopping missions in the online interface to Amazon. These activities are principally shopping on the Amazon website, but include shopping on other websites where the relation to Amazon is that the customer landed on the website due to advertising on Amazon, or the customer is using his or her Amazon account to pay for purchases on another site. In addition, the online interface to Amazon more recently has included streaming services, games, and other apps online, as well as the online functionalities of smart devices. As discussed in Chapter 1, Amazon offers primary value in Deed in the form of the convenience and richness of the experience, whatever shoppers are "doing" online or in interaction with smart devices. Setting the Deed value offer in the context of the shopping customer's own activities highlights the individual nature of this offer. Amazon does not package a solution which is right for the mass of the market, as in Degree and Dexterity. Rather, the almost infinite variety of customers and their individual situations when shopping at different times is accommodated in the Deed value offer.

Shopping customers input primary value in Deed in the form of triggered value. Amazon offers a great range of alternatives for the shopping customers (this is the stimulation or trigger for the shopping customers) and they take the time and make the effort to actually make use of them (they pull the trigger). The shopping customers get full value from the Amazon website only when they in fact utilize the many alternatives. In this way, the Deed benefits, which Amazon is hoping to transmit, are indeed taken on by the customers. As a result, Amazon's objectives to raise customer loyalty and bind them to the site are in fact realized. This input of utilizing the alternatives in turn confirms Amazon in the benefits of customer loyalty, etc. arising from offering such alternatives. The cycle of value exchange is completed in that Amazon continues to build up and extend the ease and comfort with more and more alternatives.

Moving lastly to the last column in the table above, the Delight dimension relates to the being or existence of the shopping customer, where the customer has a personal vision of what he or she wants to be(come). Amazon offers basic value via the huge variety of products, from which shopping customers can select those best fulfilling their personal vision of themselves as a consumer. Setting the Delight value offer in this context highlights the personal nature of this value. Shopping customers reflect on themselves—actively or passively—and choose from Amazon's incredible variety the items which are best for their inner selves.

In return, shopping customers input basic value in Delight to Amazon. Being able to find items which are best for their inner selves generates enthusiasm for the company and its website. The shopping customers engage in word-of-mouth recommendations, infecting their acquaintances with their positive feelings and raising the image of the brand. This input of emotion makes shopping customers and their circle of acquaintances perceive an emotional value from Amazon, as if it were Amazon creating the emotion. Thus, the input of emotion from shopping customers in turn enables Amazon to offer emotion of the same kind: the cycle of value exchange is completed.

Powerfully Coordinated Total Value Offer to Shopping Customers

In terms of managing the total value offer, it can be shown that Amazon has oriented the value offers in the three dimensions with primary value—Degree, Deed, and Dexterity—to supplement one another in a powerfully coordinated manner. The value offers conform to the generic shopping process of a typical customer. In each step of the online shopping process, Amazon addresses the most pressing demand of the customer. What's more, the different dimensions of the total value offer originate from and are managed by different units within the organization. These points are illustrated by referring to Figure 3-1.

In Figure 3-1, the online shopping process is broken down to its simplest phases: Before, During, and After. Before actually shopping, customers consider which website they want to visit. Amazon's primary value offer in Degree, rooted in the supply chain, impresses customers in a compelling manner in all its aspects like love at first sight, attracting them to its site for their shopping. During the shopping on a website, customers want to fulfill their shopping mission. Amazon's primary value offer in Deed on the website—stemming from the software teams in headquarters—enables customers to fulfill their shopping mission, such that Amazon has served them adequately. After the online shopping, customers do not want to be dissatisfied with the payment and delivery as well as the product itself. Amazon's primary value offer in Dexterity, centered in the teams managing customer experience, is generous regarding payment and delivery terms, while detailed product information and reviews give an accurate and realistic impression of the product; there should be no surprises for the customer when consuming the product. The customer will not be disappointed, such that Amazon has retained the customer.

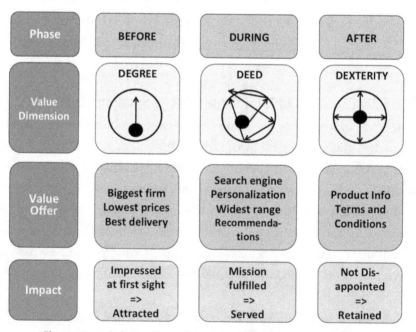

Figure 3-1: Orientation of Amazon's Primary Value Offers
to Generic Shopping Process

Thus, the primary value offers from Amazon are oriented to speak to the core of what typical shoppers seek in each phase of their generic shopping process. These primary value offers can be readily managed because they originate in different organizational units.

Cycle of Value Exchange with Business Partners

Amazon maintains business relations with principally four kinds of business partners. First, suppliers produce products which Amazon sells under its own account, generally using the brand name of the supplier. Second, affiliates are organizations running a website who direct their site visitors to the Amazon website by providing a link to the relevant page; when the visitors make a purchase on the Amazon website, the affiliate organization receives a commission. Third, partners referred to variously as "Selling on Amazon sellers" or as part of the "Marketplace" are third-party sellers who sell on their own account, but list their products on the Amazon website (for which they pay a commission on their sales) and have the option for Amazon to also handle the logistics of filling orders (for which they pay fees). Fourth, advertisers sell on their own account, but advertise on the Amazon website, for which they pay a fee.

Amazon manages a generalized value exchange with these different types of business partners in four settings, shown in the table below.

Party Type	Value Flow	Degree	Dexterity	Deed	Basic Delight
Part-ners	Area	Business setting in own market	Online retail market	Activities in the online interface to Amazon	Vision of own organizational development
	Offer	Higher standing in own market	Well-structured business relation	Platform and support to optimize online practice	Help in realizing own business development
	Input	Financial might and own standing	Market knowledge	Optimize own practice => Optimize Amazon practice	Enthusiasm and loyalty

In the first setting shown in the left-hand column in the table, Amazon offers Degree value in the form of a higher standing for the business partners in their own market: greater volumes and Amazon as a reference client. In return, the business partners input Degree value in the form of financial might by giving Amazon products (suppliers) or customers (affiliates) from which Amazon can earn a margin, or by paying commissions and fees (third-party sellers and advertisers). In addition, they input their own market standing to Amazon in that they make the Amazon website even more weighty and encompassing, enabling Amazon to maintain its own standing as a leading firm. Thus, the cycle of value exchange is completed in that the business partners and Amazon give each other a higher standing in their respective own business settings.

In the second setting in the second column in the table, Amazon offers Dexterity value in the online retail market via a well-structured business relation: well-defined processes, shaped by clear guidelines and requirements, and informed by Amazon's knowledge of what works best in the online retail market. The business partners input Dexterity value in the form of their knowledge of the online retail market: they structure and shape their products and/or websites on the basis of what they have learned works best in the onine retail market. Amazon benefits in that it can learn from the range of operations executed by the business partners, building up its own market knowledge. Thus, the cycle of value exchange is completed in that Amazon and the business partners each benefit from the others' knowledge in raising sales, as well as in the efficiency and effectiveness of the operations in the working relation.

The third setting for the business partners in the third column of the table is their own daily activities which they conduct in the online interface to Amazon. Amazon offers Deed value based on a platform: the wide-ranging functionality of its website, the online interface for the business partners, and the tools for analyzing the impact of different activities. The business partners are offered the leeway to utilize this platform as they best see fit. But not only that, Amazon provides active support to the business partners by providing tips, ideas, and information targeted at specific, concrete situations in which the business partners find themselves in their selling activities. In return, the business partners input Deed value in that they actually make use of the platform, leeway, tips, and support to optimize their own activities. In this way, Amazon discovers which functionalities and forms of support actually optimize the selling activities of partners. Thus the cycle of value exchange is completed in that Amazon and the business partners both optimize the selling activities of business partners to mutual benefit.

The fourth setting for the business partners in the rightmost column of the table is their vision of how they want to develop as an organization. Amazon offers Delight value in helping develop the business, e.g. move into new kinds of business areas, gain new kinds of capabilities, or address new customer segments. In return, Amazon's business partners input enthusiasm for Amazon and communicate more openly about their visions. This completes the cycle of value exchange: Amazon realizes how its business partners want to develop and accordingly can help them in realizing their visions, which motivates the relationship and binds them tighter to the Amazon organization in a more loyal manner.

Powerfully Coordinated Total Value Offer to Business Partners

In terms of managing the total value offer to business partners, it can be shown that Amazon has oriented the value offers in the different dimensions to supplement one another in a powerfully coordinated manner. The value offers conform to the generic elements of a business partner relationship such that in each element of the overall relationship, Amazon addresses the most pressing requirement of the business partner, as presented in the following.

In Figure 3-2, the relationship to business partners is broken down into three basic elements: the attraction to work with Amazon rather than an alternative retailer; the operations, terms, and conditions of the relationship; and the day-to-day activities of actually conducting the relationship. Regarding the attraction of working with Amazon, presumably the most important consideration for a business partner is the depth and breadth of the contact with shopping customers, as well as the reach and positioning of the online retailer in the retail market. Amongst US online retailers, Amazon will score the highest on these points by virtue of its Degree offer at the primary level for all business partners. In the operations, terms, and conditions of the relationship, Amazon's Dexterity offer places the working relationship on an efficient and effective footing for the business partners. In terms of the daily activities in conducting the relationship by means of the online interface, the Deed offer optimizes the business partners' day-to-day selling activities on or linked to the Amazon website.

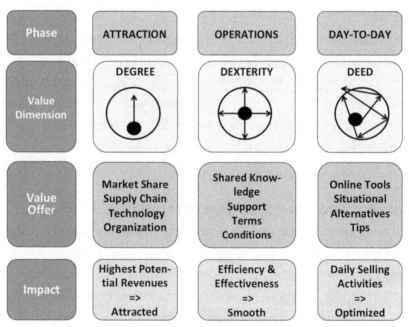

Figure 3-2: Orientation of Amazon's Value Offers
to Business Partner Relation

Value Exchange with Personnel

Amazon has established value offers with competitive advantages on the market—i.e. at the level of primary or secondary value—for shopping customers and business partners in different D's in distinct divisions within the organization. The supply chain operations offer Degree value; the website/online functionality offers Deed value; and the units responsible for the operations, terms, and conditions of the after-sales customer experience offer Dexterity value. In order to offer these kinds of value, the value needs to be generated, i.e. the personnel need to work in a manner aligned to the characteristics of the value dimension. How this is managed is discussed in detail in Part II. Here, the discussion begins by examining how the value exchange with personnel is managed in a distinct manner in each of the different divisions, aligned to the corresponding value dimension. This distinctive value exchange with personnel is summarized in the table below.

Party Type	Value Flow	Primary Degree	Primary Dexterity	Primary Deed	*Basic Delight*
Per-sonnel	Area	Working for career (in logistics) in labor market setting	Working with colleagues (in customer service) in the online retail market setting	Working on own tasks (in website / online) in the setting of employee own activities	*Working in / for firm*
	Offer	Expected career development	Material / Immaterial work conditions	Empowerment	*Professional development*
	Input	Be like an owner	Cooperation and knowledge sharing	Optimize custo-mer's situation	*Identitiy and enthusiasm*

Beginning in the first column in the above table, employees gain value in advancing their standing on the labor market, both while they are at Amazon and afterwards. Amazon offers Degree value to personnel in the form of an elevated compensation package as well as a structured path for career development. In the supply chain operations, a career ladder, attractive compensation, and an excellent reference on the resumé are systematically on offer at the level of primary value. In the rest of the organization, the Degree value offer for career development and compensation has been present in a more generalized form. Employee feedback from outside the supply chain operations shows a balance between the presence and lack of upward mobility, suggesting benefits at the secondary level. Indeed, given the unspoken but apparent policy at Amazon to keep the employment duration limited to no more than two years for the bulk of employees—discussed in the following chapter on MDW 2—several employees advised others to use Amazon as a stepping stone in their career. Turning to the elevated level of compensation throughout the organization, a key part of this has been the shares granted, for which all employees have been eligible. The personal gain from selling shares has formed a substantial part of the employee compensation, as specified in the 1997 Compensation Plan. For an individual employee, the proportion of total compensation arising from share grants is greater the higher the employee is in the hierarchy, reaching to over 90 percent of compensation for the five executive directors.

Early in the second decade of the twenty-first century, it was reported that new hires were given an industry-average salary, a signing bonus spread over two years, and a package of stocks spread over four years: 5 percent at the end of the first year, 15 percent at the end of the second year, and then 20 percent every six months over the final two years. The benefits from the share grants were, however, not evenly distributed amongst employees. Only personnel who had remained four years or more gained the full 100 percent of stocks in the package. There was the perception that a two-tier caste system within Amazon was emerging, where long-time employees had "deep ownership" with a stronger commitment to the culture and regarded themselves a bit like royalty. There is no indication that compensation policies since then have changed significantly.

In return, Amazon employees input primary and secondary value in Degree in the form of being and acting like owners. Owners are interested in raising the standing of the organization in the markets in which the organization is active. It was shown above that Degree value in the supply chain has been crucial to Amazon's ability to attract shopping customers and business partners. Accordingly, the input of functional excellence and other aspects of Degree value takes place at the primary level in the supply chain operations. This point will be pursued throughout Part II, but here the expectation of unrestricted dedication to the firm—normal for an owner—is presented. The best example of this expectation is the work schedules at fulfillment centers. Mandatory overtime is widespread and occurs so often that it has been referred to as a "killer," while the individual work schedules often change abruptly. Indeed, in 1998 and 1999, the input of Degree value in the supply chain became so critical that virtually all employees were required to input this value to the firm. Employees were expected to do whatever was good for the firm, without consideration of what was written in their job descriptions. For one month in 1998 and two weeks in 1999, almost every employee was drafted into shift work in fulfillment centers around the clock to ensure orders were filled before Christmas. The employees were expected to pitch in and follow the instructions coming down from above, while feeling motivated to input Degree value due to their share ownership. As one Area Manager from a fulfillment center wrote, "Not a place for those with no desire to work hard in a fast-paced environment."

The Degree input to be like an owner is more generalized at the secondary level in the rest of the organization. The Compensation Plan for all employees is deliberately weighted to share ownership to align the interests of the personnel with those of the owners. Quoting from the careers website in 2017: "We want Amazon employees to think like owners, and awarding equity provides an ownership opportunity to employees." This policy had been established in the earliest days of the firm. Later, at the time of the IPO, the role of share ownership in steering and forming personnel behavior in the overall interest of the firm and the shareholders was reiterated. "We will continue to focus on hiring and retaining versatile and talented employees, and continue to weight their compensation to stock options rather than cash. We know our success will be largely affected by our ability to attract and retain a motivated employee base, each of whom must think like, and therefore must actually be, an owner." The 2018 Proxy Statement repeated once again the conviction that this is the most suitable compensation model to align the interests of employees and shareholders.

An additional aspect of being like an owner is that all employees need to recognize that costs reduce profits. A clearly communicated leadership principle at Amazon is: "Frugality. We try not to spend money on things that don't matter to customers. Frugality breeds resourcefulness, self-sufficiency and invention." Personnel have needed to accept material working and employment conditions that in certain respects dip below the industry average. Furthermore, unrestricted dedication is also expected from all employees. One employee said, "Life just stopped. You were stuck in amber. But inside that amber was frenetic activity that no one else could see." Putting a more positive slant on the time to be spent at work at Amazon, Jeff Bezos himself sees work and private life as integrated parts of one circle which are reciprocal. For him, the notion of a work-life balance is counterproductive because it implies a strict separation. One should be happy at home and at work, implying that counting the hours on the job is irrelevant. Continuing, being and acting like an owner has involved accepting that an owner expects nothing less than the best. Often employees are asked to soldier on with little in the way of positive feedback; indeed, with the awareness that they could be terminated at any time. One observer reported, "Many Amazon employees live in perpetual fear. Good performance reviews are rare. Employees spend their days anticipating their termination. There are few perks or unexpected performance bonuses."

The Degree input from personnel raises the standing of Amazon on the markets where it is active, including the retail market in general, the capital market, and the labor market. Thus, the cycle of value exchange in Degree is completed in that Amazon can offer an elevated standing in the labor market by virtue of its elevated standing in all markets.

Moving to the second column in the table above, Amazon employees conduct their work in the online retail market. Relevant and prevailing in this market are certain working conditions as well as certain knowledge about performing the work which will meet the demands of the market. Indeed, for a firm to offer the most appropriate working conditions can also be regarded as a matter of knowledge: knowledge of which working conditions strike the right balance between what works well for the personnel in conducting the work and what works well for the firm in being successful on the market.

It was shown above that Amazon's Dexterity offer to shopping customers is crucial to keep them from being disappointed. Dexterity benefits are offered at the level of primary value in the call centers and other organizational units active in after-sales customer service as follows. The workplace ambience is to the liking of quite a few employees, with upbeat attitudes and a relaxed, even fun, atmosphere. The physical facilities and team events are also positively viewed. The relationship to colleagues is friendly, but, more importantly, there is a remarkably high level of helping and sharing of knowledge. Training and technical support are praiseworthy. One employee summed it up with regard to Dexterity value by remarking that the "company really cares about their employees." Further in this regard, a number of employees gushed that in the balance of pros and cons in commenting on work at Amazon, there were no cons.

In the rest of the organization, there is a generalized offer of Dexterity value. At Amazon, the team and teamwork form the basis for working conditions throughout the entire firm, and on the whole, this is regarded as a positive aspect of working at Amazon. Generalized Dexterity value is also offered via the generous minimum wage which was raised to $15 per hour in 2018, as well as the level of benefits, praised by many employees. More broadly speaking, Amazon offers employment conditions which are a benefit to the wider society such that the firm contributes to the local community. For example, Amazon runs initiatives and programs which aid and support the integration of veterans into Amazon. In 2017, Amazon pledged a commitment to the Seattle community by continuing to locate corporate headquarters in the city. This involves contributing yet more workplaces to the metropolitan area. In addition, the future corporate headquarters are intended to offer an office infrastructure and working conditions at a level above market average, a benefit to all employees at the vast headquarters. Finally, the almost desperate eagerness with which 200 cities in the US made their pitch in 2017 and 2018 to be additional headquarter locations for Amazon is an indication of the esteem with which communities regard employment conditions at Amazon.

In return, Amazon employees input strong value in Dexterity, and in after-sales customer service, at the primary level. As noted above, the Dexterity value offered to shopping customers is that they are not disappointed and thus remain loyal. Critical to achieving this customer satisfaction is for the customer service associate (CSA) to treat the customer in such a way that the customer is satisfied with the overall service from Amazon. This involves resolving the customer issue as best as possible—even if the source of the problem is a third-party seller or a logistics provider beyond the direct control of Amazon—while always being competent and friendly. Even when the CSA cannot solve the problem which the customer is complaining about, the CSA is expected to make the customer satisfied with the customer experience at Amazon. After a call, customers are sent a quick survey to rate whether the CSA made them satisfied; this is the key performance metric in evaluating each CSA. CSAs typically complain that they are being measured on aspects of the customer relation which they cannot influence or control, yet it is this customer satisfaction which they are required to achieve because it is critical to Amazon's success.

Furthermore, CSAs handle customers in all their moods and attitudes, which can be psychologically demanding. CSAs have to meet productivity requirements regarding the number of calls handled per hour. They can take no more than a two-minute break between calls, which in fact is not always a break but typically includes finishing off the mail which is part of dealing with the call from the last customer; that is, the mail should start being written already during the call. CSA staff cannot take vacation during the peak sales time, i.e. October-January, and have to work on many national holidays. Finally, customer service employees input team spirit, collegiality, knowledge sharing, and friendly support to one another, as discussed above regarding the Dexterity offer.

In the remainder of the organization, Amazon employees on the whole input Dexterity value at the secondary level in two ways. First, the employees generally exercise a kind of solidarity and team spirit, making for, on the whole, a positive relationship with work colleagues. Second, Amazon personnel are generally able and willing to share knowledge with other Amazon employees. Thus, the Dexterity inputs at the secondary level generate positive working conditions in the firm, which serve as a constructive foundation for motivating and enhancing the work performed at Amazon.

The Dexterity input of Amazon personnel is to apply knowledge such that market requirements—in particular, customer satisfaction with Amazon's level of service, and, more generally, that Amazon's offers are to some extent consistent and coordinated—are fulfilled. In fulfilling these market requirements, Amazon builds its knowledge of how to structure and steer the personnel inputs to achieve this market objective by means of the working conditions. Thus, the cycle of value exchange in Dexterity is completed in that Amazon is able to offer suitable working conditions due to the knowledgeable inputs of the personnel.

Moving to the third column in the table above, Amazon employees take on work tasks—on their own initiative, as part of being a team member or part of a process, on the basis of an assignment, as a consequence of a directive or an instruction, etc.—in the context of performing their own activities. Regarding these tasks, Amazon offers primary value in Deed to all personnel in the form of empowerment: on the one hand, the availability of large-scale, high-quality organizational resources as a platform to support what the personnel do, on the other hand, considerable individual leeway in performing the work. In particular, employees with non-routine work are free to assess each individual situation in their own way and proceed with the solution that they think best fits to the specific requirements of the given situation. Comments from employees indicate that many managers and specialists enjoy autonomy and freedom in defining their role and leading their team as they see fit.

Technical specialists experience this combination of individual leeway and organizational resources at two levels. First, for a select—or lucky—few, employment at Amazon holds open the opportunity for a simple idea to be turned into a monumental business mover, drawing on and shaping huge amounts of Amazon's resources. For example, 1-Click came out of a luncheon conversation in 1997 with Jeff Bezos, the CIO, and a new programmer; the basics for the personalization on the website were developed by one programmer in two weeks; a programmer came up with his own idea to search for books in a cache rather than in the live inventory list; and in August 2014, an operations specialist joined in discussions about how to shorten delivery times and developed an idea for rushing goods to urban customers in an hour or less. One hundred and eleven days later, she was directing the start of the new service, Prime Now. In other cases, leading technical specialists were attracted to work at Amazon by the offer to shape and define the entire new industry of online retail, or so they and Amazon thought. Second, beyond this handful of high-profile success stories, the opportunity to work with a wide scope of impact in new areas means that many Amazon personnel gain a great deal of experience very quickly and intensively. One software engineer wrote, "Amazing place to learn, accelerate your growth as an engineer or leader, and to build products that are used by thousands of customers." An operations manager points out, "The days are long, schedules are not conventional, and you will have to put in the work to get recognized! But if you are willing to put that aside and not make excuses, you will reap many rewards and grow exponentially." Bezos wanted a de-centralized organization where people could come up with independent ideas rather than subscribe to group-think.

At Amazon, there is room for individual leeway even in routine work. For example, the rigorous safety rules in a fulfillment center include the requirement to announce one's presence with the cart at every intersection of the aisles. One employee chooses to fulfill this requirement by singing, thereby making his time at Amazon "joyful and fun." An observer remarks on another employee with a flamboyant appearance and idiosyncratic movements in packing boxes, unbowed by the formal rules and programmed machines. Comments from workers at fulfillment centers have highlighted the scope for autonomy and independence on the job, in the sense of being able to take out of the job what they put into it. The individual leeway in the Deed offer to non-managerial employees includes work that the employee can individually adjust to his or her other priorities, interests, or demands in life, as shown in the following examples. Fulfillment centers offer a variety of shifts, e.g. for those who want to be free during the day, some couriers have freedom to choose when they do delivery work; and in the Virtual Contact Center, CSA employees provide customer service support while working from home. The flexibility to work at home is ideal for many employees who, perhaps because they have young children or for another reason, either cannot or prefer not to work outside the home. The Virtual Contact Center was Amazon's fastest growing "site" in the US in 2013, operating in more than ten states. Finally, the Leave Share program lets employees share their Amazon paid leave with their spouse or domestic partner if their spouse's employer doesn't offer paid leave, and Ramp Back gives birth mothers additional control over the pace at which they return to work.

Working in this Deed manner, the individual can express himself or herself in the work, which can be enrapturing for the employee. Employees working in various divisions in the headquarters can get completely caught up in the work and have it come to absorb the entirety of their life, sometimes being likened to an addiction. Another employee felt that working at Amazon was like receiving a present: "I personally consider or see Amazon as a wrapped gift containing its own little yet large world filled with possibilities waiting to be discovered by the ones hungry enough."

Bezos' pithy description of work at Amazon, which for him served as the shorthand pitch to attract personnel—"work hard, have fun, make history"— can be interpreted as fundamentally oriented to the offer of Deed value. Individuals work hard on their assignments because they are empowered, and thus individually stimulated and engrossed; the individual stimulation is perceived as positive and takes on the character of fun because one can exercise leeway on the job and employees could see their work as related to the series of ground-breaking innovations at the firm.

In return, Amazon personnel input primary Deed value in that they exercise their empowerment to optimize the situation of their customers, both internal and external customers. One employee sees it as positive that there is the expectation of "Helping customers receive products as quickly and efficiently as possible." Amazon employees methodically utilize their individual, in-depth understanding of the particulars of a given situation to systematically—throughout the organization and throughout the history of the firm—come up with a solution which is optimal for the customer. A product manager at headquarters describes the job as "Working with smart, hard-working people who's top objective is satisfying our customer." The innovations, the exercise of a managerial role, even the performance of routine work when the work schedule fits to an individual's lifestyle, are carried out with an extra zest and extra attention to the individual customer situation. Further to this point, Amazon employees often remark on how working for the firm drives them to drive themselves. "Once you have become a true Amazonian other roles outside of the company seem boring and uninteresting," explains a product manager. Another writes, "gives you ton of autonomy and ownership; work life balance is most self-directed, not micromanaged, face time doesn't matter," and a third states, "work-life balance is not easy to maintain. There's something about the work that makes you want to put in fifteen hours a day. There's no external pressure to work long hours but endless opportunities make employees extra ambitious. So the pressure is coming from the inside." The self-initiative carries over to an inner drive to improve the work of others. One specialist explains the atmosphere of giving feedback to others as, "There's no reward for not speaking up. 'Good backbone' is a compliment. It's a very seductive quality about the organization because people want to contribute."

The value exchange—offers and inputs—in the Deed dimension has been most prominent amongst personnel working on the website and other aspects of the online interface to shopping customers, e.g. the product managers, software engineers, and generally the personnel in the headquarters. The prominence of the value exchange in Deed with these employees can be related to the primary value in Deed offered by the website and online interface to shopping customers. That is, the personnel in this business area have received a strong dose of Deed value, such that they could generate a distinctive Deed value for the users of their website/online interface. The Deed value on the website was critical to Amazon's ability to fulfill customers' shopping missions, which are situational. The leeway of the involved personnel was a kind of enabler for them to generate value which could be optimized for different shopping missions. This point is further pursued in the remaining chapters of Part II.

The Deed input of performing work tasks—exercising leeway in utilizing the platform of Amazon resources to meet customer requirements—to optimize the customer situation enables these employees to gain experience in working this way, and thus be able to do it even better in the future. Furthermore, employees also "gain experience" indirectly via observation of what others are doing and can thus perform their tasks even better. Amazon management also observe how the tasks are performed, and thus design the platform and allow for leeway—i.e. manage the empowerment offer— in order to support this kind of task performance. Thus, the cycle of value exchange in Deed is completed in that the inputs of exercising leeway in the tasks form the basis of shaping the offers of empowerment.

Moving now to the rightmost column in the table above, in their professional being, the employees gain value from developing themselves towards their personal vision of gaining new technical expertise, moving to different departments within the firm, discovering and cultivating talents in themselves they never knew existed, and so forth. Amazon has offered basic value in Delight to employees in the form of the self-realization of a vision of who they are and/or want to become as professionals. At the turn of the second decade of the twenty-first century, a researcher noted that "former Amazon employees often consider their time at the company the most productive of their careers ... frequent lateral movement between departments offered constant opportunities for learning ... The pace of innovation is thrilling." Recently, it was remarked of Amazon employees that "some said they thrived at Amazon precisely because it pushed them past what they thought were their limits." Realistically, however, such attitudes were almost only to be found at the headquarters, and there only among a minority. Thus, Delight benefits have been offered at Amazon, but not in a widespread nor systematic manner. Amazon did not institute programs or policies, nor did management regularly communicate with employees, to underscore the offer of Delight value to personnel.

In return, employees input basic value in Delight to Amazon by participating in the collective life of the firm. Employees identify with the firm and work with enthusiasm at the basic level.

The Delight inputs take place under limited circumstances in the organization and workplace. Amazon management can observe these circumstances and use these observations to guide them in designing the Delight offers. Thus, the cycle of value exchange is completed in that the circumstances which lead to the Delight inputs of identification and enthusiasm can be recognized and then made the basis of the Delight offers.

On balance, regarding the value exchange with employees, there is a great diversity in the nature of the value exchanged with individual employees, i.e. the work experience at Amazon varies greatly from person to person. One employee comment on glassdoor.com gives the flavor of what many others wrote: "I have read through some of the other Amazon reviews and it seems to me that everyone has a very different experience! This is so true. Within the same team, you can have both workaholics and slackers coexisting and coworking together. I think I am more of the balanced type as I try to stay sane. The Amazon experience is basically the entire spectrum and it is what you make it out to be." Some ex-Amazon employees said they were protected from pressures by nurturing bosses or worked in slow divisions. This wide range of experiences suggests an overall Deed dimension of value in the relations to personnel, where individual managers have much leeway to shape the work environment in their teams.

In the Deed dimension, employees work in a series of one-off situations requiring initiative from each employee. In the Degree dimension, employees strive for themselves to climb up the ladder. Thus, the Degree and Deed inputs drive the organization forward. In contrast to these two rather individualistic inputs, the Dexterity input to cooperate and share knowledge and the collective Delight identity are the glue that hold the organization together. The employee engagement in cooperation with others is the underlying fundament for Amazon employees to work in the collective, both within the team and between teams. Thus, there is a certain consistency and coordination in the firm's functioning and in its outputs.

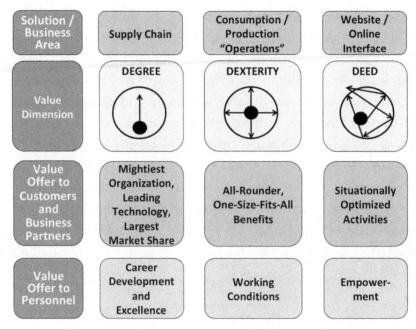

Figure 3-3: Offers to Personnel Aligned with Offers to
Customers and Business Partners

The key elements of the offers to personnel are aligned with the offers to customers and business partners. The offers to personnel are designed so that the personnel generate the appropriate value for these key parties. How the appropriate value in a given D is generated is introduced here and continued in the remaining chapters of Part II. Figure 3-3 summarizes the alignment in the value offers to customers, business partners, and personnel. The Degree offer to personnel—principally in the supply chain—of career development and excellence enables Amazon to offer to shopping customers and business partners the relation to a mighty organization, with leading market share, technology, logistics, etc. The Dexterity offer to personnel—principally in the organizational units concerned with customer experience as well as, presumably, business partner experience—of leading working conditions enables Amazon to offer shopping customers and business partners high quality in their "operations." The working conditions which emphasize knowledge sharing, teamwork, training, and respect enable the personnel to generate value marked by knowledge of the features and processes of their organization, understanding for the requirements of the shopping customers and business partners, and respect for their wishes. The Deed offer to personnel—principally in the organizational units concerned with the website and the online functionality—of empowerment around a platform and individual leeway enable the personnel to generate value by empowering shopping customers and business customers in an analogous manner.

In sum, the value offers to three key sets of parties—shopping customers, business partners, and personnel—are closely aligned with one another. The alignment enables Amazon to offer very convincing value in the D's to the parties, thereby setting the basis for Amazon to be successful in relations to all three. This in turn is the fundament for Amazon's extraordinary business success.

Targeted Primary Value Exchange with Parties

Amazon exchanges primary value with parties other than shopping customers and business partners in four dimensions, varying according to the party. It seems that Amazon targeted the value exchange with a given party in the dimension which makes the most impact on the party and which provides the greatest benefit to Amazon, as will be discussed below. The table below shows the offers in primary value to reviewers, authors, AWS customers, developers, and investors. The corresponding inputs are implied by the nature of the offer.

	Degree	Dexterity	Deed	Delight
Area	Market	Operations	Online	Development
Reviewers	Status	Guidelines and tips	Platform and leeway for writing reviews	Contribute to others and / or to community
Other party types	**Authors** Sales and prestige	**AWS Customers** One-size-fits-all functionalities	**Developers** Support to optimize online practice	**Investors** Growth stock for long-term investors

Reviewers may well be the unsung heroes for Amazon. It is impossible to quantify the contribution of different parties to the success of Amazon, but it may be suggested that the reviewers give Amazon a decisive advantage over rivals. The quantity and quality of the reviews they input are critical at the level of primary value to Amazon's corresponding offers to shoppers and, derived therefrom, to business customers. In particular, of all the inputs from parties, Amazon exercises the least influence over the inputs from reviewers, because there is in fact no contractual relationship or transaction to manage. Given this perspective on reviewers, it is perhaps not surprising that Amazon "spoils" them with an offer of primary value in all four dimensions. Reviewers are accorded a status in Degree relative to other reviewers, benefit from helpful guidelines and tips in Dexterity, enjoy the Deed leeway in building their own profile and style on the platform of Amazon's website, and gain Delight fulfillment from contributing to the consuming joy of shoppers and the community of reviewers. They are not paid and yet are critical to the success of the firm; Amazon bends over backwards, as it were, to offer them broad-based and far-reaching value in an immaterial sense. Although immaterial, the value offered is nevertheless highly structured and managed as thoroughly as possible.

Authors have the most to gain from Amazon simply as a retail channel for their books, and Amazon gains the most from authors in that their success translates into Amazon's sales. Thus, the primary exchange takes place in the Degree terms of sales on the market for books.

The market for AWS services is still young; with respect to this lack of maturity, the offers from Amazon and its rivals on the market are not yet strongly differentiated. Thus, it makes sense for Amazon to generate an all-around, one-size-fits-all offer in Dexterity in order to gain the greatest market share at this stage in the market/product life cycle. Correspondingly, Amazon is eager to learn more about this relatively new market, where the customers themselves are just finding out what it is that they want. For Amazon, it is crucial to keep apace with the customers regarding the trends and developments in demand as they appear. Thus, the Dexterity input of market knowledge from these parties is most valuable to the firm.

Developers know their apps and the benefits therefrom; how they want to profit from Amazon is largely related to what to do with their apps in the business area of distribution. They seek from Amazon Deed value regarding convenience and support in first, designing and implementing in their apps the interface to the appropriate page(s) on the Amazon website, and second, making their apps available in the appropriate distribution channel(s). Developers are best served in the "doing" in relation to the Amazon website and the other online interfaces of the firm. In return, when the developers optimize their online practices in relation to Amazon, Amazon gains the Deed input of its own website and online interface being optimized on the market.

Regarding investors, from the start Amazon was oriented to the long haul: jump-step innovations to shape the future of online retail which would take a long time to reach fruition. Such innovations by their nature involve missteps along the way, while holding out the prospect of returns well above the average—but only in the long term. Thus, the business approach of Amazon depends upon investors who can stump up significant sums of finance, and then be willing to wait a long time for their return. That is, Amazon has been dependent upon the long-term capital inputs of Delight investors at the primary level, and accordingly, has needed to offer primary Delight value to them in the form of a growth stock.

Summary of value exchange in MDW 1

This section presents a summary of the essence of Amazon's value exchange across party types, i.e. the common denominator in the value offered to each party in each D, and the common denominator in the value input from each party in each D. A detailed presentation of MDW 1 the value exchange between Amazon and each party type is available for download on www. dimensions-of-value.com. The essence is summarized in the table below.

Party Type	Value Flow	Degree	Dexterity	Deed	Delight
Across party types	Area	**Business / Societal Setting** of party	**Online Retail Market** in which party participates	**Online / Interface** of party daily activities	**Being** of party
	Offer	Standing	All-Rounder	Empowerment	Development
	Input	Reputation and stock of resources	Market knowledge	Optimize party situation	Identification and enthusiasm

In the Degree dimension, shown in the first column of the table above, each party type conducts a relationship with Amazon in the context of a broad setting in which the party is positioned: societal for shopping customers and reviewers, business for the others. Amazon offers each party type the benefits of an elevated standing in their own setting due to the relationship to the firm with the leader position. In return, each party type inputs a stock of resources to Amazon plus their reputation, the latter either singly as regarding well-known authors, named AWS customers, as well as the highly-regarded investors, such as Vanguard Group, BlackRock, and Jeff Bezos, or collectively in the dominant market share enjoyed by Amazon with respect to the mass of shopping customers, business partners, authors, and reviewers. The mass of inputs boost Amazon's standing, and the firm is then able to offer an elevated standing to any party, completing the cycle of value exchange.

In the Dexterity dimension, shown in the second column in the table above, Amazon offers each party all-around benefits in executing their "operations" as related to the online retail market. In executing these "operations," each party seeks value in being able to cover the generic market requirements established for online retail, indeed requirements which Amazon may well have significantly shaped. Parties in return input market knowledge to Amazon in the form of Big Data and other feedback regarding their preferences and behaviors. The cycle of value exchange is completed in that Amazon utilizes this market knowledge to fine-tune its own offers and stay on top of generic requirements for one-size-fits-all benefits.

In the Deed dimension, presented in the third column of the table above, parties perform activities in the online interface to Amazon, principally the website but also the smart devices. Parties are empowered in this interface in two ways. First, the online interface constitutes a huge and rich platform which the party can utilize as the party best sees fit. Second, in utilizing the platform, the party is supported with tools and information regarding how best to make use of the platform, and they are accorded the leeway to decide for themselves how to do this. In return, the parties utilize the platform and the leeway to optimize their concrete situation each time they enter into the online interface to Amazon. In optimizing their own concrete situation, they input value to Amazon in the form of sales, product information, customer loyalty, finance for organizational development, and so on. The collective inputs of the parties in utilizing the platform and exercising their leeway builds an inventory of activities. These mass inputs create the backdrop on which Amazon is able to offer to each party the opportunity to situate itself in a unique and individual manner, thereby completing the cycle of value exchange.

In the Delight dimension, shown in the rightmost column of the table above, the parties have a being—i.e. an existence—as a party to Amazon: shoppers are consumers, business partners are businesses, reviewers are reviewers, and so forth. The Delight offer from Amazon enables them to develop themselves further towards realizing a fuller and richer vision of themselves. This development takes place together with others, where the "others" can include the contact persons at Amazon or a community. Parties then input an identification with and enthusiasm for the relation to Amazon. This commitment serves as part of the basis for Amazon to be able to offer parties the means to develop themselves: the cycle of value exchange is completed.

Taking stock

A picture emerges of Amazon as a highly complex and diverse organization, operating in distinctly different ways in different markets and business areas. Behind this complexity, respectively the reason for the complexity, is a thoroughly coherent and comprehensive attention to the specific needs and requirements of different parties. Amazon is remarkable for being able to, first, understand the particular needs and requirements of different parties in their own terms, and second, translate this understanding into a convincing, targeted offer. Hand-in-hand with the understanding for the parties goes an equally coherent and comprehensive attention to understanding exactly the kinds of inputs which Amazon needs from parties in order to make the offers. As open as Amazon is to offering parties exactly what they want, it is equally demanding in requiring inputs which exactly meet the firm's specifications. With this strict attention to detail, Amazon as a firm draws a clear line between what it wants or is prepared to do, and what it does not want or is not prepared to do.

These demarcations and boundaries in the value exchanges on the market are reflected within the organization as well. There are distinctly different organizational behaviors in different parts of the organization: there is no "Amazon" but rather "Amazons." The consequence of this is that any one party experiences Amazon in a particular way; there are also multiple "Amazons" as perceived by different parties, and not one unified firm managing relationships uniformly.

There is a great diversity in the types of parties with whom Amazon manages relations, much greater than any other online retailer. Amazon even makes a success out of managing relations to competitors: third-party sellers and advertising customers. Without pre-conceived notions of what belongs to its business and what does not, the firm has identified who are the players in the business areas where it is active and defined value exchanges with the parties to mutual benefit.

It is interesting to note a certain dichotomy in the B2C versus B2B relations at Amazon. To a large extent, Amazon manages the diversity of shopping customers by treating them more or less the same, where the framework of this sameness in fact allows for many options and choices which the customers can choose, i.e. they manage their own diversity. Amazon manages the diversity of business parties, including business partners, authors, AWS customers, developers, and investors by treating them each in a specific, distinctive manner; they are channeled into a specific way of behaving. B2C is homogeneous but with choice and B2B is heterogeneous but with channeling. Personnel are channeled into one of three ways of behaving, depending on the organizational unit, linked by one underlying mode of organizational behavior in Deed.

MDW 1 Managing Value Exchanges at Amazon is characterized by extraordinary depth—intensive value offers and inputs with primary value in up to four dimensions—and breadth with a huge range of parties. In this way, Amazon is able to score very highly on Markets Value Factor 1. Indeed, the firm is in a category by itself in terms of the depth and breadth of its value exchanges.

The value exchanges represent the specific, concrete, and day-to-day transactions in the relationships which Amazon maintains with parties. These specific transactions are managed within the framework of an overall approach to the market presence and positioning. This overall approach is MDW 2: managing External Demand Interfaces, the topic of the next chapter.

| Chapter 4 |

MDW 2: Managing External Demand Interfaces

Markets Value Factor 2	Managerial Do-Well 2
The greater the number of parties with preferences in the D's in which the firm is strong	Manage demand interfaces to shift party preferences to the firm's strong D's

M arkets Value Factor 2 evaluates the weight of the party preferences addressed by the firm with its strong D's: the higher the proportion of parties with the strongest preferences in the D's in which a firm offers primary or secondary value, the greater the market success of the firm. For a firm to score well on MVF 2, it could have had luck or it could have exercised market knowledge and foresight in choosing strong D's in dimensions which were or were going to be the weightiest in the market. Managerial Do-Well 2 involves a third possibility, namely that the firm's offer in its strong D's was so convincing that it shifted the preferences of a high proportion of parties to those value dimensions. MDW 2 examines the demand interfaces of the firm to its parties.

Markets Value Factor 2 thus builds on MVF 1 to evaluate not simply how many strong dimensions a firm has, but which; is the firm operating in the most or least promising D's in the market? Managerial Do-Well 2 analogously builds on MDW 1 by considering the background to the value exchange between the firm and its parties; how has the firm influenced the preferences of the parties or how has it moved the party to prefer the strong D's of the firm? MDW 1 examines the terms of the value exchange and MDW 2 considers the background to this transaction which the party has entered into. MDW 2, if one will, may be considered akin to the marketing activities of the firm, where marketing is to be understood in its broadest sense.

The Parameters of MDW 2

The demand interfaces to parties are constituted by five parameters in the firm's activities. The five parameters are on the face of it commonplace in the management literature, and indeed in business thinking. The five parameters, however, take on particular definitions and impacts in the context of Managerial Do-Well 2, as shown in Figure 4-1. At the center of the Figure are party preferences, which from the perspective of a firm seeking to influence them can be divided into three categories: party preferences which are weighted to D's in which the firm is not strong, party preferences which are weighted to D's in which the firm is strong, and party preferences which have, in fact, led the parties to enter into a relation with the firm, i.e. to become one of the firm's parties. Success for a firm regarding MDW 2 is shifting party preferences towards the D's in which it is strong, i.e. as a result of such shifts, the firm will score higher on MDW 2 because the pool of potential parties for the firm becomes larger. Failure is when party preferences shift away from the firm's strong D's, i.e. the firm will score lower on MDW 2 because the pool of potential parties for the firm becomes smaller. The preferences of parties are formed and expressed in three contexts: the society in which they live; the market in which they participate as customer, worker, or investor; and the firm with which they have chosen to enter into a relation as customer, worker, or investor. Firms address parties in these three contexts, where different parameters of the external interface impact a different context or contexts, as presented in the following discussion.

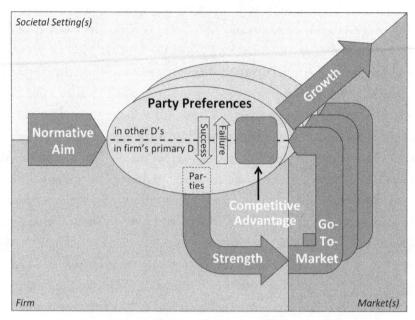

Figure 4-1: MDW 2 Party-Shifting Strong Value

The Normative Aim addresses societal needs and generates societal benefits in the societal setting(s) in which the firm operates. The societal setting for a firm can be global, individual continents or countries, regions within the country where the firm is most prominent, communities where the firm's operations are located, or the segments within the population which the firm targets. The Normative Aim is an overarching objective which goes beyond single initiatives or ventures to give a unifying rationale to the firm's activities—both business activities, as well as activities not primarily associated with business—with respect to the circumstance that the firm is part of the societal setting. The benefits therefrom arise principally from the business activities of the firm, but as well stem from flanking activities which are part of what is often termed Sustainability or Corporate Societal Responsibility. The Normative Aim demonstrates to parties in the societal setting how the strong D's of the firm generate societal benefits: The primary and secondary value dimensions of the firm are a "good thing" and therefore parties should place a greater weight in their preferences on these D's.

The Normative Aim also addresses a set of parties in the societal setting which are crucial to the firm: namely the firm's parties. The Normative Aim shows the firm's parties that the strong D's of the firm are good for society in general and for the other parties to the firm in particular. Thus, the Normative Aim generates value for the firm's parties to the extent that they value being associated with a firm which generates benefits for society, as well as for their colleagues or contacts at the firm. The Normative Aim thus is managed to motivate firm parties in generating the strong D values. The Normative Aim also serves as a steering function for the firm's parties, establishing guidelines for how to generate these kinds of benefits for society and for other parties. The Normative Aim informs the firm's parties how to think, behave, and decide in order to generate such benefits in the strong D's of the firm. The Normative Aim thus addresses the firm's parties in a double role as members of the societal setting and as parties of the firm. It forms the fundament for the solidarity between parties and the society, as well as amongst parties.

The managerial challenge of the Normative Aim is to find societal benefits which not only motivate and steer parties in solidarity, but also serve as the basis for a Strength of the firm which supports market success.

Strength is the Normative Aim translated into the internal operations of the firm, converting the normative societal benefits into the source of the firm's value offer on markets. The strong D's which are convincing to parties in the societal context become, in the context of the market, the basis for the value offer which will successfully attract parties to the firm. Although Strength is ultimately aimed at the market, it is managed entirely in the internal context of the firm. The activities are concrete and able to be grasped in the everyday work routines, and the results are readily measured and evaluated in terms of the direct and immediate daily tasks. The Strength is the value-generating essence of the internal operations. Strength is thus the pivotal parameter in the firm's external interface, the only one linked to all three contexts: derived from societal benefits, managed in the firm, and oriented to market offers. Strength is therefore the slippery aspect of the external interface for the firm: it is a challenge to keep the right balance between the three contexts for parties and not let one context dominate party behavior.

The Go-To-Market model is how the firm converts the Strength into a value offer on the market. It is the vehicle for the Strength to address market requirements and the mechanism to work the market: how the Strength is concretely expressed, communicated, and positioned on the market. The Go-To-Market model is a Janus head, with one face to the internal operations of the firm and one to the external requirements of the market. It forms the crossover from the context of the firm to the context of the market. The Go-To-Market model adjusts both sides of the Janus head to fit them together, influencing market requirements towards the firm's strong D's and re-shaping the firm's value offer to better meet market requirements.

The two perspectives of the Janus head are entirely in the world of the management. The internal operations of the firm are immediately familiar to management. The market perspective considers the features of the firm's value offer relative to those of the rivals. Both perspectives represent what management directly sees and perceives, can react to, and shapes. The perspectives are palpable and can be readily grasped, indeed often measured. Simply said, the Go-To-Market model is a realm that managers can manage, which cannot be said of the fourth parameter in the external interface.

The Competitive Advantage addresses party preferences and is the parameter in the external interface which convinces parties to shift their preferences in favor of the firm's strong D's. The Competitive Advantage addresses the parties in their own terms: the benefits they gain from the market offer. The perceived benefits are the basis on which parties perceive, think, decide, and act when adjusting the weights of their preferences or not.

The Competitive Advantage exists in the world of the parties: the benefits they perceive and their preferences regarding these benefits. It is outside the confines of the firm, and thus not directly manageable by the firm. The Competitive Advantage thus includes an element of uncertainty which the firm needs to address. The challenge of managing the Competitive Advantage is made easier for management because it is supported by the Normative Aim. The societal benefit is aligned with the party benefit, thereby reinforcing the benefit perceived by parties.

Thus, the Competitive Advantage links up with the Normative Aim. In this way, the four parameters of the external interface examined to this point—Normative Aim, Strength, Go-To-Market model, and Competitive Advantage—form a closed loop where each parameter is aligned with and supports the others.

Growth is the logic of expanding the closed loop of the four external parameters onto new markets. It constitutes the firm's development path in expanding the organization and the markets in which it is active. Although concerned with all four external parameters, Growth focuses principally on the Go-To-Market model as the vehicle to expand its value offers onto new markets. Growth functions in both the context of markets, as well as of societal settings: when growing, the firm moves into new markets and, at the same time, into the new societal settings in which the new markets are couched.

The subject of this book is value exchanged in market transactions. MDW 2 is about how firms manage demand in the markets where they are active.

In principle, a firm manages external demand interfaces to all the markets where it is active. This chapter will focus on Amazon's managerial practices in MDW 2 with respect to customer markets, as summarized in Figure 4-2. This focus is for purposes of simplicity as well as primacy: the interfaces to customers inform and shape the interfaces to all other markets and parties. MDW 2 at Amazon will be examined by considering each dimension of value on its own, with a brief, consolidated overview to close the chapter.

	Primary Degree	Primary Dexterity	Primary Deed	*Basic Delight*
Area **Mgmt. Element**	Customer as member of society	Customer as online retail market participant	Customer as shopper	*Customer as consuming person*
Normative Aim	Firm as Purpose: Leader of Internet / Technology Business Enterprise (Mission)	Firm as Function: Meet Explicit Needs of Market and Society (Values)	Firm as Enabler: Support Parties to Be the Master of Daily Activities (Goals)	*Firm as Creator: Give Everyone a Piece of the Good Life (Vision)*
Strength	Build Best of Class in the Organization	Standardized Processes	Initiative and Agility	*Realizing Modular Packages*
Go-To-Market Model	Positioned Resources	Continuous Improvement	Match Technical and Party Dynamic in "Doing"	*Address and Steer Latent Demand*
Competitive Advantage	Size	Standardized Services	Emerging Needs	*Individualistic Mass Appeal*
Growth	Extensive	Market Potential	One-Offs	*Intensive*
Summary / Essence	Best of Class in the Organization	Continuous Improvement in Standards	Operational Solutions for Situational Needs	*Holistic Solutions Uniting Opposites*

Figure 4-2: MDW 2: External Demand Interfaces of Amazon

MDW 2 at Amazon in Degree at the primary level

Amazon's Normative Aim in Degree is to be a leader of business enterprise in the internet/technology sector in two senses. First, and most significantly, the organization is to be a leader in size and scope. The Amazon river is substantially larger than any other river and, from the beginning, the firm had a grandiose perspective that it would one day sell everything. Amazon's current logo shows a curved arrow going from "a" to "z": the firm is willing to deliver everything to everyone. As formulated by an employee, "Amazon. com is a true dominator in its endeavors. Being a part of the history making behemoth is rewarding." And the firm has by no means come to the end of the expansion in its size and scope. Many employees are motivated by "thinking big and knowing that we haven't scratched the surface on what's out there to invent," as one employee put it. Second, Amazon takes on the mantle of being a thought leader regarding business excellence. Jeff Bezos has been quoted on hundreds of occasions regarding his views on how to be successful in business. And Amazon is seen on the forefront in innovation. One employee described being involved with "cutting edge technology and insight into the future of retailing and data storage."

The societal benefits of leading size, technology, and business enterprise translated readily into Amazon's Strength in Degree: to build Best of Class in the organization. Building Best of Class in the organization firstly took the form of hiring top managers with experience from leading companies in retail (Walmart), book retail (Barnes & Noble), software (Microsoft), corporate management (PepsiCo), and financial management (General Electric). In logistics, Amazon has pursued a dual policy of integrating Best of Class capabilities from outside (e.g. the insights from an MIT professor in supply chain management in 2001 and the robots from the firm Kiva Systems acquired in 2012) while building internal expertise (e.g. software to steer the fulfillment of orders, as well as large scale supply chain planning, is market-leading and developed in-house without vendor software). Already in 2003, Amazon could fill an order within as little as four hours when the industry average was twelve hours. In 2014, Amazon had 18,000 robots at work in fulfillment centers around the world, enabling a worker to complete up to three times as many orders as previously. In 2018, Amazon reported that the automation capabilities in the fulfillment centers drawn from Kiva Systems enable the firm to reduce the time between order and shipment from sixty to seventy-five minutes down to fifteen minutes.

Finally, building Best of Class in the Amazon organization also involved hiring ever brighter and smarter individuals. The idea was to raise the bar with each new employee, such that after five years an employee should think, "I'm glad I get hired when I did, because now I would not qualify." Employees often say their co-workers are the sharpest, most committed colleagues they have ever met. One comment is representative of what many wrote: "everywhere around you, brilliant people." In the recruitment process, the role of the "bar raiser" was introduced, handpicked by senior management and holding veto power to ensure the top quality of new recruits. In the firm, all personnel are constantly under review and those employees who are ranked at the bottom are eliminated every year. This approach is labeled "purposeful Darwinism" by a former top Amazon human resources executive, who explained, "They never could have done what they've accomplished without that." Another manager said, "Amazon is O.K. with moving through a lot of people to identify and retain superstars. They keep the stars by offering a combination of incredible opportunities and incredible compensation." Numerous software engineers with experience at headquarters confirmed this cycling through of personnel within two years.

The following perspective may be presented on Best of Class for personnel in the Amazon organization. It is an interpretation based on many observations, but nevertheless ultimately speculative. It seems clear that Amazon demands only the best from its employees. It is possible that there is a view at Amazon that this "best" from the employee depends on the individual work level; employee productivity is not drawn from company structures or processes. This view would be in keeping with the overall Deed approach to personnel, where individual drive, skills, and judgment largely influence work results. Furthermore, it may be that there are two assumptions about employee productivity rooted in the individual. First, productivity is maximized when the employee is wholly oriented—or better said dedicated or even devoted—to Amazon; everything else in his or her life should take on a diminished role. Second, it is expected that the work level, initiative, and drive of an employee as a new hire begins at a highly intensive level but then falls off over time. In this interpretation, the offer from Amazon to employees is that they take on a job for a particular juncture in their lives when they are open to prioritize their career above everything else. Amazon offers them a very intensive and fulfilling experience, which indeed can fill much of their life. Employees are willing to put their all into the job, which makes sense for Amazon and the employee. Amazon expects, however, that as a rule, this intensity in the employee relationship will not last: productivity falls off with time and/or employees seek other goals in life beyond simply career objectives. Thus, the employee relation is managed on the whole with something like a two-year horizon. The only exception to this rule is that Amazon scans the workforce for the high flyers and retains them. High flyers are valuable in the long term because even if their intensity falls off and/ or they have additional priorities in their life, they are extremely talented and thus will still be productive. In addition, they help with maintaining continuity to some extent.

Amazon's leading role in society, business, and functional excellence enabled it to entrench itself in the online retail market, built on what are here termed "positioned resources" in its Go-To-Market model in Degree. These are resources positioned relative to one another in the two senses of the Janus head such that they relate to one another so as to gain synergies. In this regard, Amazon reports that any one technology and content investment or capital spending project typically supports more than one product and service offering for two reasons. First, due to geographic expansion throughout the organization: scalability is key at Amazon, where in the Janus head facing internally to the operations, all solutions are able to be scaled up and rolled out in multiple offerings throughout the organization. Second, cross-functionality: the punctual delivery service is in the Janus head facing externally to the market requirements intimately linked up with low pricing, expanding product range, and convincing direct marketing. Over its history, Amazon has learned how each function gains impact by being linked with the others: fast delivery is even more impressive when it is free for all kinds of products which have been individually recommended; low prices are even more attractive when they cover a huge range of products delivered the next day; recommendations can strike the mark even better when addressing many different products with a choice of shipping schedules. Amazon continues to build up the impact of positioned resources in physical delivery by expanding its fleet of airplanes and trucks—drones would be the next step. Amazon also has immaterial resources which are positioned on the market in terms of image, awareness, and interest: The IPO would not only bring in equity, but was part of the PR effort to get the company known; the firm communicated about itself always as Amazon.com, never Amazon; interviews with Jeff Bezos gain wide attention; and press releases are carried on multiple media channels.

The massed resources of the Go-To-Market model enable Amazon to enjoy the Competitive Advantage in Degree of size. In this regard, Amazon refers to its "flywheel": a chain of parameters addressing customer preferences which boost each other yet higher and higher, where the logic can begin at any given parameter in the chain. A greater product range attracts more customers to the site, which generates more volumes, which lowers costs, which lowers prices, which attracts more customers, which generates more visitors to the site, which attracts more third-party sellers, which raises the product range—and then it all starts over again. First, size is a Competitive Advantage in offering a comprehensive selection which Amazon draws from its own suppliers, Selling on Amazon sellers, and advertisers. In India, Amazon has powered its way to a leading market position due to having the largest product range—sourced entirely from Selling on Amazon sellers. Second, size enables lower costs due to many economies of scale. The resulting everyday low prices are more important than advertising to attract customers. Similarly, AWS customers benefit from the low prices resulting from Amazon's size. For a typical company, the in-house data center has a utilization rate below 20 percent. Amazon pools the workloads across customers to attain a much higher utilization rate, lowering the average costs for serving any one customer.

Third, size is a Competitive Advantage for Amazon because the large scale significantly lowers the cost and raises the precision of fast shipping. The Prime offer of free delivery has done much to raise volumes, and raising the volume and range of products offered under Prime has enabled Amazon to attract more Selling on Amazon sellers using Fulfillment by Amazon. Amazon can then optimize the logistics of the whole, lowering costs and increasing the accuracy of forecasted delivery times. Fourth, size enables the firm to expand along the value chain, entering new areas of business and drawing the customer even more deeply into the relation with Amazon. Amazon designed and manufactured devices—from the e-book reader Kindle to Fire TV and Fire Tablet to the virtual assistant Echo—as well as developed streaming services such as Prime Instant Video and Amazon Music. The devices and services were initially boosted by the market presence of the website, and in turn drive higher engagement with every element of the Amazon ecosystem. For example, the original TV shows and cartoons on Prime Instant Video draw customers onto the Amazon website, thereby increasing the retail sales of the firm.

As summed up by the firm, there are certain things that only large companies can do. Amazon's size enables it to develop services for customers that it could otherwise never even contemplate. The huge scale and the services not contemplated by others close the circle to the Normative Aim of business and technological leadership.

Amazon pursues Growth in Degree at the primary level by means of extensive growth into ever more party markets. The initial impulse is to extend into new customer markets, which brings with it the move into new areas of personnel and supplier markets. Amazon remains in the same capital market, although by means of its growth has attracted new investor segments. The priorization of Growth was clearly formulated in the first Shareholder Letter of 1997, written for the IPO. Pursuing market leadership to establish an "enduring franchise" by investing to expand and leverage the customer base, brand, and infrastructure stood at the top of the agenda.

In the first years, this Growth took place in two ways. First, Amazon multiplied its book retail activities into more and more product categories: music CDs in 1998, toys and electronics in 1999, and so on through dozens of categories into the first two decades of the twenty-first century, when notably food was added. In parallel to this "copy-paste" approach was an extension of Amazon's market realm in the internet landscape. The Associates program in which other websites steered their visitors to Amazon, as discussed in Chapter 3, was established in 1996. In the late 1990's, Amazon paid tens of millions of dollars to be the exclusive bookseller on the popular sites of the day like AOL, Yahoo, MSN, and Excite. In this century, Amazon grew geographically with a "copy-paste" approach. The integrated operations—a website in a given language, product offerings from suppliers, Selling on Amazon sellers and advertisers, one or more fulfillment centers plus a logistics network for deliveries—as a functioning whole have been built up in multiple countries, e.g. in six European countries: France, Germany, Italy, Netherlands, Spain, and the UK. In contrast, in China, Amazon built up an integrated operation via acquisition. The service Prime Now was also grown as "copy-paste": launched in New York in 2014 and multiplied to forty cities as of 2016. Even the recent move into brick-and-mortar bookstores is "copy-paste": a visitor thought the store was the physical incarnation of the website.

Amazon has also grown by extending its ecosystem of products and services into neighboring business areas along the value chain. In 2009, Amazon established its own publishing houses which were specialized for particular genres, e.g. thriller, romance, and so on. In 2011, Amazon bought Marschall Cavendish, publisher of children's books, and in 2012, Avalon Books. As noted above, Amazon creates new movies and television shows. It also funds the publication of many books for Kindle. The Prime offer also includes music, photo storage, Kindle Owners' Lending Library, as well as a huge inventory of streaming films and TV shows.

In the Degree dimension, the closed loop of Normative Aim-Strength-Go-To-Market model-Competitive Advantage has been extended into new product categories, new "territories" in the internet, new geographical regions, and new products and services in the value chain.

MDW 2 at Amazon in Dexterity at the primary level

Amazon's Normative Aim in Dexterity is to embody the values of an internet society, where every user is treated the same and benefits equally from the advances in the internet, from which indeed the society gains. The oft-quoted customer obsession of Amazon reflects this Normative Aim to give all customers an ever higher level of service. When Amazon.com launched in 1995, it was "to be Earth's most customer-centric company," which is still proclaimed today. In recognition of societal values, Amazon strives determinedly to reduce its carbon footprint throughout its organization and operations. These two sets of values informed the Frustration-Free Packaging program, introduced in 2008 and, as of 2015, covering more than

400,000 products. The program eliminates tens of millions of pounds of excess packaging material, the packages are easier for customers to open, and both transportation costs as well as transportation emissions are reduced. In pursuit of sustainability, Amazon generates energy from renewable sources and utilizes low-pollution vehicles for the last-mile deliveries.

The Aim to give all users an ever higher level of service is the driving force behind Amazon's Strength in Dexterity: designing, implementing, and continually improving standardized processes, particularly in the after-sales customer experience. Standardized processes automatically steer the payment and delivery processes, where the human interaction with customers is reserved for the unusual situations where the customer is not satisfied. Customer Service Associates (CSAs) are schooled and supported by a knowledge center in categorizing customer concerns into standard issues so as to give the corresponding standard answers. In Amazon's "culture of improvement," the standards undergo "constant change," growing in sophistication from a list of canned answers in 1998 to a complex matrix today, which enables CSAs to reply to as many as twelve e-mails in a minute. Standardized processes also govern direct marketing. The timing of mails sent following a purchase or a visit to the site is structured in intervals. The look and feel of the mail is the same as the website: Amazon duplicates the standard of the website in the customer's inbox. Amazon sends discounts, special offers, newsletters, cart abandonment reminders, special competitions, requests for reviews, random product recommendations, and reminders to sign up for Prime. Amazon often capitalizes on current happenings or events, e.g. shoppers who have bought fishing equipment are mailed shortly before the local opening of the fishing season.

The Aim of customer centricity and the Strength of standardized processes feed Amazon's Go-To-Market model in Dexterity of continuous improvement. The internally oriented Janus face of processes and their outputs are continually tested against the externally oriented Janus face of customers and their wants. Step-by-step the former are brought in line and continually updated with the latter: processes and outputs are improved in line with market requirements. Continuous improvement in customer service was referred to above and has been a constant at Amazon right from the start. Fourteen out of 110 employees in late 1996 were answering e-mails from customers and refining the procedures, and during the firm history, managers from throughout the organization had to spend time in the customer service process in order to understand the need for continuous improvement. Bezos once declared, "It's our job every day to make every important aspect of the customer experience a little bit better." Service offerings have also been continuously improved. The depth and breadth of the Prime membership has steadily grown since it was first introduced; more than fifty "benefits" were added in the second half of 2016 alone. So too for AWS. In 2015, there were 722 significant new features and services, a 40 percent increase over 2014; in 2017, the number of new features rose to 1,400. In the retail operations, the continuous improvement takes place today using Big Data and algorithms for demand forecasting, product search ranking, product and deals recommendations, merchandising placements, fraud detection, and translations, amongst other things.

Amazon enjoys the Competitive Advantage in Dexterity of standardized services for customers. Three standardized services for shopping customers discussed above are customer reviews, the terms and conditions for payment and delivery, and the information provided as part of after-sales direct marketing. In addition, the video-streaming service Prime Instant Video was standardized after seeing how Netflix and other streaming services do it. Finally, the services in AWS are standardized, enabling Amazon to systematically improve its Competitive Advantage in prices by continually lowering them. The very nature of standardized services is that all users are equal, linking to the Normative Aim.

Amazon engages in Growth in Dexterity by means of it's management capability in standardization, which enables the firm to address new areas of market potential. On the one hand, standardizing an operation has enabled Amazon to offer it as a service to new segments. For example, as noted above, Amazon Payments was developed for its own customers and then as a standard was offered to other websites, while the supply chain was built up for own suppliers and then as a standard offered to Selling on Amazon sellers as Fulfillment by Amazon. In a similar vein, Amazon licensed the 1-Click software to Apple in 2000, and in the second decade of the twenty-first century standardized its own capability to evaluate suppliers as part of the purchasing function into the management capability to evaluate their suitability for loans as part of its lending program to suppliers. On the other hand, the capability in standardization supported the Degree growth into new market areas with corresponding standardized services.

The closed loop of Normative Aim-Strength-Go-To-Market model-Competitive Advantage in Dexterity has been grown in its own right into market spaces with promising potential, and grown as a support to consolidate the market potential in the Degree growth path.

MDW 2 at Amazon in Deed at the primary level

Amazon's Normative Aim in Deed is to be an enabler by supporting parties to be the master of daily activities. Upon launch, Amazon.com set itself the goal of being the site "where people can find and discover anything they want to buy online." With the growth of the firm since then, it supports the daily activities of a broader range of parties: "Amazon's customers … include millions of Consumers, Sellers, Content Creators, and Developers & Enterprises. Each of these groups has different needs, and we always work to meet those needs, innovating new solutions to make things easier, faster, better, and more cost-effective." The development of the virtual assistant/ speech recognition software, Alexa, built into the devices from Amazon and other producers—more than 4,000 smart home devices from 1,200 unique brands—to make them "smart" in being more easily operated, is a distinctive manifestation of the Normative aim in Deed.

Wanting to support so many different parties in so many different ways in the great variety of their daily activities has led to Amazon's Strength in Deed of initiative and agility. In the previous chapter, it was noted that Amazon employees are offered empowerment. Personnel utilize the empowerment to themselves take the initiative, which in sum makes the organization agile. Many examples can be found in the "folklore" of Amazon's earliest days: the functionality for writing reviews was coded over a single weekend; the first reviews were written mostly by employees and friends; the personalization software was written in two weeks; editors gathered extra information about books they wanted to highlight by going to bookstores and taking notes from the dust jacket; and employees scoured independent bookshops and antique book dealers to find rare and out-of-print books in order to counter Barnes & Noble's claim to have a deeper catalog. Agility is present even in the massive supply chain. At the beginning of the twenty-first century, first two-day shipping, and then the Prime deliveries, could be organized because the software for the fulfillment centers was agile enough to be able to push forward certain orders. This kind of initiative and agility is still to be found today, taking the example of Prime Now, offering one-hour delivery on an important subset of selection. It was launched only 111 days after it was first thought of. In that time, a small team built a customer-facing app, secured a location for an urban warehouse, determined which 25,000 items to sell, got those items stocked, recruited and on-boarded new staff, designed and implemented new software for internal use—both a warehouse management system and an app for drivers—and launched in time for the holidays. Just fifteen months after that first city launch, Prime Now served members in more than thirty cities around the world. The initiative of these employees in implementing Prime Now was only possible due to the underlying agility literally programmed into the organization.

Initiative and agility have also been combined in the long-term perspective which Amazon adopts when pursuing new ideas. Simply by extending the planning phases to a time frame which is unusually long for the business world—between five and seven years—Amazon believes it can pursue strategic moves which other firms would shy away from. In sowing the seeds and watching them grow for such a long time, Amazon demonstrates its commitment to initiative. During this time, the firm can be very agile in the details of the implementation, tinkering with this and that in order to find the best solution. The numerous successful innovations at Amazon, mentioned throughout the book, illustrate this mix of initiative and agility. Three may be highlighted here. First, Prime Now was successful in 2014, but same-day delivery had been thought about since 1999. Second, Prime itself was derided at launch as a charitable benefit to customers; it took several years for the service to become the cornerstone of Amazon's market positioning. Third, the offer to third-party sellers launched as Marketplace in 2000, which has evolved into Selling on Amazon today, and was preceded by not one but two initiatives, Auctions and zShops, both of which failed dismally. As noted by the firm in 2015, "We learned from our failures and stayed stubborn on the vision, and today close to 50% of units sold on Amazon are sold by third-party sellers." This long-term view on initiative and agility is reiterated in the 2018 Proxy Statement, describing Amazon as a firm that "relentlessly pursues invention across a wide range of opportunities," focused on "the long term success of the Company as a whole" by means of "experimentation and long-term thinking." Activities at the firm should not be channeled into the short-term confines of a particular service or industry, but should be open to break into new business areas wherever the opportunities lie, as has been aptly demonstrated in the firm's past.

Finally, one of the Leadership Principles is a bias for action, and the Just Do It award recognizes initiative, often outside an employee's primary job responsibilities. Two product managers agree, one writing, "Company has a strong focus on action—get a lot done," and the other describes a climate of "do it now, do it quickly."

The initiative and agility of the organization—Amazon's Strength—which pursues the Aim of creating solutions for parties to master their daily activities, is conducted in the two contexts of the Janus head forming Amazon's Go-To-Market model in Deed. In the internally oriented Janus face, product developers intensively follow the technological developments in a given functional application. In the externally oriented Janus face, these product developers immerse themselves in the world of the customer and his or her daily activities. Unlike the Dexterity customer feedback, which focuses on the mainstream and average feedback, the Deed immersion pays attention to emerging activities as signals for new, previously unmet needs and wants. The intense involvement picks up these weak signals and then develops them further, matching the emerging customer requirements to the latest technological developments in order to define the specifications for an entire, integrated, and convincing offer. Because the existing signals are only weak, the product developer has to create a mental conception of what is needed and what is to be offered, drawing on his or her intuitions which have been honed by the immersion into the customer's world. As written in 2016, "Good inventors and designers deeply understand their customer. They spend tremendous energy developing that intuition. They study and understand many anecdotes rather than only the averages you'll find on surveys. They live with the design." For example, in designing the Kindle, the team sought the "subconscious qualities that made it feel like one was reading a book." Or the convenience store concept Amazon Go, piloted in Seattle in 2017, simulates in an offline store the principles of 1-Click shopping on the website. The payment process is made effortless by Amazon's cloud computing, machine learning, and logistics know-how, supplemented by cameras and sensors which automatically record the customer's choices. The final bill is calculated when the customer leaves the store and is sent via the app in which the customer had logged in upon entering the location.

Expanding on the long-term perspective of Amazon's initiative and agility, the weak signals which the Go-To-Market model address often carries with it the consequence that the development process to the successful solution can take long. In addition, when the signals are only weak, it may take a while for customers to wake up to the realization that the offered solution actually offers them benefits which are not necessarily immediately apparent. Thus, an aspect of the Deed Go-To-Market model of matching technical dynamic with changing situational needs of customers is that it can require a long time to reach fruition. Amazon reported to shareholders that long-term thinking is one of their four principles.

The weak signals addressed in the Go-To-Market model have led to the Competitive Advantage in Deed of meeting emerging needs with targeted offerings. That is, the Go-To-Market model in Deed has produced a set of offers that each were the first to hit a huge chord amongst customers. Three examples illustrate how Amazon gained an Advantage in meeting emerging needs. First, in online retailing itself, Bezos prophesized in 1998 that e-commerce would allow the book seller to understand its customers in a truly individualized way, much better than in a shop. Targeting this unmet need in one product category after another has led to a retailing turnover in the US second only to Walmart, although having a lifetime only about half as long as Walmart's. Second, the launch of Prime was not justified in any straightforward way by a business plan, but rather based on "gut and experience." Super Saver Shipping, the first stab at low-cost shipping, had changed customers' behavior, motivating them to place bigger orders and shop in new categories. By going one step further, Prime should further raise volumes. That is, Prime—and Super Saver Shipping before it—were fundamentally innovations aimed at customer online shopping behavior, i.e. in the realm of Deed and "doing." The annual subscription fee of $79 for Prime was not the issue; rather, customers should come to the conclusion that they would not shop anywhere else. Amazon describes the decision to launch Prime as an "intuition"—as in the Go-To-Market model—that it would come on big with shopping customers.

Third, Amazon has developed strikingly original content for Prime Video. Directors and other artists for TV shows and videos with a distinctive taste and a highly singular style have stretched the conventional limits for moving image productions. The result is a set of series which as of 2015 had earned more than 120 nominations and won nearly sixty awards, including Golden Globe and Emmy awards. Since then, Amazon has continued with award-winning TV series and expanded into films, one of which received an Oscar nomination. Amazon is developing content that strides into new types of productions, akin to meeting new viewing needs of customers. In doing so, it carefully tracks the extent to which new needs are being met, listing off the following parameters for tracking the success of the new service: Prime free trial starts, conversion to paid membership, renewal rates, and product purchase rates by members entering through this channel. Noteworthy is that all of these parameters track the reactions of specific individuals, rather than cumulated parameters such as market share or growth rates.

The development of e-books, AWS, and Selling on Amazon are further examples of what Amazon describes as "bold bets that worked," which in this book are characterized as meeting needs that were without precedent, hence emerging.

In the search for meeting emerging needs, Amazon has not always hit on a winner. Indeed, Amazon argues that it is in the nature of such singular innovations that it can only rarely hit on a winner. The failure from betting against conventional wisdom—where conventional wisdom is usually right—goes hand-in-hand with success, when a firm searches for singular innovations. But the immense gains from one time being better than conventional wisdom can more than cover the losses from many experiments.

The Competitive Advantage of meeting new needs enables Amazon to keep on meeting the Normative Aim of enabling parties to master their daily activities, even as those activities change.

Amazon pursues Growth in Deed by means of one-off initiatives which grasp market opportunities, one-off in the sense of not being inherently linked to an existing business but reacting to a perceived hole in the market. The original step into books retailing was a shot out of the blue, conceived without precedent as the best venture for taking advantage of the opportunity offered by the internet. Jeff Bezos identified Prime, Selling on Amazon, and AWS as examples of innovations resting on intuition and risk-taking, i.e. examples of what is here characterized as one-off growth initiatives. Other examples are e-books and Kindle, one-offs because the former cannibalized existing business and the latter was a first for Amazon in actually manufacturing a product. The one-off nature of these ventures was underlined in that the teams were organizationally independent of any other division. Finally, Amazon's ecosystem of products and services has been characterized as being much looser than the tightly designed network of interlocking apps and services operated by firms like Apple, Google, and Microsoft. Rather, at Amazon, each area of products and services represents a platform that can operate on its own terms and is designed to serve its own customers in the best and fastest possible manner. This characterization may be interpreted as showing that each element of the ecosystem was developed as a one-off on its own, stimulated by a singular market opportunity, and is managed largely on its own terms, only somewhat after the fact becoming linked to other elements of the ecosystem.

Thus, the interlocking elements of MDW 2 in Deed comprising Normative Aim, Strength, Go-To-Market model, and Competitive Advantage are linked to one another in a specific and independent manner for a given venture only. Growth in Deed consists of coming up with a new set of all four interlocking elements for the next venture.

MDW 2 at Amazon in Delight at the basic level

Amazon's Normative Aim in Delight is at the basic level: the vision to create a world where everyone has a piece of the good life. Changing the world for the better may have been more prominent as an Aim in the early history of the firm, but is currently resricted.

To the extent that the firm seeks to share the good life with parties, Amazon's Strength in Delight is to put together packages of solutions which unify opposites, creating a harmonious whole which enriches customers' lives. Yet, as noted immediately above, Amazon's ecosystem is in some sense a package, but it is not notable for the harmonization of the elements.

Creating a bit of a better world with a loose ecosystem involves Amazon's Go-To-Market model in Delight in which latent demand is addressed to a limited extent. In Delight, a firm would delve into the depths of customer wishes to systematically ferret out wishes unknown to the customer. As confirmed by a product manager, Amazon does not conduct in-depth product testing or run focus groups. Latent demand is addressed as a kind of "side-effect."

The customers realizing latent wishes accord to Amazon the Competitive Advantage in Delight of individualistic mass appeal. Amazon's customers can be amazed and delighted—with a small "d"—by the prices or level of service, but only a few feel they are realizing a part of themselves they never knew existed. The Competitive Advantage in which these customers feel they are attaining their personal vision links up with the Normative Aim of sharing the good life: attaining the personal vision is to share the good life.

Amazon pursues Growth in Delight by means of intensive growth, serving ever more needs of the same target customers. The growing ecosystem largely addresses the same target customers, and, in this sense, represents intensive Growth to some extent. It is argued here that the drive for the Growth of the ecosystem is however mostly to grow the organization, as in Degree.

Summary of MDW 2

MDW 2 is the capability by which firms shift party preferences in the direction of their own strong D's. Amazon shifts the preferences of shopping customers primarily in three dimensions.

In Degree, the demand interfaces have been centered on "Best of Class in the Organization": elevated functional excellence and market leadership. The firm came to own the market position, resources, brand image, products, supply chain, status, and relations to business partners which were recognized to be at the top of its markets, American/global business, and society. These market-oriented resources could be readily extended into additional markets for Amazon to grow.

In Dexterity, Amazon has managed its knowledge of markets, technologies, and societal needs to know how to address clear and articulated requirements of its parties and society. Knowledge was developed in standardized processes, crystallized in standard services, and constantly applied and tested in cycles of continuous improvement aimed at business areas with the greatest potential. Amazon painstakingly managed "Continuous Improvement in Standards" in order to respond to explicit party and societal needs in promoting Dexterity value.

In Deed, Amazon has enabled parties to do what they wanted with the firm's value offer by presenting a platform from which they could optimize their varying individual practical situations. Shoppers have almost always found what they sought on the website, and the personnel were prepared for, indeed caught up in, exercising their initiative. Both parties could flexibly do what was needed in pursuing concrete opportunities of the moment. Amazon again and again struck a chord for Deed value with its "Operational Solutions for Situational Needs" couched in distinctive, "individualizable" innovations taking advantage of technological advances.

In Delight, Amazon is able to feel, and thus intensively address, the personal visions of certain parties, mostly investors, Selling on Amazon sellers, reviewers, and some personnel. In the early years of the firm, Amazon addressed the personal visions of a number of customers and a larger proportion of personnel. In addition, the firm responded to some extent to perceptions of wider needs and wishes amongst customers and personnel with regard to making society better. The "Holistic Solutions Uniting Opposites" enabled Amazon to personally appeal to parties by realizing their personal and professional visions.

Taking Stock

As the First Mover in online retail who never stopped being the First Mover, on the one hand Amazon was able to influence the preferences of shoppers and, more generally, all parties regarding the kind of value they sought in the industry. The value dimensions which Amazon promoted came to be the value dimensions on which shoppers and parties placed the greatest weight. On the other hand, Amazon has been able to recognize the trends and move with the times. In the early years of the internet, the firm positioned itself as part of the new technological wave fulfilling Delight visions of the good life for all. As online retail became commonplace in this century, it shifted its market approach to a Degree mission, Dexterity values, and Deed goals.

This adept balance between influencing and shifting reflects Amazon's deep-seated abilities in MDW 2 to position its strong D's in the weightiest preferences. The firm has thus scored extremely well on Markets Value Factor 2 in the competition "between" D's: Amazon has offered primary value in the three D's, which came to be the weightiest. The managerial practices for Amazon to be the market leader in those three D's is a matter of the competition "within" a D. This competition is the subject of MDW 3 Internal Supply Interfaces, examined in the following chapter.

Chapter 5

MDW 3: Managing Supply Interfaces at Amazon

Markets Value Factor 3	Managerial Do-Well 3
The fewer the number of rival firms exhibiting strong value offers in the same strong D's	Manage supply interfaces to offer more appealing D value than rivals

Markets Value Factor 3 evaluates the number of direct rivals faced by a firm, i.e. those offering primary or secondary value in the same D as the firm. This kind of direct rivalry is critical for the market success of the firm, because depending upon the level of rivalry, the firm can be more or less successful, or even driven out of the market. Where the firm faces no direct rivals in its strong D, it can win all the parties with the weightiest preferences in that dimension; market success is accordingly higher. The greater the number of direct rivals in the same D, the greater the extent to which the firm has to share out parties with other rivals, lowering its market success. And when one firm has a very appealing offer in a given D, it can drive the direct rivals out of the market and raise entry barriers against potential rivals, i.e. against new entrants. In this way, competition within a value dimension is more intense than competition between value dimensions and has a direct bearing on the market share, indeed survival, of the firm. A firm can influence the number of direct rivals it faces—and thereby its score on MVF 3—to the extent that it can eliminate direct rivals as well as raise entry barriers to prevent future rivals by means of more appealing offers.

Managerial Do-Well 3 therefore evaluates the ability of the firm to generate more appealing offers than direct rivals in its strong D's. This capability is determined by the supply interfaces of the firm, i.e. the internal operations: how well can the firm manage the internal operations to generate particularly convincing value offers. This chapter will focus on MDW 3 in regard to shopping customers and not consider offers generated for other party types.

The distinction between Managerial Do-Well 2 (the demand interfaces) and Managerial Do-Well 3 (the supply interfaces) can be clearly drawn. A firm which is very capable in MDW 2 may not necessarily win more parties, because after successfully shifting party preferences, the parties may choose the offer of a direct rival in the same D. For example, Walmart's advertising for the Degree dimension may shift party preferences to this D, but then the parties choose Amazon. In this case Walmart would score well on MDW 2, but score poorly on MDW 3.

Parameters of MDW 3

This chapter goes inside the firm. The many facets of the internal operations making up the supply interfaces are captured in the eight parameters displayed in Figure 5-1. The parameters cover topics regarding work and the work environment which are almost certainly familiar to the reader, but are here categorized in new ways. In this way, the familiar is taken as the basis for developing new insights. In addition, the parameters of the supply interfaces "shadow" the parameters of the demand interfaces. What the firm produces must ultimately find favor on the market; therefore, the internal operations are aligned to the demand interfaces. That is, the supply interfaces follow the path to the market which is laid down by the demand interfaces, actually generating or "filling in" what the demand interfaces promise to the market.

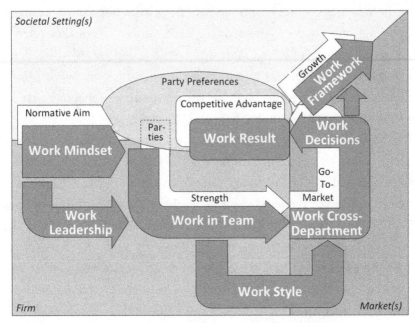

Figure 5-1: The Parameters of MDW 3

The first parameter in the supply interfaces is the mentality which expresses the Normative Aim by fulfilling it in the daily tasks. Work Mindset pinpoints the specific manner of thinking about the work which informs and governs the approach of all personnel to conducting the work. The Work Mindset straddles the society and the firm, giving the employees the sense that their tasks have an impact beyond simply the boundaries of the firm. This mentality is rooted in the perspective of a specific function which reflects the societal need addressed by the Normative Aim. That is, the Normative Aim addresses a societal need, and a specific function within the firm is best suited to represent the interests of this need. Therefore, this function is the organizational lead within the firm which steers the personnel towards fulfilling the Normative Aim in their daily work. This function is the conscience of the firm.

Work Leadership functions as the translation of the Work Mindset into the Work in Team. The Work Mindset is implicit in the company culture. Work Leadership is made up of the explicit communication acts and behavior of people managers which reinforce the Work Mindset. Work Leadership is performed only in the context of the firm; however, it makes reference, implicitly or explicitly, to societal norms and societal impacts. Work Leadership is the second (in the sense of an old-fashioned duel) for the Work Mindset, functioning to actively bring home to the personnel the message that their tasks have an impact for both the firm and the society.

On the basis of the Mindset and the Leadership, Work in Team is the actual performance of the work on a daily basis in order to realize the Strength of the firm. The Work in Team occurs entirely within the context of the firm, and is perceived and managed wholly in these terms. It is the basics of the job, constituted by the tasks which would appear in a job profile; it is what the supervisor tells/asks the employee to perform, the subject of implicit and explicit on-the-job training, and the subject which takes up the bulk of the job evaluation. Work in Team considers the relations to other employees by describing the structuring and governance of teamwork within the line unit of the employee, pinpointing the individual's function relative to his or her nearest colleagues. Work in Team is the workhorse of the firm, day in and day out.

The Work in Team conducted in an internal context needs to be formed into an offer with value on the market. Work Style turns functional work into something with "value-in-the-rough" for the customer. It builds the bridge between the internal context of Work in Team to the market context of the Go-To-Market model, making the work ready for the market. Work Style describes what the individual employees "taste" in their work day. It consists of mechanisms which shape and inform the daily activities and work procedures of the individual employees in fulfilling their tasks and responsibilities. Work Style is, so to say, the "lifestyle" of working at the firm.

Work Cross-Department puts together the Work in Team from multiple teams into a value offer for the market, where Work Style has laid the groundwork for this market orientation. The collaboration between different organizational units in Work Cross-Department is needed for value offers, because it is rare that Work in Team can directly be offered to the market; as a rule, value offers are made up of contributions from multiple teams. What's more, when departments collaborate, it normally takes place in the context of generating offers. Work-Cross Department is thus the realization of the Go-To-Market model, including both the product or service on offer, as well as how the offer is made to parties, i.e. how to work the market. Work Cross-Department is the nerve center of the firm. If not for the customer, teams could happily go their own merry way, absorbed in their own function. The customer makes teams talk with one another.

The firm's market offers can be compared to the offers of rivals in terms of features and attributes of the products and services and managed accordingly in such terms by the Work Cross-Department. The question as to what extent these features and attributes are perceived by customers as benefits is the subject of the Work Result. The Work Result specifies the output of the individual employee's work in the eyes of the customer: what is it that the employee accomplished on the job to the benefit of the customer. The Work Result is the Competitive Advantage of the firm expressed in terms of what individual employees attain—what a customer has from the employee's work. The Work Result of any individual employee's work is also the impact of that employee on the Work Result of the colleagues: how an employee influences other employees in creating benefits for customers. Thus, the Work Result has an impact both in the context of party preferences and in the context of the firm. Ultimately, the impact on the work colleagues is the same as the impact on the customers, because the net effect of both impacts is the benefit to the customer in terms of his or her preferences.

The Work Result may be likened to the simplest model of communication, where what is communicated is not what the sender intended, but rather what the receiver perceived. Until this point in the supply interfaces, the parameters have portrayed what the personnel and the firm intend. The Work Result is what the customer perceives, and as an intermediary to the customer perception, what the work colleagues perceive. The Work Result is the crowning of the employee's work; it is the underlying objective—sometimes hidden—of the employee's day-to-day work.

For the firm to grow, the entire network of activities reaching from Work Mindset to Work Result need to be applied to the context of a new societal setting and/or market and adapted to the requirements of the new societal setting and/or market. The Work Framework is the vehicle for making the adaptation take place; it is the organizational mechanism with which the firm establishes itself in and brings all the parameters of the supply interfaces to bear on the new setting and/or market. The Work Framework describes two sides of the same coin. On the one side is how the firm manages new developments on markets, i.e. the mechanisms the firm uses in gaining a foothold in the new societal setting and/or market. On the other side of the coin is the career structure and orientation for the personnel, i.e. the terms in which personnel make their career by growing with the firm. The two issues are two sides of the same coin because the framework within which personnel structure their work—e.g. an organizational unit or an assignment or a process—is the vehicle with which the firm grows. The Work Framework is the spaceship with which the firm establishes new colonies in the universe, constituting both the environment for the personnel as well as the new presence on the planet which interacts with the residents. A firm is constituted by the accumulation of the spaceships which have been launched in its history.

Two links in the network of activities making up the supply interfaces are particularly tricky. First, the link from the value generated in Work Cross-Department to the benefits perceived by customers in the Work Result is difficult because of the uncertainty regarding what customers actually perceive in the firm's offer and where their preferences lie. Second, extending the Work Framework to a new societal setting and/or market—the process of Growth—is difficult because the supply interfaces need to be adapted to the requirements of the new and unfamiliar societal setting and/or market. In both cases, the firm steps into the unknown and needs to decide under conditions of uncertainty. Managing these uncertain and therefore risky links is overseen by Work Decisions, including the context of decision-making and the steps needed to reach a decision. Decisions about the two links described above need to be taken in a decision-making process with clear contours in the firm, even when in some cases the process itself is informal. Work Decisions is the information-processing function within the firm which manages information to determine how the firm will proceed under conditions of uncertainty.

The eight parameters of the internal supply interfaces and how they are manifested in the four dimensions of value at Amazon are summarized in Figure 5-2.

	Primary Degree	Primary Dexterity	Primary Deed	*Basic Delight*
Area	Customer as member of society	Customer as online retail market participant	Customer as shopper	*Customer as consuming person*
Mgmt. Element				
Work Mindset	Budget	Production	Product Engineering	*"Instrumental Marketing"*
Work Leadership	Evaluate and Foster	Careful and Quick	Individual Development	*Identification*
Work in Team	Instructions execution	Process (step) responsible	Role	*Diplomat*
Work Style	Make the best out of instructions in your unit	Build capability in your group	Cultivate skills in your cohort	*Work to your dream with allies*
Work Cross-Department	Committees: Who	Incorporation: Which	Agreed Division of Labor: How	*Synthesis: What*
Work Result	Functional Excellence	Take / Make Account Of	Add Value	*Resonance*
Work Framework	Strategic Business Units	Team / Process	Assignments	*Stakeholders*
Work Decisions	Functional Reviews: Accretion of Positions	Unify Knowledge: Emergence of the Way Forward	Judgments in Doing: Sketch, Submit to Veto, Implement	*Commit to a Vision: Choose from Alternative Proposals*
Essence / Summary	Functional Excellence via Instructions	Process Enhancement via Knowledge Sharing	Skills and Judgment via Experience	*Synthesized Designs via Resonance*

Figure 5-2: MDW 3: Supply Interfaces at Amazon at its Best

MDW 3 at Amazon in Degree at the primary level

MDW 3 in Degree at Amazon is illustrated in Figure 5-3 and presented in this section.

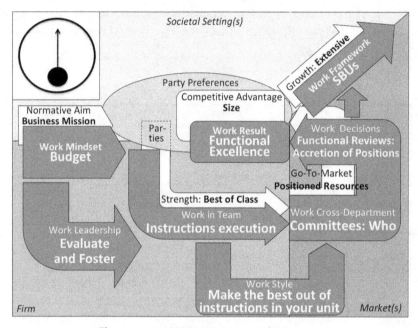

Figure 5-3: MDW 3 at Amazon in Degree

The Work Mindset in Degree is the budget relating to Amazon's positioning on markets. The budget specifies the amount of resources being expended to build and/or maintain Amazon's position in a customer market, as well as the amount of resources/revenues generated by the unit if it is customer facing. Every organizational unit has a budget which is thoroughly prepared. The leader of every organizational unit is strictly held to account to meet the budget, and this mindset/attitude is driven into the thinking of every team member. Employees are regularly informed regarding the performance to budget of their unit. The budget Mindset mirrors the Aim—the mission to lead business enterprise—in that it allocates and generates the resources at the top.

The Work Leadership in Degree is to first, evaluate and, second, foster the organization, initiatives, teams, and individual employees. Regarding the first, new product ideas, as well as every budget proposal from a team, is subject to close scrutiny from multiple layers in the hierarchy, typically very critical and very harsh. Weekly meetings examine the performance of each department. Regarding employees, managers in departments of fifty or more people are required to "top-grade" their subordinates and must dismiss the least effective performers. Regarding the second, in 2014 Jeff Bezos described his "main job" as working hard to maintain the culture, manifested in the fourteen Leadership Principles. One product manager noted, "Never in any company have the leadership principles been followed this religiously. Leadership principles are referenced every day, for every single decision," while a process assistant is enthusiastic about them: "they have an amazing principle system that most companies do not instill or encourage from their workers." The Principles are an example of fostering in that Leadership has formulated them, but their application is up to every manager and employee. Fostering is also practiced by team leadership in that clear feedback is given with regard to sub-performance, without providing advice or suggestions as to how the employee could do better. Improving performance is a matter for the individual employee to come up with.

Fostering and evaluation from Leadership will function best when they are perceived as operating at a higher level; in this way, fostering and evaluating occurs by looking down from above. This implies a certain aloofness, which indeed is seen in the comments in glassdoor.com: "Leadership is very smart but frequently treats employees as resources and not as people"; there is a "lack of interpersonal communication with the employees, everything … Is done via computer"; and, there are "brilliant and inspiring leaders at the very top." Fostering and evaluation from Leadership on high points the Work in Team upwards to the level of Best in Class, thereby linking Work in Team to the exalted Normative Aim: the mission as business leader.

The Work in Team in Degree is governed by the execution of instructions. "Instructions" as used here involve single or groups of employees being told what to do, which can take many forms: e.g. quantified targets, clearly defined criteria for the appropriate performance of a task, or IT systems specifying plans and activities. Amazon monitors the performance of employees in executing tasks with pre-defined criteria, e.g. was an Internet page appropriately coded so that it loads sufficiently quickly, or has a purchasing manager avoided out-of-stock. Amazon employees and team leaders can be held accountable for many performance metrics in business reviews, held weekly or monthly. A day or two before the meetings, employees receive printouts, sometimes up to fifty or sixty pages long. The reviews then question the reported performance data. Middle level managers and specialists are described as less and less decision-makers, but rather increasingly executors of orders.

Instructions are widely found in the supply chain at Amazon. Algorithms using dozens of metrics instruct fulfillment centers every day as to the number of customer orders they have been allocated. Pricing benefits from automatic programs that compare prices at rivals and issue instructions about Amazon's prices so as to keep to the firm's pledge to offer the lowest price anywhere, including also raising prices on items that are out of stock at rivals. Amazon proclaims that its systems steer the decisions and performance of many jobs, e.g. the global inventory planning systems decide "what, when, where, and how much we should buy to meet Amazon's business goals and to make our customers happy."

In a fulfillment center, twenty pickers (those who retrieve ordered items from the shelves) and packers (those who pack the retrieved items into packages ready for shipping) are supervised by a team leader. The large team size suggests that it is not central to the Team Leader's job to manage the team members as individuals. Rather, team leaders distribute green or yellow cards to team members based on clearly defined criteria: holding on to the railing when climbing the stairs or not; keeping out of the lane reserved for forklift trucks or not; and so on. Three yellow cards can be sufficient grounds for terminating the employment contract. Team Leaders have targets for the number of packages made ready for shipping per day; they break them down into targets for individual team members. Further, handscanners show the pickers exactly what to do: the content of the order, the location of the product, and the fastest way to get to the items on the shelves. The scanners have cameras directed both at the employee as well as at the surroundings. The movement data from the handscanners are reportedly used in feedback talks to detail the level of inactivity of the employee, although Amazon states these data are not used in Germany due to the privacy rights.

In a lengthy comment, one stower—those who store items coming into the fulfillment center at the appropriate place on the shelves—details what is expected of a stower in a fulfillment center and the high level of detail regarding what the instructions specifically call for:

> *"you have to stow a certain number of items per week. It's not a straightforward concept, as in 1000 items per day—each item has its own time limit/rate (something like—large items 30 per hour, medium items 60 per hour, small items 120 per hour), so it's not possible to personally calculate whether you're meeting the rate or not. Managers (or Problem Solvers) post a list of all working employee rates throughout the day, or sometimes once per day, and that's how you can figure out how well you're doing rate-wise.*
>
> *- There's also a QUALITY standard, where you're expected to stow about 1100 (or 1200?) items without making more than 1 error (according to the scanner).*
>
> *- And multiple rules on how items can be stored ... as in items cannot be sticking out over the shelf more than the width of your badge, items cannot be more than 50 percent above the divider (between each shelf), all items on shelf must be visible, liquid items must be placed upright, etc.*
>
> *So as a stower, your job is to stow items out of 12 'totes' (storage bins), which are located on a large cart that you push around the warehouse. The time required to remove and replace the empty totes (and cart) back to the que, find out where the full carts are located, grab a cart, and push the cart to an aisle with as much space as you can find counts against your rate. It's not necessarily Time Off Task, unless it takes you more than 6 minutes to do. However, if it does take you more than 6 minutes, or if you spend six minutes doing something else without scanning an item and scanning a shelf (such as using the bathroom which takes about 4 minutes round trip to get back and forth from, speaking with your manager or HR) you will accrue Time Off Task"*
>
> (glassdoor.com)

Individual comments confirm the centrality of instructions in fulfillment centers: "rate increase subject to change after 75% of employees are meeting rate. Work hard then rate goes up and you have to work SUPER hard to keep rate at 100%"; "Impossible goals are set, and you are expected to meet your rate or you are written up"; "Numbers are everything as a fulfillment associate"; and, in conclusion: "There's a lot of rules and regulations that one must keep in mind while doing the job. Amazon is not for the lazy."

The instructions set Work in Team at the highest level to attain the Strength of Best in Class.

The Work Style in Degree is governed by the expectation to make something of instructions: issue them, pass them on, execute them, control their proper execution by others, and/or improve them, all the while making the best out of them for the organization. "Amazon uses a self-reinforcing set of management, data and psychological tools to spur its tens of thousands of white-collar employees to do more and more. 'The company is running a continual performance improvement algorithm on its staff,'" said one former manager. One such "algorithm" is the peer-to-peer control of the Anytime Feedback tool, in which employees report on a colleague's performance to the colleague's superior. Making the best out of instructions is a central concern of Amazon. In the fulfillment centers, the best is made out of the instructions by updating them to maintain Best of Class. The instructions stem from the operations team in headquarters, who design the physical layout and work procedures in the fulfillment centers. As of 2013, Amazon was on the seventh generation of fulfillment center design. The "upgrades" to work design streamline processes and reduce defects and waste. E.g. in 2012 alone, 280 software changes in Fulfillment Centers were made. A Work Style of making the best out of instructions paves the way for the hierarchical Work Cross-Department.

Work Cross-Department in Degree is governed by who is communicating with whom in the sense of which organizational position is communicating with which organizational position. The supply chain structures are to a large extent vertically organized. The specialist teams in the headquarters issue instructions in the form of work design to the teams in fulfillment centers around the world. Within the fulfillment centers, there is a strict hierarchy of an Operations Manager at the top, to whom a handful of Area Managers report, who in turn supervise the Team Leaders. Relations between teams are governed by the next level up. The top-down Work Cross-Department ensures that those at the top of the firm, with the best overview of the firm and market, can position the Go-To-Market resources in the best way for the firm.

The Work Result in Degree is functional excellence. Numerous examples of Amazon attaining excellence in the organization have been presented above. The firm specifically refers to the "professional pride in operational excellence" found at the firm. The functional excellence in the work mirrors the high quality from the Competitive Advantage of size.

The Work Framework in Degree is Strategic Business Units. A SBU is an operation which is managed as a complete business, with—at least how it is regarded and treated in the organization, if not actually in terms of management structures—its own profit and loss account, it's own business case, and so forth. As noted above, at Amazon, every organizational unit has a budget which receives a great deal of management attention. The numbers in the budget, and the business thinking which they reflect, set the framework for employees to form their career, and the associated organizational structures constitute the firm's presence in existing and new markets.

Particularly the rising importance and weight accorded to the supply chain operations within Amazon is illustrative of the SBU as the Work Framework in Degree at the firm. Originally, this function was regarded as without strategic importance and thus outsourced. When it was realized that supply chain was indeed important to the market positioning of Amazon, the function was brought in-house. Over time, supply chain received more and more attention and was more and more closely managed with more and more tools and systems. Also, the standing of the managers within Amazon was raised. The launch of Super Saver Shipping signaled that supply chain was a key element in the offer to customers. The advent of Prime was a sign that supply chain is a revenue generator. The supply chain services and fulfillment centers are now treated as if they were SBUs.

The Growth of the firm via extension into new markets is accomplished in that new SBUs are established to solidify the presence and positioning of Amazon in the new markets.

Work Decisions will be presented further below as involving three D's in combination.

MDW 3 at Amazon in Dexterity at the primary level

MDW 3 in Dexterity at Amazon is illustrated in Figure 5-4 and presented in this section.

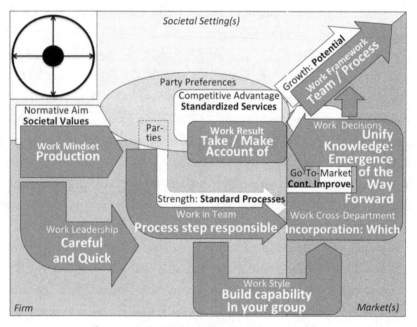

Figure 5-4: MDW 3 at Amazon in Dexterity

The Work Mindset in Dexterity is production in the context of the after-sales customer experience, i.e. performing customer service processes. Amazon employees rotate through a short stint in customer service to become steeped in the mentality of processes to maintain customer satisfaction. Customer service and satisfaction meets the Normative Aim of an internet society.

The Work Leadership in Dexterity is to be careful and quick—careful in the sense of exploring, testing, and always learning and quick in the sense that when an initiative strikes success, rapidly move to consolidate the gain. This leadership approach corresponds to what Bezos describes as "Day 1": taking each business day as if there were no preconceptions, i.e. as if one had to find out everything anew and afresh. When success is found, staying hungry to pull out all the stops and exploit the initiative. According to one observer, "Bezos believed in iteration, keep trying and be willing to wait." Careful and quick Leadership motivates the processes of Work in Team with the values of internet society.

The Work in Team in Dexterity takes the form of each team member being a process (step) responsible. The team member applies the standards by choosing which one to apply in a given situation and is thereby responsible to think for herself or himself. Work in Team in Dexterity governs the tasks of the Customer Service Associates (CSAs), where employees are given a three week introduction to operations so that they can apply their standardized knowledge when replying to customers. The CSA work is evaluated in terms of a standardized result: is the customer satisfied or not? In addition, the Mayday service allows customers to see a CSA face-to-face and was introduced as a new standardized task for all CSAs, despite resistance from some employees: taking responsibility for a process (step) is required. The responsibility for a process (step) enables Amazon to realize the Strength of Standard Processes.

The Work Style in Dexterity is to build capability in the group. In Chapter 3, it was noted that there is a strong sense of mutual help, support, and knowledge sharing amongst the CSAs: the call center employees work to raise the abilities and knowledge of their colleagues. Raising the group's capabilities enables it to better design and apply standards in the Work Cross-Department.

Work Cross-Department in Dexterity revolves around deciding which standard to apply in given circumstances. Departments work together to clarify the nature of given business circumstances and together design an appropriate standard or choose which of the available standards to apply. For example, managers from customer service interact with managers from the supply chain and the website to define the kinds of customer issues which can arise, and what the appropriate response is, so as to define the matrix of standardized responses for CSAs. Or a CSA can reach out to the support department to explain a concrete customer query and receive support in deciding which standardized response to apply. Clarifying customer issues and defining the appropriate response is the daily work of Continuous Improvement in the Go-To-Market model.

The Work Result in Dexterity is to take/make account of, best seen in the CSA processes. In the first step, when a customer contacts the service department, the CSAs are expected to take full account of the query from the customer. In the second step, they are to determine which is the appropriate response. In the third step, they are to communicate the response to the customer in a manner such that the customer accepts and is satisfied with the level of service from Amazon: the CSAs make the customer take account of Amazon's view and accept the response which Amazon regards as appropriate. The CSA takes account of the customer while making the customer take account of Amazon. In processes which run from one Amazon employee to another before ultimately ending at the customer, process (step) responsibles take account of the process step which follows their own by delivering the optimum to the next process step responsible, so that the next step can be performed optimally. Similarly, process (step) responsibles "make account," i.e. make colleagues in the process step prior to their own step take account of their own requirements, so that they can execute their process step optimally. Ensuring that the requirements for each process step are taken account of enables Amazon to gain the Advantage of standardized services.

The Work Framework in Dexterity is the team which executes a process. As the Growth of Amazon extended into new markets with potential, the CSA teams grew as well. They have been structured and managed to handle the expanding knowledge about the new operations, products, and services, while CSAs were evaluated in terms of their knowledge in the Growth areas.

Work Decisions will be presented further below as involving three D's in combination.

MDW 3 at Amazon in Deed at the primary level

MDW 3 in Deed at Amazon is illustrated in Figure 5-5 and presented in this section.

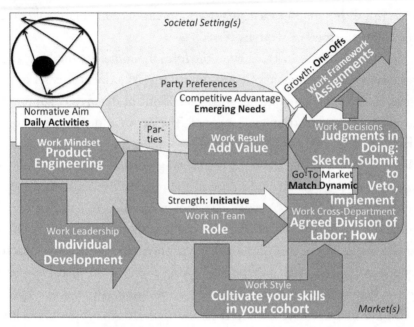

Figure 5-5: MDW 3 at Amazon in Deed

The Work Mindset in Deed is product engineering, particularly for online shopping. The design, the functionality, and the look and feel of the website are engineered to optimize shopper activities. For example, new product innovations are discussed and evaluated in terms of how customers would react to them: each new proposal is internally presented in the form of a press release announcing the launch of the innovation. The Mindset of product engineering embodies in the daily work the Normative Aim for customers to master their activities.

The Work Leadership in Deed is individual development. Leadership's task has been to see to it that individuals have been developed to reach their full potential. Numerous examples were presented regarding the value exchange with personnel in Deed in Chapter 3, where employees were given challenging assignments by their superiors from which they learned very much. Individuals were also developed by the internal procedures for internal meetings. Slide presentations are never made in meetings. Rather, employees write six-page narratives laying out their points in prose, because Bezos believes doing so fosters critical thinking. Leadership's development of individuals makes them fit to assume the roles in Work in Team.

The Work in Team in Deed takes the form of employees fulfilling a role. For the employee, each team role was simply one assignment in a set of past, present, and future assignments, such that Work in Team was approached in a pragmatic and instrumental manner. The personal distance to the role enabled the employee to take on several roles at any one time, drop any one of them, or re-orient them as needed with no great fuss. Fulfilling a role in a team has involved not only a distance to the role itself but also to the other team members. A Senior Product Manager in headquarters spelled out the implications of this: the people who are comfortable at Amazon look out for themselves and do not seek social cohesion. There is a self-selective bias that people who perform their role without being overly concerned how others perceive them tend to blossom at Amazon. In addition, Amazon hired people with the most talent rather than the most experience. Such people do not know that something "can't be done that way." Employees did not draw on their education or professional background, on "who they were" in a functional/technical sense. Rather, they assumed the role which Amazon required, and were evaluated purely in those terms. Their potential, personal development, educational, and professional background and so forth were not relevant—only the role fulfillment.

Another aspect of fulfilling a role is simply to perform the task at hand in the most pragmatic way, without concerns regarding functional instructions (as in Degree), processes (as in Dexterity), or the collective (as in Delight). For example, in Amazon's warehouses, there is "chaotic storing." A product is stored wherever there is free space, much like data is stored on a hard disk. The advantages are that Amazon can utilize more shelf space by being flexible with regard to changes in product range or stock levels and employees do not need to waste time organizing products. In a similar vein, Amazon stocks dissimilar products next to one another on the shelves of the fulfillment centers so that employees do not confuse items. Thus, it is not the case that a fixed portion of the storage space is allocated to e.g. toys, where a specific set of workers are responsible for (Degree) and/or build knowledge about (Dexterity) and/or identify with (Delight) toy storage.

Thanks to roles and their lack of fixedness, Amazon was free to handle each order and each delivery as a kind of mini one-off, to be optimized in its own terms. This was the organizational pre-condition for Amazon to move from handling orders in batches to a continuous flow, as described above. Amazon wrote algorithms which generated multiple scenarios for how to fulfill each individual order, and then chose the path which was optimal. This lack of fixedness in process orders was the basis for Free Super Saving Shipping, introduced in January 2002. For customers who could wait a few days for delivery of orders above a minimum value, the shipping was free, and Amazon shipped the order when the opportunity arose of spare room in a truck. Also, Prime was only possible due to the lack of fixedness in the organization, where individual orders were assigned priority. The lack of fixedness enabled Amazon to ultimately use delivery as a major weapon against rivals.

Work in Team in the Deed dimension is found particularly in software development. The entire division was based on "two-pizza teams"—no more than ten people in an autonomous group, such that if working late, two pizzas would feed the group. The restricted size of the team would mean that each had a significant role to fulfill, which could be readily specified. The clarity in the roles enabled the teams to work faster and more innovatively. The two-pizza concept began in engineering, and then spread into other departments within a few years. The individuality of the role enabled team members to exercise the Strength of initiative.

The Work Style in Deed is for employees to cultivate skills in their cohort. One set of skills at Amazon is cultivated by everyone at headquarters: the particular practices and organizational behaviors at Amazon which set the firm apart. New hires who after two weeks can repeat the firm's cultural values receive a virtual award proclaiming, "I'm Peculiar"—the company's proud phrase for overturning workplace conventions. Another example is the particular way in which critical thinking in internal meetings is stimulated by six-page narratives, which are silently read at the beginning of each meeting. In addition, working with smart colleagues can raise one's own skill level: "Work with mostly very smart people, and you'll be amazed at how much you can accomplish in the environment."

As mentioned above, the practice of critically commenting on other people's work is widespread at Amazon, either from colleagues (a horizontal cohort) or from supervisors (a vertical cohort in the same function). It may be suggested here that this widespread negative feedback is a method to improve skills levels, a kind of mutual improvement society involving supervisors, direct reports, and colleagues. Furthermore, Bezos himself believes strongly in the benefits of learning from failure, where failure may be seen in this context as clear, negative feedback to the work of personnel. Similarly, Amazon employees engage in substantial self-criticism. Employees talk of feeling like their work is never done or good enough. A saying around the headquarters is "Amazon is where overachievers go to feel bad about themselves." Self-criticism is a way to learn from failure. In sum, the behaviors and organizational culture at Amazon are mutually reinforcing, forming an atmosphere of criticism to make the most out of the employees' work. Two observers remark that these practices, behaviors, and culture "motivate and discipline" employees. Amazon personnel are stimulated by the negative feedback and seek to stimulate others with the same. Cultivating skills raises the ability to take on the activities which have been allocated between teams in the Work Cross-Department.

Work Cross-Department in Deed is governed by an agreed division of labor to specify how to work together. These agreements are reached in a direct manner as required between the teams involved. Amazon does not have program managers who plan, coordinate, oversee, and monitor, but has teams who develop their own solutions and communicate with others only as needed; a high level of communication is taken as a sign of dysfunction. Decentralization and independent decision-making are key to Amazon's Work Cross-Department. Software personnel at Amazon indeed report on the lack of structure in Work Cross-Department. Others say that a kind of implicit division of labor makes up for this in two ways. First, the internal, service-oriented architecture, as conceived by a few high-flyers, provides the high-quality platform on which all software adequately interfaces with other software. Second, where a team is performing poorly, loyal employees in another team pick up the slack. The demands of the Go-To-Market model, in which the dynamic of new customer situations and new technological advances are matched, is met on a daily basis by the agreed division of labor.

The Work Result in Deed is to add value. In fulfilling the role, the employee is expected to singly create as many benefits as possible for the firm. The lack of fixity in the supply chain illustrates added value: "chaotic storing" to store items simply in the most accessible place, choosing the optimal route from a number of alternatives, and shipping items when there was space in the truck are examples of adding the most value for a given task. Adding value involves doing the things people need, day-in and day-out, as explained by a software engineer: "You will work on real things that people have actually requested for, and that people will start using as soon as you are done … Most of the work has to do with solving everyday problems." Also, the requirement to add value can lead to long work hours, as declared by a middle manager: "When you're not able to give your absolute all, 80 hours a week, they see it as a major weakness." Employees with outside interests, including family commitments, are told that Amazon is not the right place for them and let go, blocked, or not promoted.

An employee described certain individuals at Amazon who epitomize added value, showing how much Amazon benefits from them and how much they like it: Amazon "has a core of incredibly loyal smart people who don't really care to leave. Seriously, I've had conversations with some highly intelligent engineers in my time at the company who could easily be very senior at Google/Facebook/etc. and they enjoy having their niche at Amazon, their problem space, and simply chugging away." Finding a niche from which to add value is widespread at headquarters: New hires are "dazzled, flattered and intimidated" by how quickly they are given an autonomous role and then expected to perform at a high level. It is made clear to them that the success of the project rests on their individual performance. A fulfillment center manager confirms this point of view: "Not many people a year out of college get to say that they lead a team of 100+ people while also getting to participate in high profile projects. Your time at Amazon is what you make it—if you can accept the fast-paced, high stakes, 'no excuses' work environment, there is no limit to what you will achieve. You will look back in disbelief over how much you have grown in a year." The "doers" at Amazon can do with elan.

Further to added value, numerous entries on glassdoor.com point out that Amazon expends few resources on software documentation. This is a further example of adding value as the Work Result. Documentation does not improve the customer experience, whereas the programming itself does. And given that the website is constantly innovated to adjust to new situations, any code may soon be re-written anyway. Thus, the emphasis is on generating code, and not documentation. The targeted nature of value add enables Amazon to gain the Advantage of addressing emerging needs.

The Work Framework in Deed is assignments. Growth at Amazon has been accomplished largely by giving personnel new assignments in the new business activities, rather than having Growth activities absorbed by existing roles. And personnel have been evaluated strictly in terms of how they perform on their assignments. The Work Framework of Assignments is most apparent in software development, where virtually the whole of the employment relationship consists of executing the assigned projects and little more. The vehicle for Growth at Amazon is new software for new functionality and new operations, and employees can advance their career principally in terms of how they perform in creating this new software.

Work Decisions

Work Decisions at Amazon take on aspects rooted in a mixture of three dimensions of value.

The decision-making process at Amazon often formally takes on the appearance of decisions in the Degree dimension, in which representatives of the relevant functions present their views as a kind of position paper and the decision represents a build-up, or accretion, of these views, one on top of another. The views of different departments and functions are collected by inviting representatives to the meeting in which a proposal is discussed.

A decision often involves stitching together different views or alternatives from different departments—a kind of accretion. The decision-making revolves around the positions—both in terms of views as well as in terms of organizational standing—of the departments, and is most applicable to allocating resources.

Aspects of decision-making in the Dexterity dimension are also present. In Dexterity, decisions are made by bringing everyone to the same level of knowledge, out of which the way forward emerges, typically in a consensus view. At Amazon, data is often used to gain knowledge on an issue, and everyone attending a meeting is expected to join the discussion without consideration of status in the organization. It may be suggested that the Dexterity elements most frequently occur in relation to operational decisions.

However, decision-making at Amazon often, in fact, involves a series of meetings on the same business issue or proposal, where the series of decisions reflects aspects of decision-making in the Deed dimension: judgments in doing. An initial proposal for an initiative (based on judgment regarding the business situation) is submitted to a meeting, and the attendees consider whether there are good enough reasons to reject the proposal (based on their judgment regarding the business situation). In principle, if one attendee wants to veto the proposal, this is enough to stop the initiative. When there is no veto, the proposal is then implemented by the manager or team, who are expected to continue to use their judgment and adjust the implementation as needed in light of what actually happens. At the next meeting on the issue, the manager or team again submits a proposal, which draws on the additional experience gained since the last meeting. And the meeting attendees make a veto or not based on the latest developments in the initiative, as well as on their own additional experience since the last meeting. That is, judgement about the latest business situation always flows into the proposal, in deciding on a veto, and into the implementation.

Examples of decision-making resting on the elements of Deed decision-making seem most weighty in the history of Amazon. Prime, Selling on Amazon, and AWS have been presented by Amazon as judgment calls. Hiring candidates is subject to the veto of one person, where the role of the bar raiser was created specifically for this purpose. This observation is in keeping with the suggestion in this book that the fundament for organizational behavior at Amazon is the Deed dimension. Indeed, Amazon has operated in the rapidly changing online retail industry, where judgement regarding the current business situation has been more relevant to decision-making than functional views or consensus. The latter are based on positions or knowledge which have built up over time, but in the online market, the past has never been particularly relevant in deciding the future.

Recently, Jeff Bezos set out the principles for the most important decisions at Amazon:

> *First, never use a one-size-fits-all decision-making process.*
> *Second, most decisions should probably be made with somewhere around 70% of the information you wish you had.*
> *Third, use the phrase "disagree and commit." This phrase will save a lot of time.*
> *Fourth, recognize true misalignment issues early and escalate them immediately.*

These four principles may be commented as follows. First, in this book it has been suggested that decision-making processes at Amazon indeed are not one-size-fits-all but adjust to the nature of the decision, e.g. allocation of positioned resources based on Degree positions, standards in customer service and operational decisions based on Dexterity data and consensus, while decisions about online functionalities and key strategic ventures draw on Deed judgments in doing. Second, in a dynamic market it lies in the nature of key strategic decisions that complete information is not available. Thus, judgment is vital to the decision and to the implementation. Third, the principle of "disagree and commit" is explained by Bezos to mean that decision-makers are often not in agreement with a proposal, but do not see sufficient reasons to reject it. Thus, they commit to stand behind the implementation, as expressed in the Leadership Principle: "Have backbone; disagree and commit." Fourth, judgment continues to be exercised when implementing an initiative. When the initiative is not running as foreseen—not uncommon in a dynamic and uncertain market—this "misalignment" needs to be recognized and escalated to the decision-makers with an adjusted proposal based on an updated judgment. The last three comments illustrate the Deed fundament to strategic decision-making at Amazon.

MDW 3 at Amazon in Delight at the basic level

The Work Mindset in Delight is what will be here termed "instrumental marketing." Employees are aware of the need to address the customer and his or her wants and needs, where the approach is not strongly oriented to subjective wishes or latent demands, but rather to straightforward, on-the-surface, "instrumental" matters of market positioning, price level, customer service, and the design for use of products and services. These aspects of the Work Mindset in Delight may be loosely, but not exclusively, associated with the term "customer obsession," which appears at times in Amazon company documents such as Shareholder Letters and Annual Reports.

The Work Leadership in Delight is identification with the leaders. A small number of employees do more than look up to Jeff Bezos, forming something like a cult around him.

Work in Team in Delight takes the form of being a diplomat within the team. To the limited extent that team members work in the Delight dimension, i.e. identify with the firm and thus are emotionally involved and/or see their professional development as being closely linked with the firm, Work in Team can involve feelings. Dealing with these feelings within the team calls for diplomacy in creating an atmosphere and finding solutions agreeable to all team members.

The Work Style in Delight is to work to your dream with allies. Some personnel have felt moved by working at Amazon as a kind of dream come—or coming—true. To a certain extent, they could find similarly motivated personnel and together work towards meeting their shared dreams.

Work Cross-Department in Delight is oriented to the features of the joint output across the departments. To a limited extent, the teams engage in a synthesis of their separate outputs to form a synthesized whole, which serves as the solution package.

The Work Result in Delight is resonance. Workers in the same team or working across teams have an impact beyond their own work because they contribute to a synthesized whole, i.e. also improve the results of what others put into the synthesized whole, which speaks to customers.

The Work Framework in Delight is stakeholders. When moving into new business areas as part of Growth, Amazon is aware that each new business area involves relations with a new set of stakeholders: not only customers, personnel, and business partners, but also national and local state representatives, unions, consumer groups, and so on. As a large employer in a community and a high-profile firm, Amazon is regarded by the stakeholders in its locations with a mix of positive and negative attitudes, as is normal. Amazon manages these stakeholder attitudes as part of doing business in a location in a normal manner, i.e. at the basic level. These issues are not particularly relevant to the performance evaluation or career development of personnel.

Work Decisions in Delight involve two or more proposals for the same initiative, presented in their entirety—in order to appreciate the unity of opposites in the whole—and the decision is to choose one of them. At Amazon, this kind of decision-making was rarely practiced.

Summary

Amazon's internal supply interfaces for designing, producing, and marketing the firm's services and products have been shaped by the four dimensions of value, principally in the three dimensions in which Amazon offers primary value to shopping customers.

In the Degree of the supply chain, functional excellence has been achieved by the "best" instructions. Every employee has had a balance between designing, issuing, passing on, and obeying instructions, depending upon the position he or she owned in the organizational hierarchy. Instructions to attain and maintain the top functionality of an excellent organization took many forms, including budgets and the allocation of resources, managerial performance reviews, targets, instructions from specialist teams, a strict vertical hierarchy in organizational units, which are managed as if they were Strategic Business Units, and functional policies.

In the Dexterity of after-sales customer service, personnel have applied what they know in a systematic manner in the form of processes. Knowledge was actively built up and shared in teams, between departments, and in management by taking account of others' knowledge and at the same time making others take account of their own knowledge. Decisions and leadership have been based on gathering, sharing, and applying knowledge in a consensual manner.

In the Deed of the website and other online functionalities, personnel have done their work as allocated within the team and divided up between departments, doing their best with their technical skill and judgment to add value by responding to concrete opportunities. Decisions were continually reviewed and adjusted in the doing, i.e. in the course of implementation, while leadership consisted of assigning and watching over what employees did.

To a much lesser extent, in the Delight of the collectivity within the whole organization, personnel felt an engagement to realize customer benefits and meet societal needs, as shared with colleagues and the firm. The shared objectives enabled two kinds of resonance, which were more marked in the first years of the firm: personnel resonated with one another to synthesize modular packages in fluidly formed teams, and the modular packages resonated with customers.

Taking Stock

In examining MDW 1 and MDW 2 at Amazon, it was shown that there are significant distinctions and boundaries in the value exchanges and market approach present in the supply chain, the website, and the after-sales customer experience. This chapter has confirmed and deepened this characterization of Amazon in that, indeed, the internal supply interfaces in these three business areas are managed in distinct ways, each corresponding to their own primary D.

MDW 3 is the capability by which firms are able to dominate their primary

D by driving rivals out of the market and raising barriers to entry. In the case of Amazon, with primary strength in three D's—and indeed the three most important value dimensions in online retail—the result has been that Amazon has dominated not only a given D in the market, but the firm has dominated the market as a whole. Externally, Amazon has dominated the market via the First Mover advantages that haven't stopped, as identified in Chapter 4. Chapter 5 has now revealed the nature of the internal supply interfaces which enable Amazon to keep on innovating, operating at the highest level in the market. Only one pure online retailer, QVC, has managed to enter the online retail market in the twenty-first century and gain a substantial market share. Other potential pure online retailers have either not even attempted to enter the market in the face of Amazon's dominance, or have gained only a very modest market share. All the other large players in online retail have leveraged their offline market presence to establish a foothold in the online market—a topic already discussed under the heading of Markets Value Factor 5 in Chapter 2 and further pursued in Chapter 7.

In closing, a noteworthy characteristic of MDW 3 at Amazon is the limited scope of Work Cross-Department. To a large extent, Amazon is organized into fairly autonomous teams and departments who do their own work. They then deliver their finished results directly to their internal or external customer with little need to coordinate or integrate their work with that of other teams or departments. Again, this reflects the fundamental orientation to Deed at the firm.

In sum, the different dimensions of value in the Work Result at Amazon illustrate the different ways in which work is conducted and results are generated by the power of the organization (Degree), the process (Dexterity), the individual (Deed), or the collective (Delight).

MDW 3 internal supply interfaces are the managerial practices to make the most out of the firm's internal resources, as examined in this chapter. Firms, however, can also draw on external resources outside the organizational boundaries to build their success. This is the topic of MDW 4, the Business Model, discussed in the following chapter.

Chapter 6

MDW 4: The Business Model

Markets Value Factor 4	Managerial Do-Well 4
Utilizing others' resources to raise the appeal of own offers	Manage a consistent business model which can utilize own and others' resources to maintain the firm's survival

F irms generate value by applying their own resources. In addition, the firm can utilize the resources of others—personnel, business partners, communities, and rivals—to raise the appeal of its own offers. However, in enhancing its value offers in these two ways, the firm needs to make sure that gaining more market share in this way in fact generates more benefits than costs; otherwise, the survival of the firm would be endangered. The firm manages the combination of others' resources with its own resources in such a way that it does not overstep itself. Managerial Do-Well 4 is the mechanism to manage the mobilization of resources—from others and from itself—in such a way that the needs of the firm as an ongoing entity are met.

MDW 4 is thus a new kind of Managerial Do-Well in that it is oriented to the needs of the firm as an institution with requirements of its own, rather than to the preferences of the parties. In MDWs 1-3, the firm is focused on meeting party preferences and, in this sense, is something like the plaything of the parties, forced to behave in the interests of the parties in order to achieve market success. In MDWs 1-3, even the firm itself is regarded as a context in which the firm has to be concerned about party preferences: those of the personnel. However, when managing party relations as in MDWs 1-3, the firm must ensure that this is done in a way which secures its own future. This "insurance policy" of the firm is the business model as embodied in MDW 4.

The five parameters of MDW 2, i.e. the five elements of the external demand interfaces, show how the firm addresses party needs. The five parameters of MDW 4 reproduce these five parameters, but in terms of the firm's own needs, i.e. in terms of the firm's own logic to survive and grow. The business model is therefore a kind of "shadow accounting" for the relations to parties, in which the business model ensures that these relations indeed serve the ongoing interests of the firm. That is, the five elements of the business model are a kind of a check, or indeed "background profit and loss account," to ensure that the relations with parties also make sense for the firm. The business model is presented in Figure 6-1, with only the single context of the firm. The parameters of MDW 4 match those of MDW 2, but represent benefits for the firm to its own purposes and ends.

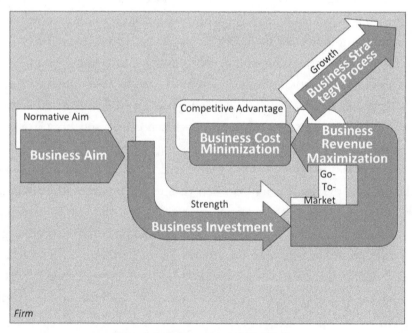

Figure 6-1: Managerial Do-Well 4

The Parameters of MDW 4

The Business Aim is the goal of the operational logic of the firm—what the firm aims for in order to survive in the long-term. The Aim is the "nutrition" for the business and its operations; achieving the Aim keeps the firm alive. The Business Aim is the mirror of the Normative Aim, which is what the firm strives for to justify, and thereby maintain, its existence in society. The Normative Aim gives the firm acceptance in the societal settings in which it operates. The Business Aim gives the firm the material and immaterial resources to survive as an institution, both the hard factors such as revenues and finance, as well as the soft factors such as the sense of success: what makes the institution worthy of continuing to exist. The Business Aim is the "reason for being" of the firm in its business activities as demonstrated to all, inside and outside the firm.

To achieve the Business Aim, the firm undertakes Business Investment. "Investment" is not used here in the conventional accounting sense. Rather, in this book, it refers to the business activities conducted in one time period which are expected to generate a return in a future time period. The effort is made today to achieve the Business Aim, while the return comes tomorrow in the form of the hard and soft factors. In addition to this transformation in the time dimension relating to the Business Aim, Business Investment builds up and develops the internal Strength of the firm in the direction of marketable results. Business Investment activities may well be booked in the accounts as running expenditures; therefore, the term "investment" needs to be understood in terms of the business logic of the operations rather than in terms of accounting principles.

The crystallized results from Business Investment form the basis for Business Revenue Maximization. This is the logic of how the firm realizes and increases turnover—the "formula," so to say, by which turnover and the increases therein are calculated. Both the underlying thinking, as well as the activities within the firm regarding how to earn and raise turnover, are structured by this formula. The Business Revenue Maximization is the result of the Go-To-Market model of the firm, representing what the Go-To-Market model achieves for the good of the firm.

Business Revenue Maximization is offset by Business Cost Minimization in order for the firm to generate a profit. Business Cost Minimization steers the parameters of the business model so that they are conducted according to an operational logic which limits outlays. This Cost Minimization arises from the Competitive Advantage of the firm: the firm generates a Competitive Advantage in a way which limits its own costs. That is, the Competitive Advantage in MDW 2 is defined in terms of party preferences, yet is achieved in such a way that in MDW 4 it generates a cost advantage for the firm. The business model thus ensures that the way the firm meets party preferences is also the way the firm minimizes costs. The two separate worlds of party preferences and firm costs are made into two sides of the same coin in the Business Cost Minimization.

The Business Strategy Process is the process for formulating strategic initiatives. Strategic initiatives constitute the changes in the operations with which the firm survives and grows. The Business Strategy Process thus defines the Growth path of the firm.

The business model channels firm activities with both a restrictive and an expansive tendency. It tends to restrict the firm to engage only in business relations which are based on the operational advantages of the strong value dimensions, the "home" territory of the firm. The business model also enables, indeed pushes, the firm to extend business relations to any given party type when this benefits the firm. In this expansive tendency, the successful business model is pliable regarding the types of parties with whom the firm enters into business relations, allowing for divergences from the firm's "home" territory when this helps. In terms of these two aspects, the business model channels the activities of the firm towards chances and away from dangers.

The elements of the business model are not readily observable in the day-to-day activities at the firms, but rather are in the background. The parameters of MDW 4 are therefore not directly associated with concrete activities and organizational behaviors of firms. Rather, the parameters represent the logic in approaching the business which is often unspoken, but implicitly followed. On one hand, the business model is a mental framework of the parties which accompanies their activities. On the other hand, the business model is also an underlying structure of the activities which ensure that the firm's balance on value offered and received remains positive. Thus, the discussion in this chapter of MDW 4 proceeds largely at a logical level, on the whole derived from the observations in the preceding chapters of Part II. The five parameters of the business model and how they are manifested at Amazon are presented in Figure 6-2. The summary/essence of each dimension is presented at the end of the chapter.

		Primary Degree	Primary Dexterity	Primary Deed	*Basic Delight*
	Area	Customer as member of society	Customer as online retail market participant	Customer as shopper	*Customer as consuming person*
Mgmt. Element					
Business Aim		Market Share	Productivity	Utilization	*Share of Wallet*
Business Investment		Centers of Excellence	Knowledge	(Long-Term) Plans	*Modules*
Business Revenue Maximization		Share of Market Spend	Expected Value	First Mover	*Customer (Segment)*
Business Cost Minimization		Economies of Scale	Opportunity Costs	Activity-Based Costing	*Economies of Scope*
Business Strategy Process		Resource Allocation	Increment-alism	Endorsed Initiatives	*Bandwagons*
Summary / Essence		Market and Cost Leader	Sweet Spots	Bull's Eye	*Infectious Engagement*

Figure 6-2: MDW 4: The Business Model at Amazon

The Business Model of Amazon in Degree at the primary level

MDW 4 in Degree at Amazon is illustrated in Figure 6-3 and presented in this section.

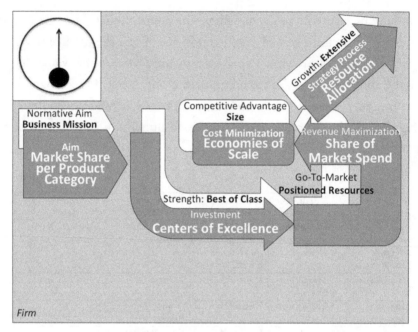

Figure 6-3: MDW 4 at Amazon in Degree

In the business area of supply chain, Amazon's Business Model is oriented to the Degree dimension of value in that it strives for a dominant position on the customer markets in terms of image, positioning, and market share. Customer markets in which Amazon seeks a dominant position are, in the first instance, product categories in retailing, and more recently expanding to include AWS and streaming offers. The Business Model in Degree utilizes the resources from a number of external parties: in retailing, the Selling on Amazon sellers, advertisers, and affiliates; in streaming, the owners of the content. AWS is operated almost entirely from its own resources and thus relies almost entirely on internal parties, i.e. personnel and investors. Amazon manages the relations to these parties, as described in the previous chapters, such that their activities are aligned to the Degree business model and thus contribute to its success.

The Business Aim at Amazon at the primary level in Degree has been to increase its market share in each product category in which it has been active. This Aim has fit to the operational logic in that dominating the sales in a given product category, e.g. electronic goods, has enabled the firm to soak up revenues and status in the category—and prevent rivals from gaining the same. Greater market share has meant a larger size, and size has come before profitability in the Amazon operational logic, because size has been key to the organizational strengths and competitive advantages in customer markets. Amazon has designed the relation to Selling on Amazon sellers, advertisers, and affiliates such that their activities serve to raise the status and market share of Amazon on customer markets. The Business Aim to dominate product categories mirrored the Normative Aim of being a symbol of successful business enterprise in internet/technology.

The dominating market shares of the Business Aim at Amazon have been attained via Business Investment in Centers of Excellence which raise the level of functional excellence throughout the organization, i.e. realize the Strength. The Centers of Excellence are the functional organizational units at headquarters which research and develop market-leading systems and technologies and then roll them out throughout the global organization, e.g. the team which designs fulfillment centers. Another example is the widespread use of systems to drive the retail operations throughout the world, e.g. the purchasing systems, which are developed in headquarters. Furthermore, Amazon's central teams investigate how to best meet the requirements of customers, Selling on Amazon sellers, advertisiers, and affiliates using big data and algorithms, and then design and operate the systems and working relations accordingly.

The investment into the Centers of Excellence positions Amazon in each product category to best understand and respond to the behavior of customers and the other relevant parties. This understanding leads to the highest—or at least a leading market share—in each product category. As Amazon became involved in ever more product categories, its orientation shifted from the market share in individual product categories to its market share of retailing/consumer spending in total. Managing the ecosystem as a whole is a sign that Amazon has moved to thinking about market share of consumption spending in general. The positioning of the Amazon brand as a whole, as represented by the ecosystem, underlies the Business Revenue Maximization at Amazon.

Amazon positions itself as all-encompassing in the market, where each market position in image, distribution, product range, etc. boosts the market position of the rest of the firm. The contribution of particularly the Selling on Amazon sellers, but also other businesses with whom Amazon has a relation, have been substantial in attaining this all-encompassing market position. This aggregate brand image reflects the interdependence of the positioned resources in the Go-To-Market model.

High market share, and thus size, has led not only to higher revenues for Amazon, but at the same time has created the so-called flywheel, causing a downward pressure on average costs. Business Cost Minimization has been accomplished via the volumes/economies of scale as well as synergies in the operations coordinated by the Centers of Excellence and the massive volumes, to which external businesses contribute. The flywheel not only reduces costs, but reflects the Competitive Advantages in Degree of size: broader product range, cheaper and faster delivery services, as well as an expanded ecosystem of products and services.

Market share is attained via positioned resources, and the Strategy Process allocates these resources to Grow the organization based on market criteria: where is growth most likely to occur? The growth path began with the extension of product categories from books to other products and services in the US, and then, in parallel, the operations were extended to other geographic regions. Similarly, relations to other businesses have been built up via the allocation of appropriate resources. In this way, Amazon's extensive Growth into new markets has been managed by allocating resources to position them in the most promising business areas. These Growth activities and resources have been organized in the structures of Strategic Business Units, each with its own combination of products/services and target market, as in Amazon's Growth in Degree.

The Business Model of Amazon in Dexterity at the primary level

MDW 4 in Dexterity at Amazon is illustrated in Figure 6-4 and presented in this section.

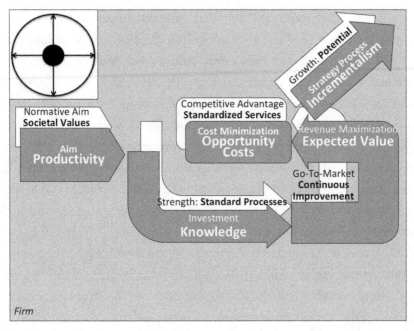

Figure 6-4: MDW 4 at Amazon in Dexterity

In the business area of after-sales customer experience, Amazon's Business Model is oriented to the Dexterity dimension of value in that it strives to improve standardized processes with regard to three major elements of the customer experience after a shopping selection is made: customer service in the terms and conditions of pricing and delivery; direct marketing in working the relation to the customer with regard to reminders, recommendations, etc.; and customer consumption of the item. Regarding the terms and conditions of pricing and delivery, it is crucial to Amazon that the Selling on Amazon sellers operate in line with the same policies established by Amazon. The two key elements of managing customer expectations regarding the consumption of the product are the product information provided by Amazon and the Selling on Amazon sellers and the product reviews written by customers. Managing the relations to sellers and product reviewers to orient them to Dexterity value is crucial to Amazon's Business Model in Dexterity.

In this business area of after-sales, the Business Aim at Amazon has been to raise productivity. Productivity is measured by the ratio of two parameters:

output divided by input. The firm has lowered input by optimizing the processes such that they absorb less resources and/or can be accomplished faster. For a given customer interaction, Amazon has reduced the amount of resources and/or sped the process of answering calls, answering mails, sending marketing mails and requests for reviews, and managing the process whereby customers write reviews. The firm has also raised productivity by raising output via a greater number of satisfied customers, achieved in three ways: First, improvements in customer service; second, in working the market—how best to send recommendations, requests for reviews, reminders, info about sales actions, and so forth; and, third, in product information. The higher productivity, in particular more satisfied customers, enables Amazon to better meet the values of an internet society in its Normative Aim.

The driver of higher productivity at Amazon has been Business Investment in core competences, where the investment takes on three forms for customer experience. First, considerable resources in personnel time, data collection, and data analysis have been expended to develop and document standard processes. Second, CSAs expend considerable time—in training and then on-the-job—learning how to choose the appropriate standard for a given customer query. Third, personnel expend considerable time continually questioning the current status of knowledge and further developing the standards, or even create new ones. An analogous build-up of knowledge into core competences takes place regarding the other after-sales processes, as well as managing the interaction with Selling on Amazon sellers and product reviewers. The personnel time used in developing, documenting, distributing, and applying knowledge in order to root it in the organization has been far in excess of the time needed to simply execute the task at hand. This "investment" in knowledge enables the Strength of standardized processes.

The Dexterity market knowledge thereby attained has been applied to systematically manage the interaction with customers, product reviewers, and Selling on Amazon sellers—the latter with regard to terms and conditions only. That is, Amazon assesses the Expected Value of the impact of different standardized processes in terms of customer and product reviewer satisfaction and implements those processes with the highest Expected Value, e.g. Amazon fine-tunes the General Terms and Conditions for shopping on the website, as well as the order in which product reviews are shown. Selecting and applying the processes with the highest Expected Value forms Business Revenue Maximization at Amazon in the Dexterity area of after-sales. Continually assessing Expected Value informs the Go-To-Market model of continuous improvement.

Thanks to the mass of market knowledge, Amazon has pursued Business Cost Minimization by minimizing opportunity costs through minimizing the loss of customers in two ways. First, by providing leading standards in the after-sales customer experience, Amazon minimizes the loss of customers due to disappointment with customer treatment. Second, by providing the leading set of product information and reviews, Amazon minimizes the loss of customers due to disappointment with the item purchased. Amazon minimizes the opportunity cost of lost customers by providing standardized services, reflecting its Competitive Advantage.

In a business area oriented externally to clearly defined customer requirements and internally to standards and productivity, the Business Strategy Process at Amazon in after-sales has been one of incrementalism: step-by-step refinements to optimize the existing strategies in meeting well-defined customer requirements and, derived therefrom, managing the relations to product reviewers and Selling on Amazon sellers. The incremental way in which Amazon strategically manages after-sales reflects the step-by-step Growth of these activities and the required knowledge in line with the market potential in Dexterity.

The Business Model of Amazon in Deed at the primary level

MDW 4 in Deed at Amazon is illustrated in Figure 6-5 and presented in this section.

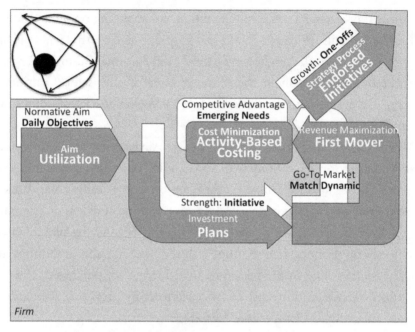

Figure 6-5: MDW 4 at Amazon in Deed

The Business Model in the area of the online experience—shopping, reading books online, "consuming" AWS services, streaming music and shows, as well as the activities of app developers—has been one of Deed. In addition, the Business Model for the overall development of Amazon has been one of Deed. The discussion will proceed at these two different levels regarding Amazon.

The Business Aim at Amazon in Deed has been a high utilization rate of the online infrastructure: hardware, software, and personnel time. Each of the features on the website should attract as much attention as possible, and offer a shopping experience as appealing as possible, in order to induce as many visits as possible. The Aim of the coding conducted by the software engineers has been to directly draw customers onto the website; all other objectives regarding the coding had a much lower priority. As a rule, the programming work was organized such that software teams wrote code constituting a direct interface to the customer and not interfacing to other software. Software was written to generate customer utilization of the software.

As the range of online services widened, the underlying Aim of raising utilization of the online experience remained. The Growth of Amazon has always been linked to the online experience, directly in the case of e.g. retail product categories, AWS, and Prime streaming, and indirectly as in the case of Prime delivery (following from online sales), book publishing (providing the things which are sold online and which, to some extent, are read online), and in the form of products such as Kindle/Fire and other smart devices which are an interface to the online services. Each of these one-off ventures has its own specific set of circumstances and characteristics. The common denominator in managing the diverse ventures has been to measure the extent to which the venture directly led to an improved online experience and thus to greater customer utilization of Amazon online resources. In recent years, the apps contributed by external developers to the Amazon ecosystem have contributed to widening and deepening the online experience.

Finally, to the extent that the Deed dimension informs culture, practices, and behavior at Amazon, the Business Aim has been to raise the utilization of each and every employee. Employees have been empowered to exercise individual leeway to optimize particular situations of, in the first instance, the online experience, and, in the second instance, of all Amazon operations. Optimizing the particular situations should lead to a higher utilization rate of online resources respectively of all Amazon resources. Thus, the Aim of the employee activities responding to these millions of individual situations has been to raise the utilization rate of their activities: in exercising their leeway, employees have been responding to a concrete situation of an internal or external customer and thus should raise their utilization in serving that customer.

The Business Aim in Deed of utilization has involved activities which directly address a concrete customer situation and so raise the appeal of the online experience, leading users to spend more of their daily time in the online experience. The Business Aim has mirrored the Normative Aim of adding value to others' activities so as to support them in mastering their own activities: the attractive online experience enabled the users to utilize their own online time more effectively.

The high utilization rate of the online services of Amazon required a considerable Business Investment in the planning for software development. Each team had to program from the underlying software architecture all the way to the user interface, and each team had to program more or less the entire functionality for the feature it was working on. Typically, such work was performed from scratch because each feature functioned in a unique context and thus was optimized for its own particular circumstances without drawing on existing code for other functionalities. Going from scratch to user interface needed to be planned thoroughly.

At the level of Amazon as a whole, as well as at the level of each employee, each of the one-off ventures in the organization, respectively each of the one-off activities of the personnel, took place in a unique context. Each venture or activity required a considerable Business Investment in personnel time to plan it from scratch in order to make the most out of the particular circumstances and opportunities of the venture. Plans were made not only for ventures, but even for each employee: given the latitude allowed employees, each employee has needed to formally or informally develop an individual plan for performing assignments. The fulfillment of all plans, whether for ventures or employees, were monitored and supervised by management and regularly updated. Furthermore, a number of the huge, innovative successes at Amazon involved initial failures, where several iterations of market launches had to be fully planned before actually coming to success, e.g. Auctions and zShops were planned and implemented before Marketplace, which was then reworked to Selling on Amazon. Thus, plans have absorbed a sizeable amount of non-productive time, but have enabled Amazon to exercise its Strength in initiative and agility. The initiative had to be planned as a whole, while the agility in refining the details also required minutely detailed plans.

Business Investment in Deed has also included investments in personnel, software, infrastructure, and reporting tools to enable app developers to interface with the Amazon website. These investments have needed to be planned by Amazon personnel. More importantly, the functionalities of the interface needed to be designed such that the app developers could plan their own activities in relation to Amazon.

Business Revenue Maximization at Amazon in Deed is realized in two steps. First, the high utilization rate—i.e. the huge, accumulated mass of shopping time, plus later in the firm history the consumption time on the website—would translate into higher sales. It is like traffic in a physical shop: the more of it, and the longer people linger in a shop, the more likely they are to buy. So too with the online shopping on the website. Second, in stimulating the high utilization rate, Amazon has been aware that utilization rate is best raised by the blockbuster hits as first mover, which generate a thousandfold return. That is, these blockbuster hits have resulted from Amazon being the first to make a given kind of market offer, such as Selling on Amazon, Prime, or AWS. Where the firm is the first mover, it enjoys a quasi-monopoly position: there are no direct rivals. As the first mover with an overriding appeal, it captures all, or at least a large share of, the customer interest and thereby allows no or only restricted room in the market for rivals to enter. The time horizon for the revenue impact has been long-term in acknowledgement of the fact that a first move into a new business area requires a long time for the offer and the demand to reach their full potential. The potential for long-term maximized revenue justifies the up-front expense for planning and setting up the operation. Maximizing the revenue for each separate venture or activity on its own reflected Amazon's Go-To-Market model of matching customer and technical dynamic, in which the most was made out of specific opportunities as they arose, rather than addressing systematic market developments or certain target segments. Amazon made the most out of opportunities at the micro level in many features on the website, and at the macro level in terms of new ventures, e.g. streaming. The impact of the app developers to date fits rather into the micro level, although the idea to interface to app developers in the first place was a macro level initiative.

In channeling its activities as much as possible to directly generating the highest volume of online time and/or sales—where the former ultimately leads to the latter—Amazon has exemplified the logic of Activity-Based Costing, where all costs are allocated to a revenue-generating activity. Business Cost Minimization has been attained by tolerating only costs which have led directly to online activity and/or sales. In software development, teams which were largely de-coupled each focused on their own specific functionality for the user interface, expending little effort in interfacing with other teams, integrating their functionality, or generating documentation. In development efforts in general, teams were kept small—the famous two-pizza teams—until market success was confirmed. Overheads which do not address the customer have been "reduced to the maximum," i.e. no more than what has been absolutely necessary. This logic of incurring costs only where they generated online time/ revenues reflects the Competitive Advantage of addressing emerging needs, where activities have been focused on those offers which Amazon believes have not been spotted by rivals but which will grow to become significant sources of demand. For example, the logic of distribution at Amazon was that the content of each order was a one-off. Each order is handled in a way involving the lowest level of resources possible, reflecting the approach of Activity-Based Costing. At the same time, handling each order individually enabled Amazon to promise specific delivery dates and prioritize some shipments, etc., i.e. to give the customer the best cost-benefit ratio—which became a blockbuster aspect of Amazon's offer, reflecting what had been, at the time, the Comparative Advantage of emerging needs in the new industry of online retail. Activities are undertaken at Amazon, and thus costs are incurred, only where online time and/or sales are generated. In the same vein, the time and resources expended by app developers for apps which are not successful do not take up Amazon resources in bandwidth, server capacity, etc.; apps require resources only to the extent that they are, in fact, used.

Given the "intrapreneurial" and one-off character of business ventures at Amazon, the Business Strategy Process has been one of "endorsing" initiatives. As noted at numerous points in the previous chapters, initiatives have sprouted up throughout the intrapreneurial organization, some of which have garnered support from senior management. Resources have been granted to the initiatives endorsed from above and they have assumed a strategic impact. The Business Strategy Process thus reflected Amazon's Growth consisting of one-offs. Successful apps are implicitly endorsed in that they gain more attention on the website.

The Business Model of Amazon in Delight at the basic level

At the basic level in Delight, the Business Aim at Amazon has been the share of wallet of the customer. To be sure, the ecosystem of products and services has covered more and more needs of individual customers and segments. This expanding share of the wallet has generated material and immaterial rewards for the personnel and the firm in the form of revenues and satisfaction in making customers' lives better. However, the former was rather the result of the business model in the other three dimensions, and the latter has not been widespread at Amazon, where the personnel are self-selected to downplay "social cohesion."

Meeting more and more needs of the customer has been accomplished at Amazon by Business Investment in modules which each have met a targeted customer need. To a certain extent, the ecosystem may be regarded as a set of modules all harmonized to the Amazon website—although the ecosystem is rather more a set of one-off ventures, as in Deed—where Amazon has "invested" a certain amount of non-productive time in the synthesis of these many individual modules into a unified, holistic design. Without synthesis, at least to some extent, it would not be possible for the different elements of the ecosystem to run on one website.

Intensively meeting more and more needs of customers has led to the Business Revenue Maximization at Amazon of raising revenues per customer. These higher revenues have, however, been overwhelmingly generated from the business model in the other three value dimensions. The higher revenues per customer have been drawn only to a limited extent from meeting the latent demand of specific customer segments in realizing their personal visions of themselves.

With this limited understanding of the latent demand of the customer, Business Cost Minimization at Amazon has been accomplished by the business model in the other three value dimensions. Cost Minimization occurred only to a restricted extent by means of economies of scope: using and re-using this understanding of the customer in many different products and services to efficiently address customer needs. Rather, as noted above, each team drew on its own resources, knowledge, and judgment in addressing customer needs.

Thus, at Amazon, there has been little in the way of emotional employees striving to meet the latent demand of the customer. The Business Strategy Process involved tending bandwagons in the interest of the customer only to a limited extent, where management orchestrates strategic moves by coalescing interest from organizational units around a given idea, who then resonate with one another to develop a well-rounded and synthesized strategic proposal.

Summary

The summary/essence of MDW 4 in each D is presented in the last row of Figure 6-2.

Amazon's Business Model in Degree has performed extremely well; the firm has assumed a leading position regarding market presence and cost levels. The Centers of Excellence have pushed Amazon to the top of almost all market categories and, at the same time, spread out the firm's presence in each market category to achieve high market shares and significant economies of scale. Amazon is both market leader in online retail in terms of quality and features—the "best" service—and cost leader. Its resources are widely spread and firmly established throughout the market.

Amazon's Business Model in Dexterity has performed extremely well at finding a "sweet spot"—that part of the tennis racket which seemingly effortlessly imparts the greatest force and accuracy to the tennis ball—where after-sales customer experience and the customer demand "click" with one another. Customers are again and again pleased with the level of service offered by Amazon and they remain loyal customers. In this state of harmony between internal and external, productivity is effortlessly high and well-anchored knowledge steers the incremental adjustments which represent optimum improvements.

Amazon's Business Model in Deed has also performed extremely well in managing a "bull's eye": identifying a precise and concrete business opportunity and mobilizing the organization to target a value offer exactly to this market chance. The entire organization is attuned to recognize opportunities and then plan the utilization of agile resources as variable costs to directly generate long-term sales from the endorsed initiative. Prime has been Amazon's most prominent bull's eye, but other innovations like Selling on Amazon have been extremely successful.

Amazon's Business Model in Delight has, at a basic level, managed infectious engagement amongst the different parties for designing, realizing, and consuming the value offers. The engagement leads parties to input a greater quantity and quality of resources, the infectious nature of which enables the impact of the resources to be spread out and intensified when combining and working together. Infectious engagement has coalesced around the ecosystem, personnel motivated by realizing a vision of internet technology to improve society and investors by a long-term view on the impact of online retail.

Taking Stock

The three primary D's for shopping customers, respectively the three areas of business, each have their own Business Model and indeed their own set of resources. They vary in the importance of external resources. The Business Model in Degree, i.e. in the supply chain, draws a considerable amount of resources from outside the organization in the form of relations to other businesses. The Business Model in Dexterity, i.e. in the after-sales customer experience, crucially relies on resources from two types of parties: managing other businesses to offer the same terms and conditions for pricing and delivery, as well as managing product reviewers to generate appropriate reviews. The Business Model in Deed has only recently begun to make use of significant external resources in the form of the apps from developers.

Underlying the way in which the firm as a whole has met its needs as an institution, i.e. has survived and grown, is the Deed Business Model. Hitting the Bull's Eye when being the First Mover into a market area is the fundamental basis for the firm's dramatic success. The business area of the website and other online services are the core of the firm: Amazon is first and foremost a technology firm operating in the internet environment. It has been shown throughout the book that this business area of the firm is characterized by the aspects of the Deed value dimension. In addition, key elements of the

Degree and Dexterity businesses were initially created in the terms of being a First Mover. Prime, the flagship element of the logistics operations, was the last in a sequence of one-off attempts to create an offer in logistics operations which no rival could match, and which, in fact, in a number of ways initially ran counter to the Degree character of the logistics operations. Many of the Dexterity features, such as customer reviews and the importance of product information, were also initially one-off plunges that hit the bull's eye and thus were subsequently standardized. The predominance of the Deed Business Model parallels the predominance of the Deed value offer to personnel, as well as the predominance of Deed in MDW 2 and MDW 3. Examining the Business Model has once again confirmed that the driving force in the organizational behavior of Amazon is fundamentally that of Deed.

The Business Model demonstrates how Amazon ensures the viability of its different business areas. The viability of the entire business enterprise is the subject of MDW 5 the Steering Logic in the next chapter.

Chapter 7

MDW 5: The Steering Logic

Markets Value Factor 5	Managerial Do-Well 5
Targeting systematic value offers in multiple channels	Practice a steering logic to align the market fit in different channels

Markets Value Factor 5 evaluates the success of a retail firm in systematically directing offers in different channels. MVF 5 shows the extent to which a retailer is able to make a convincing offer in multiple channels on the market. Success in more than one channel enables a retailer to address a wider range of shopping missions of any one customer, as well as address a wider range of customers with differing preferences for different channels, as discussed in Chapter 2.

The first demand on the retailer with regard to the corresponding Managerial Do-Well, MDW 5, is an organizational logic which is successful in one channel. This is a pre-condition to score well on Markets Value Factor 5; to be successful in multiple channels, the retailer first has to be successful in one channel. In the four previous chapters regarding MDWs 1-4, it was shown that Amazon shapes and organizes the activities and thinking of the firm in a very particular way so as to generate value in online retail. MDW 5 will show how these different managerial practices in MDWs 1-4 mesh together to form one, consistent organizational behavior suited to online retail.

The second demand on the retail firm with regard to Managerial Do-Well 5 is an organizational logic which does not block a second channel; this is the second step in scoring well on Markets Value Factor 5, i.e. to be successful in multiple channels. MDWs 1-4 need to be steered by MDW 5 to mesh together to form one, consistent organizational behavior without barriers to a second distribution channel, or, for that matter, to a third or fourth distribution channel. Thus, in its entirety, the second demand on the firm with regard to MDW 5 is to attain an organizational logic without barriers to further distribution channels. The organizational logic involves some mix of organizational resources and units which are shared between the operations in the different channels, and organizational resources and units which are dedicated to only one channel.

Finally, regardless of the amount of organizational resources and units which overlap or are distinctive, the operations in the different channels need to gain benefits from each other such that it makes sense that they are operated within the same firm. This is the third demand on MDW 5: that there are some synergies—lower costs and/or higher revenues—between the operations in the different channels. Otherwise, there is no reason for the firm to be active in multiple channels.

The examination of MDW 5 at Amazon in this chapter will be restricted to the first demand on a retailer: steering the meshed organizational logic which is suited to the online channel. This focus arises because Amazon's retail activities were conducted almost entirely online until the firm acquired Whole Foods Market in summer 2017; as noted in Chapter 2, Amazon scored the worst among leading online retailers regarding Markets Value Factor 5. The history of Amazon's managerial practices were conducted almost exclusively in the online context up to summer 2017, and this substantial body of managerial practice will be evaluated here. Amazon's first steps into offline distribution with Whole Foods Market will be evaluated in Chapter 9. That is, Amazon will be evaluated in the terms of the second and third demands on MDW 5 in Chapter 9, which examines Amazon after the acquisition of Whole Foods Market in the context of the near-term future developments in the retail market.

MDW 5 impacts all the activities involved in generating value, i.e. it steers all the other MDWs. For each of the MDWs 1-4, there is a parameter of

MDW 5 that steers and structures the value generation activities. MDW 5 is the command headquarters for directing the value offers and operations in different distribution channels. MDW 5 oversees the choice of channels in which a firm is active, determines the party types and segments to whom a systematic and institutionalized offer is addressed, and oversees the choice of which strong Ds are to be included in the offer.

The five parameters of the steering logic are presented in Figure 7-1. The parameters in the steering logic of MDW 5 are termed "constructs" to indicate their dual character: the constructs are built into the minds of the managers and shape how they think, decide, and communicate and the constructs are also built into the organization and mold the organizational processes, behaviors, and cultures.

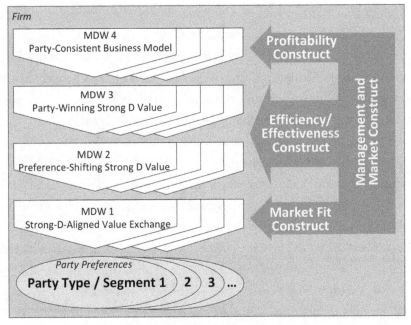

Figure 7-1: The Steering Logic of MDW 5

The Market Fit Construct in MDW 5 steers the value exchange in the market of MDW 1. Market Fit Construct is the managerial mechanism whereby the retailer ensures that the value offers and inputs in each channel are indeed appropriate to the market. On the one hand, the steering mechanism involves conceiving/designing/structuring/producing/marketing/controlling—in a word: managing—the value offers so that they indeed fit to the preferences of the target parties. On the other hand, the mechanism involves conceiving/designing/structuring/assembling/controlling the inputs so that they indeed constitute the means whereby value offers are generated which fit the preferences of the parties. The Market Fit Construct shapes on the one hand a consistent market positioning and profile in each channel, such that the inputs and offers are aligned, forming the pre-conditions for operational synergies within each division. At the same time, the Market Fit Construct creates a degree of uniformity in the market positioning and profile across channels, which is the underlying pre-condition for the retailer's synergies between channels.

The Efficiency/Effectiveness Construct steers the demand and supply interfaces of MDWs 2 and 3. The Efficiency/Effectiveness Construct is the managerial mechanism whereby the retail firm ensures that the operations are performed efficiently and effectively. The steering mechanism involves conceiving/designing/structuring/running/controlling the operations according to the intertwined duality of "doing the things right" and "doing the right things" in generating value. This Construct realizes the synergies in operations within and across channels.

The Profitability Construct steers the business model of MDW 4. The Profitability Construct is the managerial mechanism whereby the retailer ensures that there is a positive difference between revenues and costs, both within a distribution channel and between them. All methods of calculating profitability are mathematically equivalent, and all of them are derived from the simple equation: Profit = Revenues – Costs. However, the underlying way in which profit is conceived/designed/structured/controlled differs according to the logic of the Profitability Construct. This Construct steers revenues and costs apart, within and across channels.

The Management Construct steers the other three Constructs of MDW 5, aligning the three with one another and steering them in the direction of the primary D or D's. This Construct is internally oriented and shapes the value configuration of the retailer, i.e. in which D or D's does the firm systematically offer primary value. It forms the basis for internal synergies in the organization.

The Market Construct is externally oriented and consists of the mental terms in which managers perceive, think, and decide regarding the market and the organizational terms in which managers shape, structure, and steer activities. It is the basis for external synergies on the market.

The five parameters of MDW 5 the Steering Logic and how they are manifested at Amazon are summarized in Figure 7-2 and presented in this chapter. The openness of MDW 5 at Amazon in each D to managing and gaining synergies from an offline channel will also be briefly discussed, as well as the Steering Logic between the Ds offering primary value for shopping customers.

	Primary Degree	Primary Dexterity	Primary Deed	Basic Delight
Area Mgmt. Element	Customer as member of society	Customer as online retail market participant	Customer as shopper	Customer as consuming person
Market Fit Construct	Top-Down	Consensus	Intrapreneurship	Coalitions
Efficiency / Effectiveness Construct	Build and Eocnomize on Positions	Explore and Exploit Standards	Stimulate and Operate Networks	Develop and institutionalize visions
Profitability Construct	ROCE	DCF	Long-Term Margin	Contribution
Management Construct	Building Blocks	Evolution / Mutation	Agile Platforms	Pooled Forces
Market Construct	Product Categories	Market Spaces	New Market Development	Lifestyle Demands

Figure 7-2: MDW 5: Steering Logic in Four Value Dimensions at Amazon

MDW 5 Steering Logic in Degree at the primary level

MDW 5 in Degree at Amazon is illustrated in Figure 7-3 and presented in this section.

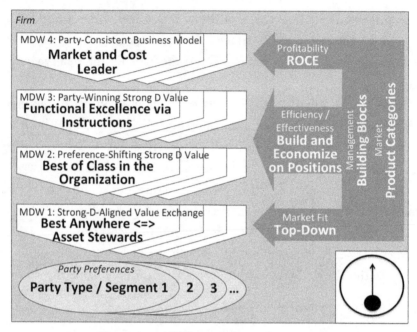

Figure 7-3: MDW 5 at Amazon in Degree

The Market Fit Construct in Degree at Amazon has been to position the firm in the online market at the top, as steered by top management with the overview of both the market and the firm. The firm name "Amazon"— denoting the world's largest river which, indeed, is larger by far than the second largest river—signaled from the start the firm's intention to be massive on the market. Top management has steered the value offers and inputs in MDW 1 towards the "est" offers: the"biggest" (organization), "largest" (product assortment), "most" (watched retailer in the media, responsibility on the job, particularly for new hires), "lowest" (prices), "best" (technology), "fastest" (delivery)—all oriented to attaining a dominant market share in online retail.

In the retail market, being at the top, i.e. the market leader, involves actually being at all vertical levels of the market. For customers, prices are systematically low, and, at times, the lowest, but when the rivals are out of stock, Amazon can raise the prices. The product assortment ranges from luxury to staples, from specialty items to mass articles. Delivery times are the fastest, but can also be one of the slowest, if that is what the customer wants. For personnel, the range of jobs varying from first, those suffused in soft factors to those dominated by hard factors; second, those with wide-open scope lacking boundaries to those with pure routine; third, those of temporary workers with compensation of only hourly wages to senior executives with modest salary and huge bonus; fourth, those with the chance to rise within the ranks—often limited to a certain level—to those where vertical moves upward are ruled out. For business partners, addressing a niche market or a mass market with an offer that can change by the minute or remains the same for years. For investors, a stock to hold for decades or for minutes. In the retail market, building volume to be the market leader involves offering a range. The parties themselves are positioned at a range of different levels, and Amazon has a range of offers, such that the parties can take the offer which addresses them where they are on the totem pole and moves them a notch upwards.

The "est" offers have involved technologies which already existed in business, and the cutting edge of these technologies were taken on by Amazon. Thus, the Market Fit Construct has been a matter of scanning the range of technologies which have existed in the supply chain and selecting the ones that are Best of Class for the logistical operational requirements of Amazon. Once established, the supply chain operations require updating as the Best of Class technologies advance. Updating involves a kind of cannibalization, i.e. bringing in the new to replace the old. This is part of the reason why the steering has to be top-down: there can be no consideration of existing interests in existing structures, jobs/functions, or technologies. Rather, Amazon wants to maintain its "est" position in supply chain operations, for which it hires new personnel to replace the old, installs new technologies, revises the process and procedures in the fulfillment centers, plans to replace trucks with drones for delivery, etc.—all without consideration of existing interests.

The drive to keep up-to-date in supply chain operations with the Best of Class technologies has jettisoned Amazon into further logistical operations which are new to the firm, although not new in the market. Best of Class involves technologies which have been proven to be leading the market. Two examples of updating come from online retail for perishable food. First,

Amazon Fresh is operating in New York, London, and other cities, and, for Berlin and Munich, Amazon has entered into a partnership with the logistics firm DHL for deliveries. The firm is apparently organizing a fulfillment center for food in the Munich area. Second, in purchasing Whole Foods Market, Amazon is not only moving into offline retail, but has acquired a leading online shop for perishables with delivery organized in multiple cities. Amazon is introducing a new logistical feature for itself which is not new for the market; Amazon Fresh is following and building on what other online shops have implemented.

In the more recent expansion of services into e-books, the Kindle reader, AWS, streaming services, and the production of moving image content, the same principles apply with regard to the involved logistics. Amazon adopted existing technologies and applied them to its own business areas and the associated functionality of the applications in order to gain the position of a leading innovator. The range of the service or product is being scaled up in order to address huge volumes on the market and thereby gain the position of market leader in each one of those business areas which are new to Amazon. As part of the position of market leader, Amazon has been the innovation leader in the sense of consolidating and applying Best of Class technologies at a mass volume, i.e. making technologies available to a mass of customers for the first time, rather than itself discovering breakthrough advances. That is, these new services have been each introduced with an "est" market position in the supply chain nearly already built-in. Indeed, Amazon has gained the position of market leader regarding e-books, e-book reader, and AWS. In streaming services, Amazon is "merely" one of the few market leaders, rather than the uncontested market leader.

The offers to and inputs from parties in supply chain operations are managed by the Efficiency/Effectiveness Construct at Amazon. The build-up of new locations/markets, features, technologies, or business areas—i.e. the assumption of an additional position on the market as part of MDW 2—benefits from synergies with the existing positions of the firm, e.g. the supply chain, server network, image/reputation, and the fundament of the existing technologies. The capital resources for developing and rolling out the additional position are thereby used efficiently (expenditures are lower to attain a certain position) and effectively (the market impact is greater). The new features, technologies, or business areas are developed in the internal supply interfaces of MDW 3 by a thorough orientation to appealing to the mass of parties, and are thus effective. The mass volumes are at the same time a source of economies of scale and other synergies. E.g., as noted above, Amazon maintained its commitment to the Prime offer because it was convinced that a huge volume of customers would take up the offer, which indeed happened. Exactly the huge volume of interest in Prime would enable operational costs to be reduced in that the high volumes would bring down average costs for logistics and transportation, as, in fact, occurred.

So too with the more recent new services: their efficiency and effectiveness have been raised by leveraging the existing supply chain resources. E.g. Amazon already had huge server capacity, IT systems to manage relations to millions of customers, and the bandwidth to enable the latter to access the former; the AWS offer was able to readily build on these existing infrastructural resources. The same is true of the streaming services. All the services together form the ecosystem in which the supply chain operation for each service is positively linked to other supply chain operations; in total, the supply chain operations are mutually beneficial in managing MDW 2 external demand and MDW 3 internal supply.

The cumulated positions on the many markets have raised Amazon to the market leader in online retail and other online services, from which the Profitability Construct has steered the ROCE of Degree regarding supply chain operations. Each new facility or functionality in the supply chain has shown a heightened impact due to leveraging on the existing operations, thereby requiring less capital and, once running, serving as a base to be leveraged by other activities. Two examples in the build-up of the supply chain operations for online retail illustrate this Profitability Construct. First, the relationship to Selling on Amazon sellers involved additional costs in handling more product information and orders online. The additional costs were, however, kept low because the additional resources could build on the existing resources, and the higher volumes in the supply chain as a whole raised synergies and economies of scale for all orders. In 2007, Jeff Bezos revealed that the commission Amazon earns when third-party sellers sell their products on the website is roughly equal to the margin on a product sold by Amazon. Second, a Prime subscriber buys goods for an average of $1,224 per year, compared to $505 per year for non-Prime customers. The average Prime member yields $78 more in profit than other customers, very nearly equal to the $79 membership fee. In other words, a Prime customer is just as profitable as a non-Prime customer due to leveraging the economies of scale and other synergies from existing resources. In general, the market position gained from integrating new offers with existing resources in the supply chain is stable over a long period of time, thus representing a stable and long-term return, as in Degree. The business areas, the technologies, and the operations in the supply chain are all collectively managed to enhance the market leading position—and, in turn, the collective power of the market leading position enhances the profitability of each of the services, technologies, and operations to generate the high ROCE.

The same Profitability Construct applies to the more recent services. The capital employed to launch AWS and streaming services has been lower than would have been the case for a stand-alone business, and the capital employed in launching a new service has an enhanced return because it later serves as a lever to boost the business performance of further new services.

The Management Construct in Degree at Amazon has been building blocks. Organizational units in the supply chain at Amazon have been, to a large extent, treated as separate organizational "blocks" that simply have been positioned, metaphorically speaking, next to or on top of one another. Each unit is by and large managed as a separate unit on its own, with its own resources and targets, while the technologies, processes, structures, etc. which are current in the firm are simply rolled out to yet another unit. The best example is the network of fulfillment centers, where an additional fulfillment center is simply added into the network. The interfaces to the other fulfillment centers are minimal, while the interfaces to the systems are the same as for the other fulfillment centers. Another example is the organizational unit to manage the relation to third-party sellers, which was simply added to the entire supply chain organization as a further source of orders. The building blocks share the objective of building the logistical organization and serving the customer, and, as shown immediately above, mutually rely on each other to raise their profitability. Nevertheless, each building block, or organizational unit, is managed in its own terms to reach its own objectives for which it is responsible and, ultimately, accountable.

Similarly, the supply chains of the new services could be added on without re-structuring. AWS involves access to software packages, while streaming involves access to audiovisual content, but it is all ultimately simply more hardware, software, and bandwidth. The logistical operations of these online services have each functioned as an add-on within the Amazon ecosystem. The interfaces to the existing infrastructure of resources are relatively straightforward and have involved little re-organization of the existing infrastructure.

The organizational blocks for each of these functionalities or services have been created and added to the organization from above. There has been limited need for buy-in or change management activities within the organization, because there has been limited need for defining new interfaces or re-adjusting the organization. The changes can be introduced smoothly from on high.

The Market Construct in Degree at Amazon has been product categories. The "products" in the supply chain operations—i.e. the features such as product range, delivery times, and so forth—have been defined in terms of the other "products" on the market from rivals. In particular, Amazon has defined the features of its supply chain operations to be the "est" features on the market, i.e. to be positioned at the top of the market relative to the other offers.

The supply chain operations at Amazon began working the market with a single product category: books. From a logistics point of view, the product category was managed as a single whole, in that Amazon simply aimed to offer every book possible, where books had particular logistical requirements regarding packaging, timing, and so forth. Then toys were managed as a single category: when Amazon moved into toys, it moved into all toys. Toys had their own logistical requirements, for example the challenge of the huge volume of orders in the Christmas season which needed to be filled before December 24th, calling for special logistical measures in the first two years of toy sales. Progressively, Amazon has moved into retailing numerous additional products and services, plus AWS and streaming, where each category has exhibited its own logistical requirements. Relevant for working the market has been to treat each extension of the product range or business activities as a single new category to be positioned relative to other offers—both from rivals as well as its own offers—as a single, massive block on the market.

MDW 5 Steering Logic in Dexterity

MDW 5 in Dexterity is illustrated in Figure 7-4 and presented in this section.

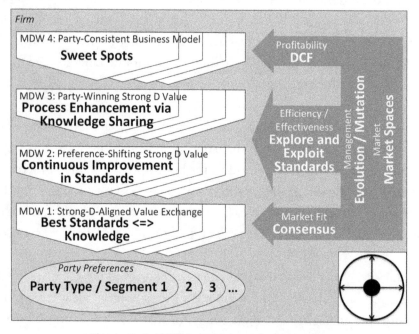

Figure 7-4: MDW 5 at Amazon in Dexterity

The Market Fit Construct in Dexterity at Amazon is consensus. The Dexterity offer applies to the customer experience which, strictly speaking, relates to activities after selecting an item:

- the terms and conditions for payment, delivery, returns, rebates and so forth;
- product information regarding the actual consumption of the item bought;
- technical support for how to use the item, repairs, and maintenance; and
- direct marketing to customers, including requests to review the item, information about related items, or special bargains on sale, and so forth.

Of course, the vast bulk of shoppers will have considered these elements of the customer experience before or while shopping on the website, but the actual activities involved only occur after the customer has selected an item: the after-selection customer experience.

The markets in which Amazon is active are complex and dynamic. In the early history of Amazon, there were no standards regarding the after-selection customer experience, because online shopping was new. The Market Fit Construct has been based on consensus in the sense that the collective organization for after-selection customer experience has fed insights, information, and other forms of knowledge into the formulation of the standardized value offer. To generate these standards, corresponding inputs reflecting technical and market knowledge have taken the form of competences oriented to meeting explicit demand. The Dexterity market knowledge has enabled Amazon to identify, collect, and work with the range of explicit party preferences for after-selection customer experience across its markets. The knowledge about standards in one market has been, to some extent, applied in another, e.g. from books to toys. There is less scope for synergies between markets for wholly different product categories such as AWS, streaming, or Kindle. Nevertheless, not the knowledge of the market, but the managerial practice to identify, collect, and design standard offers and competent inputs has been shared across the markets between the organizational units managing after-selection customer experience.

In the design and operations for standard offers and inputs, Amazon's Efficiency/Effectiveness Construct in Dexterity has been to explore and exploit standards. It took some years of trial and error—i.e. exploration—for Amazon to hit on the right features in online book retail, which, when confirmed, were consolidated and repeated in the offers, i.e. exploited in a recurring manner in the daily business. Amazon then explored rolling out this standard for books to other product categories, one after the other, moving into the exploitation mode when confirmed.

In the external demand interfaces of MDW 2 for the after-selection customer experience, exploring standards has enabled Amazon to discover the design of the standard that is most effective in covering explicit demand in the market. Amazon has then been able to quickly scale up this standard to a huge volume and maintain it over time in order to operate efficiently. In the internal supply interfaces of MDW 3, when a new product category or service was introduced, the team responsible for defining after-selection customer experience sought explorative knowledge about customer reactions in the context of the new service, market, technology, and operations to find the most effective standard. Once the standard had been defined, the team rolled it out into an efficient operation, in that the knowledge was formed into standard operating procedures.

The Profitability Construct in Dexterity at Amazon has taken on the form of a discounted cash flow (DCF) calculation. A DCF is calculated from a stream of costs and revenues over time. However, none of the activities in after-selection customer experience at Amazon actually generate revenue; the activities simply generate costs. Thus, the DCF calculation for after-sales customer experience involves simply costs. The negative discounted cash flow is to be minimized. There are three phases of costs over time for the after-selection customer experience. In the first phase, costs for "product development," or, in this case, "process development," are accumulated for initially exploring the appropriate standard before it goes into operation. In the second phase, the average costs of the standard following launch should fall over time for two reasons. First, as the standard scales up and achieves higher volumes, economies of scale and other synergies can be gained. Second, due to "learning by doing" and accumulated experience, the activities should be performed more and more efficiently. In the third phase, the standard needs to be "updated" in order for it to continue to meet explicit demands. In this third phase, there are both the costs of continuing to operate the old standard, as well as the costs of exploring the new standard. Once the updated standard is defined, then the costs go back to purely operating costs, as in the second phase. The movements up and down in cost levels over time are best reflected in a DCF calculation which can allow for these sequences in the stream of higher and lower costs over time. The future stream of varying cost levels can be discounted to express the logic of "profitability"—i.e. cost reduction—at Amazon with regard to the Dexterity operations of after-selection customer experience.

The Management Construct in Dexterity at Amazon has been Mutation/ Evolution. Knowledge and practices regarding activities in after-selection customer experience first flowed into the definition of the initial standard. This definition represented a mutation from the previous experience of management and/or from practices in comparable industries. Once established, the standard evolved over time on the basis of consensus regarding fine-tuning the design of the offer—in keeping with market knowledge—and evaluating the "profitability," i.e. the cost levels. At certain junctures, this gradual process of evolution was not adequate to keep up with the market: the consensus based on market knowledge reached agreement that a mutation in the standard was needed. An example is the re-definition of the matrix used in the call centers. Once the mutation was accomplished, there was a return to evolution, and so on in recurring cycles.

The Market Construct in Dexterity at Amazon has been market spaces. To work the market, the firm divides it up into different product-segment spaces, based on knowledge of both the product/service and the customer segment. Features of the service are matched with serving the specifics of a given customer segment. For example, Amazon has a variety of mechanisms for payment, matching the service features to different customer profiles regarding e.g. income, customer sophistication in banking services, having a credit card or not, and creditworthiness.

MDW 5 in Deed

MDW 5 in Deed at Amazon is illustrated in Figure 7-5 and presented in this section.

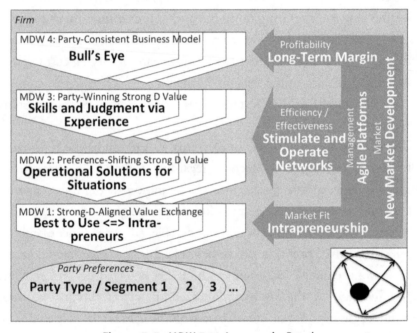

Figure 7-5: MDW 5 at Amazon in Deed

The Market Fit Construct in Deed at Amazon is "intrapreneurship" to detect market opportunities and, following that, to steer and shape the offers and inputs, principally regarding the website and other online functionalities. Time and again throughout its history, the entrepreneurial approach at Amazon has hit on online retail offers which have addressed market opportunities in the form of market holes, i.e. previously unaddressed demand. Amazon managers and specialists have managed each opportunity like a separate venture, exercising their abilities to detect the holes, formulate the offer to cover the holes, and organize the inputs accordingly.

The first market hole to be addressed by Amazon was book retail online, followed by toys online, then electronic goods, and so forth. The retail market for these product categories already existed; the "intrapreneurial" task was to draw customers to the new distribution channel, i.e. to "buy" the new online retail service. Then, Amazon addressed market holes where the market hole included the product and the distribution channel, i.e. the intrapreneurial task was to draw customers to a closely linked online product and online distribution channel. The first such market hole was e-books, supplemented by Kindle, which itself was a product and a distribution channel—when it was online—in one. Following e-books, AWS, streaming services, and shows are also ventures which are online "products" closely linked to an online distribution channel. The inputs—time and initiative from personnel, finance from investors, etc.—were steered accordingly.

To shape and steer the principally online offers in Deed, the Efficiency/ Effectiveness Construct at Amazon has formed and re-formed teams—which will here be likened to engaged networks—for each venture. In the external demand interfaces of MDW 2, the solutions in each venture have offered rewarding situational singularity—for both the customers and the personnel involved—as developed by a team of engaged personnel newly formed afresh for the venture. The teams may be likened to networks given their loose structure and the membership typically drawn from different functions. Amazon management stimulated these networks with a loosely defined objective, where the solution was developed by means of an orientation to the specific customer needs of given situations (a further example of the oft-remarked "customer obsession" at Amazon). Once the solution was designed and approved, more stable "networks" of employees performing the same function then implemented the elements of the solution which belonged to their function: i.e. the programming was performed by programmers, the marketing by marketing specialists, and so forth. The individual ventures in the online business area have been effective due to addressing situational needs and efficient due to implementation by functional specialists.

Regarding the internal supply interfaces of MDW 3, the members of the design network cross-fertilized ideas from their different functional backgrounds to design new and innovative—i.e. effective—solutions. The entrepreneurial thinking and creativity in finding the solution arose from the invigorating interaction when employees with different backgrounds stimulate one another with different ideas. Regarding the implementation networks, they served as an arena within which the functional skills and judgment of employee cohorts have been developed by means of experience, both their own, as well as what they have seen or heard about others' experiences. The solutions have been efficiently implemented in the daily activities of the stable networks: specialists exercised their function with familiarity.

The Efficiency/Effectiveness Construct in Deed at Amazon involves technologies and features which are created, developed, and implemented internally. The innovative impulse comes from the special way in which the teams are managed as networks.

The creative, invigorating, and stimulating offers developed by the networks have created novel market categories in which the Amazon online products and services have faced little or no direct competition. As a quasi-monopoly building barriers to entry by virtue of being the first mover, Amazon has enjoyed a high margin in the long-term in these areas of business. Thus, the Profitability Construct in Deed at Amazon has been Long-Term Margin. Amazon works with planning phases of five to seven years for its online products and services. This long planning horizon has enabled the firm to move into new business areas which do not necessarily reach fruition quickly, but which have a high promise in the long-term of the new market category.

In order to move into different, novel ventures as they are developed, the Management Construct in Deed at Amazon has been agile platforms. The organizational resources in the online business areas at Amazon—networks of personnel, IT systems, hardware, etc.—are crystalized into platforms which can be drawn upon to develop and implement innovative solutions. The platforms are agile in that they can be directed and re-directed in one direction or another depending on the solution. Thus, Amazon not only offers platforms as solutions to parties, it, in fact, utilizes organizational platforms to realize the solutions: it takes platforms to make platforms.

The Market Construct in Deed at Amazon has been new market development. Throughout the lifetime of the firm, it has approached the market by making a new one. In most of its innovations, Amazon was not literally the first to invent the service or product. But it was the first to develop the market for the service or product into a proper market, i.e. to manage the service or product in a manner which was viable to build demand and supply to a significant volume. Most of the "firsts" were in the Deed business area of online services. Even Kindle is as much an online service—functioning as an interface to online services—as a product.

MDW 5 Steering Logic in Delight at the basic level

The Market Fit Construct in Delight at Amazon has been coalitions which shaped managerial practice at the level of basic value. To a limited extent at Amazon, and most particularly in the early years, personnel entertained visions regarding the features of offers and the characteristics of inputs which they felt were right for the firm, for the customers, and for themselves in developing to "a better world." To realize these visions, coalitions have been formed under a loose steering by management in order to bring together organizational support and momentum to agree on the design of offers and inputs. The common denominator within the coalitions was the Delight in fully serving the customer as an entire person, and not "simply" meeting in an isolated manner a status (Degree), standard (Dexterity), or situational (Deed) customer demand. The spirit of Delight coalitions at the basic level have helped form separate Amazon offers into a synthesized package. To the limited extent that the spirit of coalitions existed, they could be formed equally within or across divisions, because the basis of the coalition, fully serving the customer, was not restricted by organizational boundaries.

The Efficiency/Effectiveness Construct in Delight at Amazon has involved developing visions at the basic level of value that were effective and could be efficiently institutionalized. Regarding the external demand interfaces of MDW 2, there has been the thrill and excitement within the firm of gathering engaged contributions to a heady vision for a new customer offer (effectiveness) matched by the need to then institutionalize the operational nuts and bolts of the offer so that it was anchored in the organization (efficiency). Regarding the internal supply interfaces of MDW 3, the team leader needed to manage a balance between the employee's Delight in working towards his or her own wishes on the job—e.g. in contributing to an effective vision—and the need for the employee to efficiently meet the requirements of the firm. To the extent that individual teams/employees oriented their work to a collective vision, moving in the same direction towards the same objective generated certain synergies within Amazon.

The Profitability Construct in Delight at Amazon has been, at a basic level, the surplus of revenues over costs for each targeted customer segment. Delight activities to fully serve the entire person of the customer have, to the limited extent they existed, been channelled to fully serve a given target segment. The attendant costs and revenues were implicitly or explicitly attributed to serving that given segment. Subtracting the costs from the revenues has represented the segment's contribution to covering overheads and gaining profit at Amazon.

The Management Construct in Delight at Amazon has been the organizational forces—coalitions, visions, and contributions—pooled around the Delight of serving customers in general, as well as of serving given target segments in particular. These forces have aligned themselves within the organization to realize the vision, or visions, which at any particular time was or were in favor.

The Market Construct in Delight at Amazon has been the lifestyle demands of segments. To the extent that Amazon, or, more accurately, a number of its employees, has been active in Delight, the market has been divided up into the needs and wishes of different segments to live their lives to the fullest. Amazon has met these wishes and needs with services and benefits in terms of the customer seeking the good life in society, e.g. shoppers coming into contact with other national cultures by means of the products offered for sale on the website.

The Steering Logic between the Ds

In addition to the MDW 5 Steering Logics of separate divisions within Amazon and their orientation to a primary D, there is a Steering Logic between the divisions and their Ds which steers the functioning of the entire organization. After having examined the different D's separately in MDW's 1-4, the Steering Logic to unite the whole organization will be presented in this section. Figure 7-6 shows the Steering Logic between the three D's at the level of primary value at Amazon.

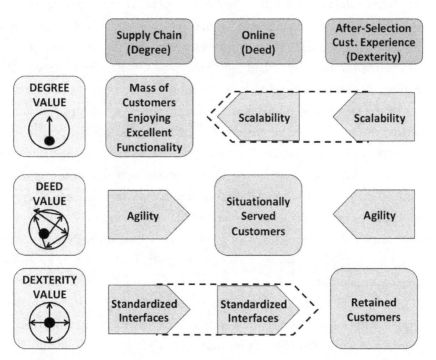

Figure 7-6: Steering Logic between Primary Value Dimensions at Amazon

The gravitational pull of the "est" offers in Degree, which in fact are not just at the top of the market but involve a range, has enabled Amazon to build a supply chain which attracts massive quantities of customers, and thus inputs, as shown in the upper left-hand corner of Figure 7-6. The benefits of the volume and functional excellence extend across the top row of Figure

7-6 to the rest of the organization, i.e. online services and after-selection customer experience. Externally, the firm's position at the top of the market has served as a Degree boost for the image and reputation of the other divisions, who could reckon with a high volume that would at least look or test, if not buy. Internally, the firm's functionally excellent operations boost the impact of each individual organizational unit: e.g. the functionality of the website is enhanced by the excellence and status of logistics—product information from multiple sources and several delivery options—while the customer service organization can steer and structure its activities around the fact that Amazon's logistics deliver world-class performance. In order to take advantage of this benefit, the rest of the organization always had to think and act in terms of the scale and excellence of the market leader. Whatever the rest of the organization did, it had to be able to be scaled up and operate with a range of features in keeping with the high level of functional excellence, as shown by the two arrows pointing to the Degree offer in the supply chain.

In the online Deed offer, customers find a solution offered by Amazon for the variety of their concrete situational needs, as shown in the middle of Figure 7-6. Deed thus gives the rest of the Amazon organization customers who are able to cover their situational demand, and, in this sense, they are appropriately served. As shown in the middle row of Figure 7-6, the mass volumes attracted by Degree will not go lost, but will be adequately served by Deed in their shopping missions such that Dexterity need not worry about the online experience but can focus on the after-selection customer experience. Deed requires that the rest of the organization is able to be agile inasmuch as the supply chain and after-selection customer experience can form and operate the new interface to the changes/innovations in Deed. This agile ability to accommodate the changing situational needs of customers, shown by the two arrows in the middle row of Figure 7-6, is particularly valuable in the new market of online retailing, where requirements change over time.

The Dexterity standards in the after-selection customer experience prevent customers from being dissatisfied, and thus they are retained, as shown in the lower right-hand corner of Figure 7-6. Dexterity gives the rest of the organization a base of loyal customers they can count on. As shown in the lower row of Figure 7-6, the supply chain and the online services are given more freedom in pushing forward into new areas, with less concern about their innovations possibly making customers dissatisfied. Dexterity is valuable as the safety net for the rest of the organization. In return, whatever Degree and Deed drive forward and launch has to be representable as standardized information and processes, as shown by the two arrows in the bottom row of Figure 7-6. Dexterity can then handle customers in a standardized manner.

Not included in Figure 7-6, but included here for the sake of completeness, is the steering logic between Delight and the rest of the organization. The Delight offer at the basic level is a unified whole forming a package. The benefit of Delight to the rest of the organization is to give a certain amount of consistency in the designs of offers and inputs. In particular, the interfaces between the different elements of the offers or the different elements of the inputs appear to have a minimum level of internal coherence. In return, Delight has required from the rest of the organization that, in the designs of their own solutions, to a basic level they take account of the interfaces to other solutions and departments in together serving the market.

Taking Stock

In online retail, the three Ds, respectively the three areas of business, each have their own steering logic. The organization has been trimmed for success in each D, both the coherence within the D as well as the straightforward and readily managed interfaces to other D's/business areas. Amazon is remarkable for being able to manage three different parts of the organization in three distinctive ways. Indeed, the management practices in each of the D's are among the best in business; Amazon is a market leader in each one of the D's/business areas.

Underlying the way in which the firm as a whole has steered the organization, i.e. has built and managed conceptual and organizational constructs, is the Deed Steering Logic. Cultivating intrapreneurship to identify, develop, and address new market categories is the fundamental basis for the firm's success. The business area of the website and other online services are the core of the firm: Amazon is first and foremost a technology firm operating in the internet environment. It has been shown throughout the book that this business area of the firm is characterized by the aspects of the Deed value dimension. In addition, key elements of the Degree and Dexterity businesses were initially created out of the intrapreneurial spirit to form new market categories. Prime, the flagship element of the supply chain operations, was a new kind of market offer that no one had conceived of before. Many of the Dexterity features, such as customer reviews and detailed product information, were also originally an intrapreneurial leap into the unknown.

The Steering Logic of MDW 5 highlights what is remarkable about Amazon: not only being able to operate three different steering logics within one organization that are each at the top of the industry, but getting them to work together and accommodate, and indeed on the whole support, each other in a more or less smooth manner. In contrast with this overwhelmingly positive picture of Amazon, the following chapter will expose the negative side of Amazon by presenting its built-in drawbacks, termed inherent weaknesses.

Chapter 8

Inherent Weaknesses in MDW's

Chapters 3-7 in Part II have presented the internal success story of Amazon: what Amazon does so remarkably well in its management practices which have led to its outstanding business performance. The presentation of Managerial Do Well's 1-5 at Amazon will be rounded off in this chapter by considering their negative side: the extent to which they do not generate value. Pinpointing what are here termed the inherent weaknesses of Amazon will demonstrate how the management practices have placed a constraint, however limited, on the business performance.

There are two sources of inherent weaknesses at a firm in terms of the dimensions of value. First, in their day-to-day activities, firms will stray from strictly adhering to the precepts of their strong D's; this is part of daily business. More serious is a second source of weakness, where firms can go too far in practicing their strong D. The firm can follow a dynamic rooted in the internal organizational logic instead of meeting external market requirements. This weakness of "overdoing it," derived from the very strength of the firm, can take an extreme or mild form.

In its extreme form, the "overdoing it" takes place when a firm is oriented to a single dimension of value, a rare situation for a successful firm. The bulk of successful firms have one primary and one secondary D, as shown for Costco, Macy's, and QVC in Chapter 1. In such cases, the operating principles of each value dimension offset each other, like checks and balances, creating a healthy balance within the organization. However, the value offer and managerial practices of a firm can become oriented to a single D. The logic of this single dimension, unchecked by another operating logic, can become "too much of a good thing" and weaken the organization. This kind of weakness can become systematic and impact the entire operations, and thus the performance of a firm, even driving it towards bankruptcy. In this regard, the case of Kmart was discussed briefly in Chapter 2. Other examples are General Motors, Ford, and Chrysler in the middle of the first decade of the twenty-first century, as presented in my book about the US auto industry referenced earlier in the Introduction.

The mild form of "overdoing it" comes from the circumstance that no managerial practice is perfect. There are always some disadvantages from operating in a certain way; it is inescapable. This mild form is more like the "limits to success" of a firm; there is an inherent, internal boundary to the success of the firm simply because, to a certain extent, there is a downside to operating in a given manner. Amazon exhibits this mild form of inherent weakness to date. This is not surprising, given that the history of the firm has been overwhelmingly marked by success. The inherent weaknesses at the firm have had only a limited impact.

The mild form of inherent weaknesses at Amazon will be examined, for the twinned purposes of simplicity and focusing on the essence, in terms of MDW 5 Steering Logic, which informs and steers all management practices. Furthermore, Deed was identified as the underlying dimension of value for the firm as a whole. Continuing in the sense of simplicity and focus, the inherent weaknesses in MDW 5 in only Deed at Amazon will be examined in this chapter.

Inherent Weaknesses at Amazon

The inherent weaknesses at Amazon arise when Deed is unfettered and is allowed to dominate the organizational behavior without offsetting practices from other Ds, as summarized in Figure 8-1. In this chapter, only the weaknesses exhibited in the course of the twenty-first century will be examined. Weaknesses in a young firm in a young industry are no longer relevant.

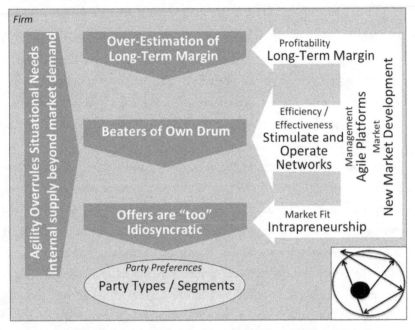

Figure 8-1: Inherent Weaknesses in Deed at Amazon

The Market Fit Weakness at Amazon has been offers which are too idiosyncratic in the benefits offered. In this century, this weakness has been exhibited principally in the value exchange with personnel. As discussed above, the offer to employees includes the substantial room for maneuver accorded to individual managers, the "purposeful Darwinism" of seeding out only the very best, and a demanding role that is so absorbing it is expected to override everything else in the life of the employee. Creating this "gladiator environment" throughout the organization is intended to bring out the best in everyone as they fight for success: the internal synergies of all employees behaving in the same way. However, this offer did not address the preferences of a substantial number of employees, who, rather, under-performed and/or quickly left. This weakness was derived from "overdoing" intrapreneurship in managing people and the associated leeway to steer the value exchange with personnel in distinctive directions—indeed such approaches were encouraged as the basis for market success—but there was no systematic guarantee that employees would favor such offers, and, indeed, many did not. In the sense of this weakness being simply a limit to success, however, to date, Amazon has not been significantly harmed by its idiosyncratic offers to personnel. For the bulk of employees, the pros of working at Amazon have outweighed the cons. Furthermore, although the personnel turnover at Amazon seems high, the firm continues to attract sufficient quantities of capable candidates to replace those seeded out. Indeed, the total number of employees at Amazon continues to expand.

Given that inputs and offers have been steered individually, the Efficiency/Effectiveness Weakness at Amazon arose from managers who each marched to the beat of their own drum. This lack of alignment was derived from the self-steering networks, where self-steering managers could choose to go their own way. Employees refer to siloed thinking, redundancies between teams, and a lack of collaboration between teams—particularly regarding software development. That is, each team had its own view of what was the "right thing" for its functionality and was not willing to budge from this perspective of the individual intrapreneur to consider what others regarded as the "right thing" for the market. In addition, the focus on "doing the right things" could override the need for "doing the things right": programming was often performed under time pressure to meet an immediate opportunity at the cost of poor quality code and lack of documentation. As a result, software engineers are continually on call to patch poor quality code to keep the systems running, and software reviews are often undertaken to simply find out how the code functions, as noted in an entry in a Google forum from a former high-level software engineer at Amazon, which has come to be known as "Steve Yegge's Google Platforms Rant." This weakness is also simply a limit to success, because the outside world sees only the functionality of the systems, which are regarded as leading in the market. Indeed, one ex-employee claims that there are "tons of mission critical code whose original author is long gone, no documentation exists, and in fact the code isn't owned by any team. I've seen many hacks to work around these problems, though I doubt they'd be super apparent to the common Amazon shopper." As he himself notes, even if he is correct with his critique, there is currently little market impact.

The Profitability Weakness at Amazon has been to over-estimate the extent to which the long-term revenue of a given venture exceeds the costs, as derived from the Profitability Construct of long-term margin. Possible examples of this weakness may be found in the expansion of the Amazon ecosystem into publishing, movies, television shows, and streaming services for music, film, and TV shows. To date, these ventures have not performed particularly well as a source of profit, but in the sense of a limit to success, Amazon's business performance has not suffered.

Although targeting—or over-estimating—long-term revenues, the Management Weakness at Amazon has been that the firm has been at times too focused on agility and not enough on significant and lasting needs. Customer Service Associates, who perhaps more than anyone else at Amazon are interested in stability in order to meet standardized customer requirements, point out that the organization has been re-directed "too often." This weakness is derived from the agile organization which oriented and re-oriented its activities to market developments which appeared to be taking hold and hindered the organization from settling down to address significant needs. In the sense of a limit to success rather than a weakness, the history of Amazon is remarkable for the ability of the firm to shift and change direction in responding to new and different market opportunities. It may well be true that this business approach has resulted in one or two shifts too many, but any negative consequences arising therefrom have been restricted.

In the vein of "too much" agility, the Market Weakness at Amazon has been that the creativity and innovativeness of the intrapreurial employees have gone beyond what the market was ready for. That is, Amazon has developed offers which have represented new market categories—true inventions for which no rival offers existed—but for which, in fact, there was scarcely any demand: a new offer which did not attract parties.

In the discussion about MDW 2 at Amazon, reference was made to the Shareholder Letter 2015 in which failure and invention are presented as going hand-in-hand; indeed, for new market categories, it is to be expected that there will be many more failures than successes. This is the sense in which the Market Weakness has been merely a limit to success. Amazon has developed numerous offers which ended in losses, but they have been more than compensated by the successful innovations which have boosted business performance.

Taking Stock

The essence of the inherent weaknesses is that the firm becomes too inward-looking rather than oriented to the market and other external settings. Amazon can become too caught up in its own institutional concerns and pay less attention to external interfaces, including where the "external" interfaces involve the relations to the personnel within the firm.

This inherent weakness lies in the nature of business, particularly in large organizations. The issues, concerns, requirements, etc. of the firm have a concrete immediacy; they are graspable, and often measurable, and are the subject of daily business. Therefore, orienting activities to the internal priorities of management lies close to hand and is straightforward to accomplish in day-to-day activities. In contrast, responding to party preferences in the market, the societal setting, and even in the environment of the firm itself is inherently more vague, less immediate, less concrete, more difficult to grasp, and harder to stick to repeatedly over time. An "orientation drift" towards the institutional/internal and away from the organizational/external is intrinsic to large firms.

This chapter closes Part II, examining the managerial practices of Amazon as it was constituted before the acquisition of Whole Foods Market, i.e. as a leader in online retail and internet technology services. Part III addresses the future of Amazon in a re-constituted form, beginning with the next chapter to understand the sale of services and the move to omnichannel.

PART III

The Future of Amazon:

After Whole Foods Market and Beyond

Chapter 9

The Ongoing Present in Services and Omnichannel Retail

This chapter examines the near-term future of Amazon by evaluating its prospects to be successful in the context of the retail market developments to be expected in the ongoing present. The two major developments considered in this chapter are the sale of services and the shift from multi-channel retail to omnichannel retail.

The sale of services would be an additional build-up of Amazon's ecosystem. Selling services such as travel tickets, hotel bookings, insurance policies, banking services, or tickets to concerts and other events would represent a major step for Amazon for two reasons: the services would not draw on Amazon's superior supply chain infrastructure, yet would involve physical activities in the offline world, which is different from the streaming services and e-books.

The market requirements and advantages which are relevant to multi-channel retail were discussed in Chapter 2 with regard to Markets Value Factor 5. Omnichannel retail is a further step in the maturity of the retail services in that the customer is offered seamless and integrated shopping services across all channels. Amazon's acquisition of Whole Foods Market is a decisive step in the direction of overcoming its weakness in Markets Value Factor 5 by developing a second channel for omnichannel retail; the move will be evaluated in this chapter. The evaluation will be made by considering what Amazon can do for WFM, as well as what WFM can do for Amazon. The former involves looking at how the strengths of Amazon could alleviate the weaknesses of WFM and improve its business performance, from which Amazon as owner would also profit. The latter involves looking at the extent to which the acquisition of WFM furthers the growth path of Amazon, in particular the openness of the Amazon organization to offline distribution and the organization's scope for synergies between online and offline. The first actual steps taken by Amazon as new owner of WFM will be evaluated in terms of these two sources of potential benefits to establish how far Amazon has come in realizing them.

It will be shown that many factors support Amazon's potential success in selling services online and in developing omnichannel retail. It will, however, be suggested that the success potential for both of these developments would be considerably improved if Amazon revived secondary value in Delight. The benefits from re-introducing Delight managerial practices in the organization and the path to realizing this organizational development will be briefly sketched.

Sale of Services via Online Retail

Amazon has been active in the sale of services online, ranging from travel to banking and now including added-value services in pharmacueticals. In the travel industry, Amazon partnered with Expedia in 2001 for hotel and travel bookings and then in 2006 with Sidestep for the same. In 2015, it offered hotel bookings with discounts on its own account. All of these ventures were stopped; as often the case in the history of Amazon, the firm is searching for the right success formula. Certainly part of the challenge for Amazon is the massive presence of Expedia in the market, which, via its various subsidiaries, holds three-quarters of the global market in online travel bookings.

Amazon has had much more success in financial services. The services increase the number of customers and sellers and the volume of their activity in the ecosystem by enabling them to sell and buy more and reducing any buying/selling friction. Amazon has been experimenting with payment functionalities since 2006, going through several alternatives before the current set of promising solutions. Amazon Pay is a digital wallet, Amazon

Cash allows customers to deposit cash, and Amazon Allowance is an account for children controlled by their parents. Amazon partners with Synchrony Bank for the Amazon Prime Store Card and with Visa for the Amazon Visa Credit Card. Amazon Lending provides finance to many third-party sellers on its website. In Europe, Amazon Protect provides accident and theft insurance on various consumer goods in partnership with a UK insurer. Amazon is reportedly in contact with several banks to develop something like a checking account, which could be pushed primarily through Amazon Cash.

The move into services can also involve the sale of products with added-value services: e.g. in June 2018, Amazon acquired Pillpack, an online retailer of prescription medicines who packages them in the patient's daily doses, typically involving several drugs. Further examples of possible added-value services could be user support and advice for complex consumer products or the installation and configuration of apps and other software performed by an online service. Sales of services could also include tickets to museums, concerts, or other events. There are many possibilities.

Amazon's organizational readiness to move into the online sale of services can be evaluated in terms of the MDW 5 Steering Logic in each of the four dimensions of value, identifying the parameters which support and those which hinder the online sale of services.

With regard to Degree in the supply chain, in the Market Fit Construct of Top-Down, the senior managers would identify the developments in the market and arrange for a new kind of supply chain as market leader. The "suppliers" would be firms new to Amazon—insurance companies, banks, airlines, hotels, restaurants, event organizers, and so forth—requiring new working relations, organizational units, and processes. Organizational shifts and changes in priorities would be undertaken top-down, without consideration of established interests. Amazon would move into services retail in a decided and determined manner. The Efficiency/Effectivenss Construct to Build and Economize on Positions would come into play only in a restricted manner. The market positions to be drawn upon would be merely the brand image and the internet infrastructure; the market positions in the supply chain are not relevant. Accordingly Amazon's particular strengths in the Profitability

Construct—ROCE which draws upon synergies between resources positioned on the market—would only minimally come to the fore in the sale of services. The Management Construct of Building Blocks would simply place the required teams in the organization and the Market Construct of Product Categories would add the sale of services as simply an additional "product" category.

In Degree, the Market Fit, Management Construct, and Market Construct would readily accommodate the online sales of services, while the Efficiency/Effectiveness and Profitability Constructs would not be able to particularly play out their strengths. Considering other Managerial Do-Well's in Degree, Amazon's MDW 2 would support the move into selling services. The Normative Aim to be Leader in Internet Technology/Business Enterprise would support the organization in staying on the forefront of market developments in online retail, while moving into services would fit the extensive Growth of taking on new product categories. In MDW 4, Amazon's Business Model to be Market and Cost Leader would induce the organization to sell services in order to raise its revenues and market share by selling yet another product category, although there would be little impact on Cost Leadership. In conclusion, Amazon in Degree is moderately well situated to be successful in the sale of services.

Turning to Deed and the online functionalities, the novelty of selling services online should play to Amazon's strong points in this area. The Market Fit Construct of Intrapreneurship would identify market opportunities and oversee the appropriate offers and inputs; the Efficiency/Effectiveness Construct to Stimulate and Operate Networks would develop and implement the new ideas; the Long-Term Margin of the Profitability Construct would give Amazon the time to manage the features of the new functionalities until the benefits successfully meet market demand; the new operations would form Agile Platforms under the Management Construct; and the New Market Development of Amazon's Market Construct could be played out to the full in building up this new business.

All the Constructs in the Deed Steering Logic would be able to take advantage of the sale of services. In addition, in MDW 1, Amazon could link the purchase of goods with individualized recommendations for services—

jewelry and household insurance, or books about wild animals and safaris—and vice versa. Customers would gain greater value from their shopping missions and business partners would gain greater value from Amazon's ability to link services and goods in individualized recommendations. In Deed, Amazon is well suited to be successful in the sale of services.

With regard to Dexterity and product information, as well as terms and conditions, Amazon would face considerable challenges in the new realm of services. The Market Fit Construct of Consensus would find it doubly difficult to design the offers and inputs, given that little knowledge of services markets is available in the organization and the "product information" for services is complex and subject to many regulations. The Efficiency/Effectiveness Construct would be almost entirely Explore and very little Exploit, while forecasting the cash flows for the Profitability Construct of DCF would be very difficult. The Management Construct would be largely Mutation in the manner of jumping around to find the appropriate solutions, with very little Evolution. Finally, the Market Construct of Market Spaces would be caught up in simply trying to find the services and customer segments that match. These challenges may be part of the explanation why Amazon has moved carefully in the sale of services.

Finally, turning to Delight and serving the customer as a whole person who consumes goods and services, the Market Fit Construct of Coalitions would bring together personnel from different departments to offer innovative and comprehensive packages of goods and services, e.g. a tour of Aztec sites in Mexico with appropriate clothes, the most suitable insect repellent, and the book written by the tour guide. Under the Efficiency/Effectiveness Construct of Developing and Institutionalizing Visions, the coalitions would conduct intensive market research into the implicit demand of customers. For example, focus groups for Aztec tours would reveal the weight of interest in aspects such as romantic Mexican culture, knowledge of the Aztec political and economic developments, touching the hearts and minds of the Aztecs who lived there, and so forth. The coalitions would accordingly institutionalize, i.e. implement as well-established and recurring features, tours with elements that could include reading selected books in advance and wearing fashion from Mexican designers while attending an evening show, all bought on Amazon. The Profitability Construct of Contribution would enable Amazon to properly calculate the return on such packaged activities for target segments. The Management Construct of Pooling Forces would bring together enthusiastic employees from throughout the organization to creatively drive the Market Construct of Lifestyle Demands, in which the packages would address the implicit lifestyle needs and wishes of customers.

Summing up, the potential for Amazon to be successful in selling services online is moderately boosted by its primary value in Degree, substantially boosted by its primary value in Deed, while the primary value in Dexterity represents demanding challenges. Introducing Delight—or rather reviving it out of Amazon's past (see Chapter 2)—is likely to be most suited to raising the potential for success in the sale of services online.

Further considerations with regard to the revival of secondary or primary value in Delight at Amazon are made at the end of this chapter. The next sections turn to the retail market development in omnichannel retail and in this context evaluate the acquisition of Whole Foods Market.

Whole Foods Market: Primary Value in Degree and Dexterity

In this section, the WFM acquisition will be evaluated in the terms of WFM alone, i.e. how Amazon can—or cannot—raise the performance of the WFM organization. In the next section, the WFM acquisition will be evaluated in terms of the combined organizations in omnichannel.

In 2018, WFM operated over 470 stores, almost all of them in the US. The chain is firmly positioned as the leading retailer of natural and organic foods in the US. Its focus is on perishables, either sold in raw form or made into ready-to-eat dishes. Whole Foods Market prides itself on having the highest quality standards in the market and has gained numerous certifications for its products and processes. In 2017, WFM was one of only eleven companies to have made the "100 Best Companies to Work for in America" list every year since the award's inception by Fortune magazine in 1999. WFM has been active far beyond the retail market, supporting both the spread of organic standards in sustainable agriculture, as well as many NGOs. WFM itself has founded and operates three foundations acting to the benefit of the planet, children, and cities.

As summarized in Figure 9-1, an overview of Whole Foods Market will be presented in terms of the five elements of MDW 5 the Steering Logic, the key managerial practices in the firm. A detailed presentation of all five Managerial Do Well's at Whole Foods Market is available for download on www.dimensions-of-value.com. WFM exhibits primary value in the Degree and Dexterity dimensions (see Chapter 1), which unlike Amazon are not organizationally separate but are combined into overall value elements throughout the firm. The inherent weaknesses of WFM in the mild form, i.e. more like the "limits to success," will be discussed. The potential for Amazon as the new owner to introduce Deed practices and thereby overcome the weaknesses will be evaluated and compared to the actual actions taken through the end of 2018. Amazon's actions at WFM will be presented in more detail further below in the discussion of omnichannel retail at Amazon.

Construct	Combined: Overall Value Elements	Overall Combined Weakness	Potential Combination of WFM and Amazon	Steps Realized by End 2018
Market Fit	Centralized standards and decentralized implementation agreed by structured consensus	Offers are "too" fine-tuned into mini-standards	Manage only logos, brands, etc. which truly add value in addressing market opportunities	More centralized purchasing of mainstream brands
Efficiency / Effective-ness	A store and an own brand are economical and exploitable positions, built-up / explored via diversity	Multiple organizational cross-currents in conflict	Parallel functional networks with own operating logic	Functional-specific processes in purchasing, marketing, pricing, customer experience and human resource management
Profit-ability	Earnings Per Share (EPS)	Over-estimation of durability of existing brand(s) image(s)	Only build-up market positions with viable long-term margin	Too soon to evaluate long-term success
Manage-ment / Market	Uniform organizational culture for all units and their interfaces, mutating nationally and evolving locally; Standards defining core product categories within the context of developing the entire market space	Over-estimation of the ability of culture alone to direct the operations	Enhanced organizational infrastructure for personnel to draw on	More infrastructure to serve the market

Figure 9-1: Steering Logic at WFM and Improvements via Amazon

In the Market Fit Construct at WFM, the principles for the quality standards and values found in the offers and inputs have been defined centrally, largely top-down with select bottom-up participation. The quality standards and values have then been de-centrally implemented in the regions and stores in a manner combining the top-down hierarchy of regional and store managers with the consensus view from the teams. The product range for own-branded products has been established by centralized purchasers and product managers, while each store could develop a consensus and team-based view on local products to be sourced. The weakness may be suggested to be the high number of own brands, logos, trademarks etc., each being something like a mini-standard. The marketing messages of the many brands may overlap and confuse the customer, while it is possible that the cost-benefit ratio of this fine-tuning has not been favorable. Introducing the Market Fit Construct of Amazon in Deed, focusing on offers and inputs which are concretely oriented to a clear market opportunity, could potentially pick out those logos/brands which really add value and eliminate the rest. Amazon indeed has already increased the share of mainstream brands in the WFM product range and reduced the share of own brands and locally-sourced products.

In the Efficiency/Effectiveness Construct at WFM, a store and an own-branded product both represent a position in the market, feeding on each other: the stores are interesting because they offer the own-branded products, and the own-branded products can be launched and managed while benefiting from the context of an own store. In this duality, there has been space to explore a diversity of new possible standards in store formats and own brands. The weakness lies in the diversity and decentralization in the organization: too many different sources of organizational culture within the firm, lack of alignment in organizational initiatives, and regional and store management pursuing their own agenda. Introducing the Efficiency/Effectiveness Construct of Amazon, where functional networks are managed to operate in specific areas of the business in certain ways which make sense for that part of the business alone, has the potential to create different functional networks co-existing side-by-side, each in their own part of the business. In fact, Amazon has introduced processes which are specific to certain functions within the organization.

The Profitability Construct at WFM is Earnings per Share (EPS), rewarding a block of finance passively placed in a shareholding while generating a flow of income out of running operations. Indeed, EPS is one of the central financial targets defined by WFM. The weakness has been to over-estimate the profitability of market positions relating to reputation and image. The values and practices which formed the basis for WFM's success have in recent times been watered down, seemingly in the expectation that the personnel and customers would nevertheless continue to behave as before. Yet, in the past five years, business performance has fallen off and the voluntary turnover rate of personnel has nearly doubled. Introducing the Profitability Construct of Amazon to assess the long-term margin of market positions could discover which offers and business practices really are viable in the long-term and ensure that they gain sufficient managerial attention. At the end of 2018, it was still too soon to evaluate whether Amazon has been able to introduce this long-term thinking.

In the Management Construct at WFM, the organization is managed as building blocks in that the teams are simply placed next to one another, with little management of the interfaces. It is assumed that the shared culture and values are enough to govern the processes and interaction. The culture and values mutate thoroughly at the national level as part of regular internal initiatives, and they evolve gradually over time at the local level. In the Market Construct, WFM works the market regarding its standards and quality for clearly defined product categories, dominated by perishables and targeting organic food. WFM also works the market space in which the value chain operates, educating customer segments and suppliers about the benefits of sustainable agricultural practices and working with all market participants to agree, e.g. national standards for labeling organic foods. The weakness has been to think that spreading and deepening the organizational culture was enough to optimally steer the operations for the market without e.g. standardized IT systems, aligned processes, and robust procedures. The Management Construct at Amazon of agile platforms could provide more infrastructural resources to the organization. Indeed, Amazon has beefed up the infrastructure for serving the market, e.g. with methodical marketing campaigns and systematic shelf stocking.

Omnichannel Retail: Amazon's Openness to and Synergy Potential with Offline Retail

As discussed in Markets Value Factor 5 in Chapter 2, the future of retail lies in omnichannel retailing. Omnichannel is more than just having multiple channels; it's integrating them with a "seamless" experience for the customer.

The evaluation of Amazon in omnichannel will proceed by first assessing the potential for the firm to fulfill what was described in Chapter 7 as the second and third demands on a retailer: the organization's potential to allow for another distribution channel and be open for synergies to that second distribution channel. Then the steps towards realizing this potential, which Amazon has taken with WFM and, where relevant, in other areas will be evaluated. The assessment is conducted predominantly at the level of MDW 5 Steering Logic in order to assess the actual and potential improvement of Amazon's score on Markets Value Factor 5. The assessment proceeds in each dimension of value.

As summarized in Figure 9-2, the only relevant steps towards omnichannel taken by Amazon in Degree are in connection with the WFM acquisition. In this value dimension, the Market Fit Construct of top-down enables senior management to look from above in both channels regarding the entire market and the entire organization and make decisions accordingly. Upon acquiring WFM, the Amazon leadership introduced price reductions on a small number of high-profile items, which in 2018 was extended to 10 percent price reductions on selected items for Prime members. WFM has, however, not lost its image of high prices.

Construct	Primary Degree	Openness / Potential	Actions at WFM by End 2018
Market Fit	Top Down	Management considers both channels	Selected lower prices, especially for Prime members
Efficiency / Effectiveness	Build and Economize on Positions	Different positions of the supply chains	Structured position of suppliers in supply chain plus stores as locations for supply chain
Profitability	ROCE	Few synergies	Sales continue to be flat
Management	Building Blocks	"Tack on" new units in organization	470 WFM locations; Short-term deliveries of groceries ordered online using WFM and Amazon resources side-by-side
Market	Mass offer of entire product categories	Offline involves subsets of products and segments	1,000 WFM products on Amazon website and 100 pop-up stores for Amazon devices in WFM locations

Figure 9-2: Steering Logic in Degree at Amazon and Openness to Omnichannel

The Efficiency/Effectiveness Construct to build and economize on positions requires overlaps in operations to generate synergies. The supply chain operations at Amazon are centred on individual orders filled with individual deliveries via fulfillment centers and vehicles, or servers and bandwidth for streaming services. The supply chain for offline stores is radically different: batches of shipments to fixed points to maintain stock levels. Overlaps are found, for the most part, in purchasing greater volumes and using stores for online customers to pick up orders or drop off returns. Indeed, regarding the former, in 2018, Amazon has introduced more structured relations to WFM suppliers to make WFM's supply chain somewhat more similar to Amazon's, including a greater proportion of central purchasing, lower prices, and placement fees. A survey of 2000 shoppers by Yahoo Finance showed mixed feelings about the centralized sourcing: there was appreciation for the increased availability of mainstream brands, while disappointment at the loss of regional flavor. Regarding the latter, one of the first steps by Amazon was to install Amazon lockers at WFM stores for Amazon customers to collect their online purchases of WFM food only, making use of a password given to them online. The Amazon lockers at WFM stores can also be used to return Amazon purchases.

A high ROCE in Degree is generated by the favorable impact of synergies in the Efficiency/Effectiveness Construct. Given the restricted scope for synergies in an omnichannel supply chain, there is little potential for boosts to ROCE. Amazon does not release detailed numbers for Whole Foods Market, but Second Measure, a company tracking consumer spending, calculates that WFM sales continue to be stagnant as they have been since 2015. Any improvement in ROCE would have to come from lower costs. In general, however, it is too soon to evaluate the performance of ROCE in omnichannel.

The Management Construct of building blocks allows for the new channel to be "tacked on" to the organization. The 470 WFM locations are operated largely as before in parallel with the online channel. WFM has operated an online distribution channel since 1999, and since 2015, in selected cities, WFM has offered same-day delivery of fresh groceries in alliance with the firm Instacart. WFM and Instacart made more same-day deliveries of fresh food than any other firm in 2016. Building on this leading operational base, in the middle of February 2018, Amazon announced it would offer free, two-hour delivery of WFM groceries in four US cities, with plans to expand to further cities later in 2018. This expansion will use a mix of Instacart and Amazon resources, the latter being PrimeFresh, Prime Pantry, and Prime Now, operating side-by-side. Also, as noted above, there is a certain overlap in that online orders of WFM food can be collected from Amazon lockers in the WFM store. On the whole, it appears that, for the time being, the two organizations will stay as building blocks next to one another, fundamentally continuing their paths in parallel.

In the Market Construct at Amazon, each product category is a uniform, mass offer, directed in principle at everyone. An offline channel is, in contrast, a set of specific, physical locations serving a concrete target market which is geographically bounded, where a store cannot stock the huge range of items offered online. In other words, Amazon has worked the online market in wholes, while the offline market deals with specific and small subsets of product ranges and customer segments. The steps taken so far in this regard are that the product category of food on the Amazon website has been increased by roughly one thousand WFM products, while in roughly one hundred WFM locations there are now pop-up stores selling Amazon devices and promoting Prime membership. The product categories on the website and in the stores have been enhanced to a limited extent.

In sum, omnichannel generates limited potential benefits for Amazon in Degree at the level of MDW 5 Steering Logic. In addition, there can be benefits at three other levels of management practices. First, Amazon's MDW 4 Business Model is to be Market and Cost Leader. The higher market share in the entire retail market due to an offline channel enhances Amazon's position as Market Leader. And the higher volumes can improve purchasing prices for Amazon and WFM, thereby improving Amazon's position as Cost Leader. Second, in MDW 2 External Demand Interfaces, Amazon engages in extensive Growth in product categories. An offline channel enables growth into product categories which are best suited to offline shopping, e.g. fresh food. Finally, in MDW 1 Value Exchange with customers, to the extent that Amazon can lower costs in the offline channel, it could offer lower prices. Overall, it seems that, in Degree, Amazon has taken steps to realize most of what can be gained from the WFM acquisition, with room for further substantial benefits only with regard to further price reductions.

With regard to Deed, Amazon has taken a number of steps towards omnichannel in addition to the acquisition of WFM, all of which will be evaluated in this section (see Figure 9-3). In this value dimension, the Market Fit Construct of intrapreneurship draws on the ability to simulate what customers want, particularly given the possibilities made available by technological advances. Intrapreneurs at Amazon can utilize their understanding of the customer and technology to identify new opportunities in offline retail, as well as in the integration of the two different channels. Intrapreneurship offers the potential for unique advantages offline and in the combination of the two channels.

Construct	Primary Deed	Openness / Potential	Actions by End 2018	
			WFM	Other
Market Fit	Intrapreneur-ship	Unique opportunities in two channels	Amazon lockers and pop-up stores in WFM locations; food items on Amazon website; short-term food deliveries	Returns to Kohl's; Calvin Klein pop-up stores; Amazon Books; Go supermarkets; Instant Pickup
Efficiency / Effective-ness	Stimulate and operate networks	Functional specialists in the two channels together design solutions	Functional specialists in each channel implement the solutions in their channel	
Profit-ability	Long-Term Margin	Time to find right solution	$1.3 billion in physical stores sales in 2017	
Manage-ment	Agile Platforms	Re-directed to new opportunities; resources more fixed in offline	No re-structuring and more robust infrastructure	Pilot phase
Market	New Market Development	Pursue new opportunities	Open to new opportunities as they arise	Disruptive format of Go?

Figure 9-3: Steering Logic in Deed at Amazon and Openness to Omnichannel

Changes in the Degree supply chain for WFM and Amazon noted above have improved the Deed offers regarding shopping missions. Shoppers in WFM stores can purchase Amazon devices, while the Amazon lockers in the WFM stores increase the options from which customers can choose in the "doing" of their shopping. Soon after Amazon acquired WFM, over one thousand WFM food items were offered on the Amazon website and via AmazonFresh, Prime Pantry, and Prime Now. Amazon has made membership in AmazonFresh, its grocery delivery service in a number of cities which costs Prime members an additional $14.99 per month, a requirement to order WFM foods. An additional feature for Prime Now was launched in two cities in August 2018, where, within an hour, food orders could be collected at a reserved parking spot at the designated WFM store.

Amazon has introduced initiatives regarding the "doing" of shopping mssions beyond WFM. Amazon agreed with the department store chain Kohl's that Amazon customers can hand in their returns to Kohl's stores in two cities; presumably, this will be extended to further stores. Amazon agreed with Calvin Klein to run pop-up stores in New York and Los Angeles offering exclusive fashion and a unique experience: customized fitting on the spot, plus fitting rooms serviced by Alexa to answer questions about the fashion as well as control the music and lighting. Amazon Books stores were opened in thirteen urban locations. The firm is experimenting with small Amazon Go supermarkets, where, via an app plus sensors and cameras in the store, the customer can walk in, select the purchases, and walk out with automatic check-out and payment via the customer's Amazon account. Finally, on several college campuses, Amazon runs the Instant Pickup service. For a very restricted range of "need-it-now" items such as snacks, drinks, and phone chargers, customers who subscribe to Prime can order the items online and then collect them within five minutes from a locker. In these five examples, the omnichannel approach is evident: the ease for customers to (later) visit one of the many Kohl's stores reduces the reluctance to purchase online items such as clothes which may need to be returned; the pop-up stores offer a "phy-gital" experience; the Amazon bookstore has been described as an offline version of the website; in the experimental Go supermarkets, Amazon is deploying in an offline setting what it has learned about payment procedures online, i.e. paying as with 1-Click; and, on Instant Pickup, customers can order conveniently online yet have the item within minutes.

Considering Amazon's initiatives by the end of 2018 for supporting shopping missions in omnichannel, the advantages of omnichannel retail for customer "doing" are limited. The differences in the offers for shopping missions are evaluated as follows. In the MDW 1 Value Exchange with shopping customers in Deed, a key benefit of the Amazon website is the extremely broad product range from which shoppers can fulfill a huge variety of shopping missions. To fully gain the advantages of operating two different channels in omnichannel retail, Amazon would need to offer in its offline channel a correspondingly broad product range at numerous locations. However, the product range at WFM and the other pilot initiatives is quite limited and WFM's network includes 470 stores. These are encouraging developments, but do not come close to e.g. the product range offered by Walmart in its over 2,000 stores located within ten miles of 90 percent of the American population.

In the Efficiency/Effectiveness Construct, team members who develop new solutions come from different functions. In Amazon's omnichannel initiatives in 2017 and 2018, it can be assumed that representatives of offline functions, e.g. WFM personnel or project team members from the Go initiative, were included. The implementation of the solutions were presumably performed by the functional specialists on their own in their own channels, as in keeping with Deed at Amazon. In this manner, the solutions identified in the Market Fit Construct are designed and implemented in much the same way as before Amazon was active in omnichannel.

The Profitability Construct of a long-term margin allows Amazon to spend time and money before hitting on the ideal solutions. Yet, already in 2017, Amazon recorded $1.3 billion in physical store sales. However, it is speculated that the infrastructure in the Go stores currently costs up to $1 million, which, at the moment, considerably dampens the profitability of that initiative.

In the Management Construct of agile platforms, organizational resources can be re-directed to new opportunities, which include the offline channel. However, it may take some time for the organizational resources to become familiar with the offline business. Furthermore, Amazon has steered its platforms in the virtual world of online business. The resources in offline retail are by their nature less agile and mobile, including e.g. specific stores, the personnel assigned to the specific stores, and fixed logistical routes. Nevertheless, stores can be opened and closed, and personnel and logistics routes can be re-shuffled. The organizational resources in omnichannel can indeed be re-directed as needed. By the end of 2018, there still had been no re-structuring of the WFM chain of stores and the other initiatives were still in the pilot stage. Whereas, as noted above, the infrastructural resources and platform at WFM have been rendered more robust.

In the Market Construct of new market development, the thinking and the processes oriented to new market development support the new opportunities identified by the intrapreneurs in the Market Fit Construct. Indeed, particularly the new format of the Go supermarket may represent the beginnings of the future disruption of offline retail.

In sum, at the level of MDW 5 in Deed, an offline channel at Amazon can generate many organizational benefits with some practical barriers only in the beginning. However, this evaluation in terms of MDW 5 may overlook barriers and problems which could arise at the level of MDW 3. Internal supply interfaces in Deed rest on skills and judgment gained via experience. Amazon personnel lack experience and, therefore, lack skills and judgment in offline retail. To the extent that the required skills and judgment are significantly different, there may be barriers in Deed to the successful integration of an offline channel into the Amazon organization, limiting the omnichannel benefits for Amazon.

In Dexterity, without going through each Construct, it can be concluded that the Steering Logic in Dexterity is in principle a hindrance to an offline channel. Dexterity relies on the market knowledge which is entrenched in the organization, and the Amazon organization has essentially no expert market knowledge regarding the offline channel. However, to the extent that readily identifiable, generic terms and conditions such as pricing policy or loyalty programs can be extended from the online to the offline channel, there would be an openness to gaining synergies in Dexterity between online and offline channels. "Obvious" terms and conditions would not require expert market knowledge to exploit. Indeed, on the basis of the synergies in the Degree supply chain and the Deed distribution channels, Amazon has introduced synergies in the Dexterity standards regarding terms and conditions. Amazon is working on making Prime the centerpiece of WFM's customer rewards program. At the end of February 2018, it was announced that WFM shoppers using the Amazon Prime Rewards Visa card would receive 5 percent cash back on purchases. Cardholders who are not members of Amazon's yearly subscription service would get 3 percent cash back. These cash-back rewards mirror the offer to cardholders for purchases on the website. And Amazon included Whole Foods in its Prime Day event last month, giving Prime members a $10 Amazon.com account credit if they spent $10 in the store. This kind of synergy in Dexterity terms and conditions is generic to retail and does not require expert knowledge of offline retail; yet, it can boost the omnichannel success.

Turning lastly to Delight, although management practices in this D are not present at Amazon beyond the basic level in MDW 5, the Delight value exchange in MDW 1 with investors takes place at the level of primary value. The acquisition of WFM, as well as the pilot initiatives in offline channels, has opened up the perspective for Amazon to be the dominant force in all of retail. Such an offer to investors should accordingly attract a large volume of inputs. From the summer of 2017, when Amazon announced the acquisition of WFM, to November of that year, the share price remained stable at around $1,000; no positive reaction from investors. The share price then shot up to over $1,500 by March 2018, and, as noted above, rose even higher to September 2018. Thus, it seems that, upon mature reflection, the capital market has been convinced of the benefits of the acquisition, or at least does not see it as hindering the further development of Amazon as the most dynamic force in retail today.

Amazon and Delight

The previous section demonstrated that there are limited benefits in omnichannel to be expected in Degree, Deed, and Dexterity. The brief discussion in Chapter 7 regarding MDW 5 Steering Logic in Delight and the remarks above in relation to selling services suggest that the management practices of this D are particularly suited to making the most from retail in two contrasting channels. Pursuing this point by stepping away from Amazon and WFM for the moment, success in omnichannel retail may be defined as an even-handed balance in earning revenue in both channels rather than in the total volume of revenue. Figure 2-6 in Chapter 2 shows that Macy's is the traditional offline retailer which by far is the most successful in balancing the share of revenue it earns offline and online. Macy's gains one-fifth of its revenue online; Walmart and Costco do not make it over one-twentieth. Even Apple, the high-tech firm par excellence, gains less than one-tenth of its revenue online. Macy's exhibits primary value in Delight. The managerial practices in this D may be the recipe for success in omnichannel retail today. Reviving Delight value at the secondary level in the selling operations seems to be a promising way for Amazon to make the most out of two channels. The differences between the channels, which in Degree, Deed, and Dexterity constitute barriers to collaboration between the channels, can be a stimulating source of creative tension in Delight.

A further reason to integrate Delight practices into the organization is that it could serve as healthy checks and balances and thus help alleviate the inherent weaknesses in Deed. In this section, it will therefore be proposed, with all modesty, that Amazon would be better able to respond to the challenges and more fully take advantage of the potential benefits in its ongoing present by augmenting its management practices with elements of the Delight dimension. Given the background at Amazon of operating in different primary D's in different business areas, the integration of Delight would generate the most benefit by introducing it predominantly in the selling operations: the combination of the online website and the offline stores. This section examines the changes in the MDW 5 Steering Logic if Amazon were to augment its management practices with Delight at the secondary level, combined with primary practices in Deed, into its selling operations, as summarized in Figure 9-4. The proposal is illustrated with two examples of possible innovations in the selling operations introduced via Delight practices.

Construct	Primary Deed and *Weakness*	Second-ary Delight Practice	Augmented Practice	E.g. Shopping Online => Offline	E.g. Shopping Offline => Online
Market Fit	Intrapreneur-ship *Offers are too idiosyncratic*	Coalitions	Intrapreneurs mobilize resources and people to generate offers addressing the whole person	In-store system-based individual recommend-ations for further purchases	Online chat with a customer viewing the same item
Efficiency / Effective-ness	Stimulate and Operate Networks *Beaters of own Drum*	Develop and Institu-tionalize Visions	Networks develop mini-visions for solutions and their implementation within firm-wide collective vision	Specialists develop vision of data integrated into customer conversation and implement it in training	Simulation and focus groups to design the features meeting situational and implicit demand
Profit-ability	Long-Term Margin *Over-estima-tion of long-term margin*	Contri-bution	Long-Term Margin calculation considers costs and revenues per target segment	Identify and estimate revenues from key target segments	
Manage-ment	Agile Platforms *Agility overrules situational needs*	Pooled Forces	Align resources and employees to shared views of lasting needs and wants	Specialists and store employees gather and communicate encouraging anecdotes	View becomes shared to engage the entire person of the customer on the website via skills in online interaction
Market	New Market Development *Internal supply goes beyond market demand*	Lifestyle Demands	Develop new markets for lifestyle demands	Recommend-ations enhance customer lifestyle	Lifestyle of shopping online with friends and family or deliberately with the freshness of strangers

Figure 9-4: Steering Logic in Selling Operations at Amazon augmented with Delight

The introduction of Delight would adjust the view of the customer in the selling operations. In Deed, the customer is seen as someone who has a shopping mission to fulfill, whereas, in Delight, the customer is a consumer with a broad range of wishes and requirements related to the entire person of the customer. The combined business area would view the customer as a shopping consumer.

Considering the Market Fit Construct, intrapreneurs in Deed mobilize organizational resources to grasp market opportunities with the Weakness that the solutions can be too idiosyncratic. By introducing Delight, intrapreneurs would also engage groups of employees to form coalitions for creating solutions which offer shopping consumers a piece of the good life, coalescing feelings, perceptions, and trends amongst shopping consumers. For example, the key online benefit of individualized recommendations could be synthesized into the personal interaction in a store by installing small screens throughout the store; when a customer purchases an item in the context of a conversation with an employee, the employee could enter into the screen the product number of the purchased item and see the three items most commonly purchased together with that item. The store employee would introduce the recommendation into the conversation fitting to the entire person of the customer, e.g. the employee could take account of the relation to the customer, the style of speaking favored by the customer, other interests of the customer which the employee may have discovered, and so forth. This kind of synthesis from online to offline would be identified by a coalition of specialists in the technical features of online recommendations and specialists in training store personnel in customer interaction. Another possibility goes in the other direction of an offline practice being translated into the online website functionality. WFM positions its stores as offering a Third Place between home and workplace, where customers feel comfortable to converse with one another. This kind of welcoming and familiar environment in the offline store could be translated into the online experience by offering what could be named "Shared Shopping Stroll." For online customers who have registered for this functionality, when they have an item on their screen, a window for chatting would open up to another customer who is viewing the same item and who has also registered for the service. The shoppers could share personal perceptions and impressions within the impersonal online context. Thus, the shopping mission would be enriched by the expression of feelings. This kind of synthesis from offline to online could be identified by a coalition of specialists in store and website interaction.

Turning to the Efficiency/Effectiveness Construct, the cross-functional networks in Deed develop solutions which take account of shoppers' daily activities and technological developments, with the weakness that managers can each beat their own drum. The Efficiency/Effectiveness Construct in Delight would help in that the development and institutionalization of a vision would generate a collective view of the solutions for shopping consumers and lead to more alignment in the selling operations. For the individual recommendations in the store, the network of specialists in online recommendations and store trainers could develop visions of how to synthesize statistical data with personal conversations, and then institutionalize the visions into role-playing exercises in training sessions. For the imagined "Shared Shopping Stroll," the network of specialists would design the feature by simulating the situational needs of the customer when moving through the phases of joining and using the feature (as in Deed) as well as by drawing on focus groups to investigate the implicit demand for the look and feel of the window, the sounds associated with the feature, how the customers are identified to each other—what else beyond the name—and so forth (as in Delight). The implementation work would be divided amongst functional teams, as in Deed. Yet, as in Delight, each implementing team would be charged with developing two visions for their assigned daily work: a vision of the concrete solution to be implemented, as well as a vision of how it will be implemented, i.e. how will the work be performed in the team and how will multiple teams collaborate.

In terms of the Profitability Construct, in Deed, the calculation of the long-term margin bears the weakness to overestimate the extent to which the long-term revenues of a given venture exceed the costs. Augmenting this practice with Delight would make the profitability calculation more accurate by taking into account the costs and revenues associated with key target segments. For the two examples of innovations in the selling operations, the estimation of the increased sales would be calculated in terms of identifying the key segments responding most enthusiastically to each innovation.

With regard to the Management Construct, in Deed, agile platforms of organizational resources are formed from which intrapreneurs are empowered to draw on as they see fit. The weakness at Amazon is that the firm has been at times too focused on internal agility in responding quickly to market opportunities and not enough on significant and lasting needs externally. Introducing Delight would support the pooling of forces—both people and resources—within the organization to focus on what shopping consumers genuinely demand. Employees would engage in discussions about the needs and wants which are truly lasting, out of which a collective view would emerge to align resources. For the recommendations in the store, the pooled forces would include the specialists and the store employees, who would gather and communicate anecdotal stories about the wider impacts of the initiative, e.g. that customers express their enthusiasm for the individual attention in the store or indicate that they feel encouraged to look themselves for associated items when making purchases. In the example of the "Shared Shopping Stroll," the view would be spread amongst the personnel in the selling operations that more needs to be done on the website to engage the person of the shopper, and the training, shared job experience, and recruiting for personnel would place more weight on the skills needed to design and program more interaction on the website.

Turning to the Market Construct, in Deed, Amazon has been oriented to new market development, with the weakness that the creativity and innovativeness of the intrapreurial employees have at times gone beyond what the market was ready for: inventing offers for which no rival offers existed, but which did not attract sufficient customers. By augmenting the management practice with Delight, the approach to the market at Amazon would take greater account of the lifestyle demands of shopping customers. For the recommendations in-store, the personnel would be trained to take account of the lifestyle demands of the shopping consumers when explaining the individual recommendations. Enhancing the customers' lifestyles would

for and consuming goods and services. They would perceive themselves as being personally addressed, which would lead to their full engagement in Amazon's shopping process.

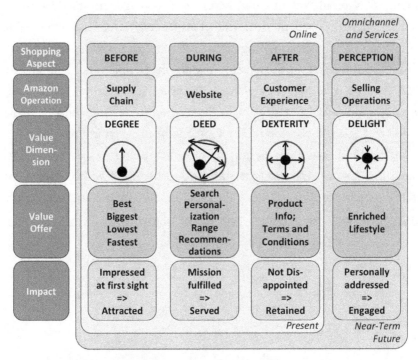

Figure 9-5: Engaging Total Value Offer including
Delight to Shopping Customers

Taking Stock

Amazon is the driving force in the retail industry. What does the ongoing present hold for such a firm? This chapter dared to answer how the management practices at Amazon could make Whole Foods Market more shipshape, as well as how Amazon could operate in two distribution channels to raise the success of the entire enterprise. These internal organizational developments were set in the context of two expected external developments in the retail market: the rise of online retail for services and omnichannel retail. It was demonstrated that Amazon is well prepared and can utilize many of its capabilities in responding to the expected developments in the ongoing present of retail. However, it was suggested that it would be able to take fuller advantage of the acquisition of WFM, as well as better respond to today's challenges in retail, by integrating Delight managerial practices into its organization, most particularly in the selling operations, but also in the entire organization. Thus, the ongoing present of Amazon was examined largely within the framework of the existing management practices of Amazon and WFM and the potential they offer. An additional analysis was provided to show that managerial practices in Delight could be revived out of Amazon's past to create even more potential for success in the ongoing present.

The next and final chapter examines more far-reaching aspects of the future of Amazon. A prospective long-term future for Amazon will be speculatively sketched in the context of developments in the retail market which will transform society and thereby disrupt the retail market.

| Chapter 10 |

The Long-Term Future in
Societal Transformation

Amazon has succeeded beyond probably its own wildest dreams. What does the long-term future hold for such a firm? This chapter sets broad horizons by taking as the context a number of trends in the retail industry, in business, and, indeed, in society. These trends are only beginning and the full flowering of any of them will only take place in the long-term. Furthermore, it will be suggested that the management practices of the emerging fifth dimension of value, Deep-Connect, will be the basis for success in driving/responding to these long-term trends. Thus, for Amazon to continue on its meteoric path of success, it will be speculated here that the firm will include the management practices of this D in order to stay ahead of rivals.

The discussion in this chapter picks up where the last chapter left off by considering long-term societal transformation and the corresponding disruption in retail and how Amazon has already begun to respond to the first traces of such trends. The chapter then considers how Amazon could more successfully respond to—even lead—these changes by adopting Deep-Connect value into its offers. This perspective for radical change at Amazon is proffered with all humility from a single author writing about one of the most successful firms in the world.

Societal Transformation and Disruption in Retail

There are trends already present today in a limited form which could potentially gain weight in the future of retail to ultimately disrupt business and transform society. Or, better said, retail and retailers could actively seek and take on the function to disrupt business and transform society in a number of fundamental ways. These potential future functions of retail can be foreseen speculatively as a further development of trends which are already present, as summarized in Figure 10-1.

Current Trends		Prospective Disruption / Transformation
Source	**Trend**	**Extension to All Online Retail**
Food Retail	Show ingredients relevant to health and environment	Raw materials in all products
	Farming practices, e.g. worker rights, organic practices, conditions for animals	Production conditions, e.g. working conditions, worker rights, environmental impact, automation, artificial intelligence
	Location of farm	Location of steps in value chain, including transport
Logistics	Customer chooses pick-up or delivery	Supplier and customer choose collection point or individual address
	Customer chooses delivery time, location and package placement	Supplier and customer choose timing, location and placement
	Supplier packs own packages	Individual agreement with every supplier regarding packaging
Crowd-funding	Showcase the firm	Showcase all supplier firms
	Present range of offers, including experience beyond product	Present range of offers from all supplier firms
	Option to contribute to firm development, e.g. as creditor or test customer	Present options to contribute to all supplier firms
Online Retail	Product reviews from customers	Customer stories of how they feel / how they experience themselves when consuming the product: what it means to consume the product
	Owners and potential purchasers of products chat with one another	Community of customers: shoppers and owners
	Community of product reviewers built by online retailer	Customer community built by retailer
Sharing Economy	Lending products for short-term use or trying out.	Lending organized in communities
	Selling used products	Selling organized in communities
	Businesses offer repair or recycling services	Businesses advertise in communities

Figure 10-1: Potential Disruption/Societal Transformation via Retail

The trend in food retail to give shoppers comprehensive information about the ingredients and their impact on consumer health and the environment could be extended to all products sold by retailers. Shoppers should be able to choose how they influence their own health and the state of the environment with their purchases. Retail would take on the role of actively informing and educating shoppers about the consequences for their health and for the environment of different raw materials and components. This principle could be further applied regarding the practices and working conditions under which goods are produced. What has begun regarding organic farming, child labor, and treatment of animals could be extended to all aspects of production. E.g. if shoppers are offered transparency on whether a product has been produced by hand or machine, whether human or artificial intelligence has steered the production process, etc., then shoppers can influence the spread and impact of human versus non-human production in business and the associated consequences for society. Continuing in this vein, the practice in food retail to name the country from which fresh food has been sourced could be extended to all products, including the location of the steps in the value chain. This issue can be relevant to the shopper as a matter of e.g. where jobs are supported, as a matter of taste regarding the culture of a given country, or as environmental concerns about emissions and energy use in transport.

Moving on to issues in logistics, the current trend for customers to determine the timing and placement of deliveries could be extended to offering the sender the analogous choices. The sender could also have greater freedom in determining the packaging to fit to its own requirements to offer value in a given D, e.g. packages could be more colorful and informative. The supply chain would be open to individual agreements regarding shipping and packaging.

Firms today compete for parties on the basis of their sustainability profile. Taking this a step further, firms could compete on the basis of their entire approach to work—one is a globalized corporate with a clear vertical hierarchy, the other a local collective with a completely flat hierarchy, and so forth. In this way, firms would sell themselves in their entirety and not just their products, taking on aspects of practices in crowdfunding. Retailers would sell products and showcase the firm. Shoppers could influence the success or failure of different ways that firms organize and manage themselves since they would include these factors in their purchasing decision. Furthermore, as in crowdfunding, firms could make offers to shoppers which go beyond the product, e.g. a "subscription" to receive certain products on a regular basis, a tour of the firm, or a personalized product. Again, as in crowdfunding, a shopper could take part in the development of the firm, inputting e.g. finance or ideas or the willingness to be a test customer. Online retailers would enable shoppers to gain a personal involvement in the supplier's business.

Turning to trends in online retail itself, it was this distribution channel which developed customer reviews of products for the masses to a fine art. In a transformed world, the reviews would discuss the experience of consuming the product and the meaning thereof in various contexts: personal, business, industry, national, environmental, societal, etc. Furthermore, Amazon offers the feature "Ask an Owner," where potential buyers can chat with owners of products. Building on this trend, the owners and shoppers of special kinds of products could communicate with one another online permanently in the form of a community. Online retailers have built up a community of product reviewers; in a transformed world, they could steer customer communities.

A further step in such communities would be into the Sharing Economy. Community members could lend/borrow products amongst themselves, while newcomers to the community could try out a product from an existing owner. Community members could sell used products and businesses offering repair or recycling services could advertise in the community.

First Steps towards Societal Transformation at Amazon and WFM

Amazon already engages in certain practices and has already undertaken certain initiatives which represent steps in the direction of realizing the kind of speculative societal transformation outlined above. Whole Foods Market has done the same. Figure 10-2, split into two tables, summarizes the developments at the two firms which, if further developed, could lead to the transformation via retail outlined above.

Current Trends		First Steps at Amazon and WFM in Driving / Responding to Societal Transformation
Source	Trend	
Food Retail	Show ingredients relevant to health and environment	Amazon: Detailed product information for Amazon Elements items: baby wipes and vitamins WFM: Detailed labeling and certificates for entire product range
	Farming practices, e.g. worker rights, organic practices, conditions for animals	Amazon: Short description of design and manufacturing process including role of animals WFM: Training and information for personnel in general and knowledge about local suppliers in particular
	Location of farm	Amazon: In supplier description for Amazon Elements WFM: Part of training / information / knowledge
Logistics	Customer chooses pick-up or delivery	Amazon: Logistics for pick-up being further developed WFM: Purchase or pick-up in store
	Customer chooses delivery time, location and package placement	Amazon: Broad choice on website WFM: Broad choice on website
	Supplier packs own packages	Amazon: Supplier packs "inside" packaging WFM: For all Instacart deliveries

Figure 10-2a: Steps at Amazon and WFM towards
Societal Transformation via Online Retail

With regard to ingredients and labeling in food retail, Amazon has taken a significant new step with the Amazon Elements items, including two product groups at the end of 2018: baby wipes and vitamin pills. Detailed information about ingredients, safety, healthiness, and care of the products is shown. Every product has a unique QPR code which, when scanned, allows customers to track its specific ingredients, date and place of manufacture, date of delivery, and "best by" date. WFM is one of the leading retailers in the US—and indeed in the world—regarding the depth and range of product information provided, ranging from ingredients to certifications. Indeed, it is a pioneer and market leader in this aspect. Concerning work practices behind a product, the Amazon Elements items include information about the design and production process, including the role of animal testing. WFM has throughout its history placed a great weight on training and information for personnel with regard to general aspects of organic farming and the different variants thereof, as well as particular knowledge about the practices of local suppliers. Finally, the location of the producing firm is part of the background information for Amazon Elements items and part of the training and knowledge given to WFM personnel.

Turning to trends in logistics, Amazon is the best in the business for delivery and is building up the possibilities for customer pick-ups in WFM stores, as well as its chain of Instant Pick-Up locations. At WFM, customers can of course buy products when they choose to be in the stores as well as pick up in stores the items which they ordered online. Customer choice in defining the delivery has a high priority at Amazon and the InstaCart delivery service used by WFM for online orders. Amazon needs its external packaging for shipping in order for the item to move smoothly through the logistics process, and WFM packs the packages which InstaCart delivers.

Current Trends		First Steps at Amazon and WFM in Driving / Responding to Societal Transformation
Source	Trend	
Crowd-funding	Showcase the firm	Amazon: Short description of supplier for Amazon Elements WFM 1: Knowledge about local suppliers WFM 2: "Prosperity campaign": showcase supplier WFM 3: "Five percent days": showcase NGO
	Present range of offers, including experience beyond product	WFM: "Five percent days": showcase NGO
	Option to contribute to firm development, e.g. as creditor or test customer	WFM: "Five percent days": showcase NGO
Online Retail	Product reviews from customers	Amazon: Some customer reviews include how they feel / how they experience themselves when consuming the product: what it means to consume the product
	Owners and potential purchasers of products chat with one another	Amazon: "Ask an Owner"
	Community of product reviewers built by online retailer	Amazon: Blog for product reviewers plus Aspects thereof on page for Amazon Elements items
Sharing Economy	Lending products for short-term use or trying out.	
	Selling used products	Amazon: Selling used products
	Businesses offer repair or disposal / recycling services	Amazon: Businesses can advertise on website

Figure 10-2b: Steps at Amazon and WFM towards
Societal Transformation via Online Retail

Drawing on trends in crowdfunding, the webpage for Amazon Elements items includes an abbreviated showcasing of the supplying firm, including why Amazon chose the firm. At WFM, personnel have knowledge with which they can "showcase" local suppliers in a conversation with the customers. Showcasing of suppliers also occurs in WFM's "prosperity campaign," where for six weeks in a year customers are encouraged to donate to WFM's Whole Planet Foundation, which finances microcredit loans in six countries. A small number of suppliers donate as well, and their products are featured prominently in the store and receive better placement in the shelf space. Customers come to know the supplying firm and its products better. Also at WFM, during the "five percent days," a NGO receives five percent of the turnover on a given day. The NGO can set up a table in the store to showcase itself, present a range of offers to the customers, and inform them how they could contribute to the development of the NGO as an active member, via donations and so forth.

In online retail, Amazon has developed new content and formats in which customers communicate online about products. Some product reviews on Amazon include feelings and perceptions from consuming products, e.g. product reviews of the Amazon Elements baby wipes include the good feeling from knowing that they are good for the baby and the planet. "Ask an Owner" enables Amazon shoppers to chat with owners. Amazon has created a blog site where all product reviewers can discuss amongst themselves, and the webpage for the Amazon Elements items has a community feel where product reviewers can respond to one another in their reviews.

In terms of the sharing economy, neither Amazon or WFM are active in short-term lending of products. However, Amazon sells a huge volume of used goods, giving a new owner the benefit of a lower purchase price rather than burdening the Earth with more waste. Furthermore, businesses who offer repair or disposal services are free to advertise on Amazon.

Thus Amazon and WFM are already active in a number of areas which point in the direction of the societal transformation outlined in the previous section.

Responding to and/or Driving Societal Transformation and Disruption: Amazon's prospective Deep-Connect Offer to Shoppers

The trends and potential future outlined above involve a kind of individual collectivism in contexts. Individual consumers become aware that their choices influence which firms survive and prosper in the market, which in turn influences many additional parameters. The organization and working conditions of the firms which survive and prosper, where they are located, and their impact on parties, stakeholders, and the environment, will influence how the business world functions, as well as impact the associated societal setting and the natural environment. This kind of disruption and societal transformation gives shopping choices a deeper meaning beyond simply an act of consumption. The value that shoppers gain is that their choices are given meaning for themselves, their communities, the regions and countries with which they identify, the human race, and the planet.

The Deep-Connect dimension of value is suitable for realizing this kind of value. Thus, it is suggested here that for Amazon to be successful in a business world of deeper meaning arising from individual collectivism in contexts, it would be helpful for it to offer Deep-Connect value. That is, in the prospective future for Amazon presented here, each of the pillars for its current success would be developed further to constitute offers which are Best for Mankind, as in Deep-Connect value. This prospective future for Amazon is summarized in Figure 10-3 and presented below.

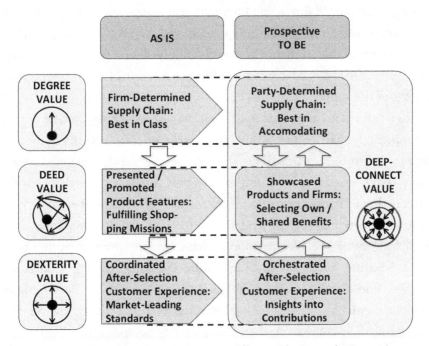

Figure 10-3: Prospective Future Amazon Offer to Shoppers in Deep-Connect

Amazon's supply chain is currently "firm-determined" to be Best in Class, in that Amazon defines the requirements on senders in order to be able to make the "best/most" offers. In Deep-Connect, these operations would rather be "party-determined" in that the parties involved as senders and receivers would choose many aspects of the shipping. Amazon would offer many options so that senders and receivers could individually and transparently design the shipping to gain value in a number of their own contexts, as they—and not Amazon—see it. There would be a wider variety of packaging materials, forms, colors, and designs so that the package itself could transmit messages related to the value and contexts of the offer. And receivers of packages would be able to exercise more control over the timing and nature of the delivery. For example, Amazon deliveries can become a celebration of the neighborhood: neighbors feel a sense of belonging to a local community when they accept deliveries for a neighbor and/or know that another neighbor is standing ready to accept a delivery for them; the meeting of the neighbors to hand over the delivery can become the occasion for a chat, a coffee, etc. Thus, those senders and receivers choosing to adjust the supply chain due to their own considerations would gain Deep-Connect value in that their considerations would take account of the multiple wider contexts of the supply chain.

The "party-determined" supply chain would, of course, not be entirely determined by parties but would ultimately operate according to what Amazon determines to be viable. There would still be the core of a Degree supply chain, operating according to the Best of Class technologies which Amazon deems necessary for the "best/most" features. Indeed, it is quite possible that the majority of senders and receivers would choose the "best/most" features of the Degree supply chain, which would continue to be very compelling for many kinds of online shopping. Even if senders and recievers choose the "best/most" shipping, it would involve Deep-Connect value for them because they will have actively chosen this based on their meaning in their contexts, rather than passively accepting the Degree offer of Best of Class, as is the case today. Thus, the supply chain offer as Best for Mankind would consist of being the most accommodating supply chain, individualistically customizable within the terms of a deal to which both Amazon and the parties can agree.

Amazon's website in Deep-Connect would provide much richer information by showcasing the products, the firms producing them, and

Amazon itself. The website would enable shoppers in three ways to select from a wide range of benefits on offer in multiple contexts. First, they would "shop" for benefits to themselves, both from the product itself (how does it impact one's lifestyle, how does it make existing activities more fun or faster, how does it make possible new kinds of activities, etc.) and from the supplying firm (e.g. touring the firm, participating in a user group or taking part in a firm event, and so forth). Second, Amazon customers would also "shop" for benefits to others in that they would evaluate the impact of the supplying firm on its parties and stakeholders, e.g. working conditions, how are the firm's suppliers screened and selected, the carbon footprint of the firm's operations, the communities and region within which the firm is embedded and how it interacts with its surroundings, etc. Third, Amazon customers would "shop" for benefits related to the development of Amazon as an organization, who they may well want to support. Amazon would showcase its supply chain operations: the transport modes, the working conditions, the environmental impact, new technologies or organizational developments, regions that it wants to promote for the supply chain operations, and so forth.

The act of purchasing would take on deeper meaning for the shopper since the shopper would be aware of the impact of his or her selection in multiple contexts. The content, search functionalities, and personalized recommendations on the website would include the wider benefits. Nevertheless, it is quite possible that the majority of visits to the website would be to fulfill a shopping mission, e.g. simply to find out about product features or to make a repeat purchase. Thus, the Deed offer to shoppers of fulfilled shopping missions would remain. However, for all customers, both those seeking wider benefits and those fulfilling shopping missions, the potential to inform themselves about further benefits offers Deep-Connect value to the shopper. The website offer of Best for Mankind would involve selecting own or shared benefits from showcased products and firms.

With regard to the after-selection customer experience, in Deep-Connect, Amazon would orchestrate insights into contributions to the self and others in four ways. First, the content about contributions to the self would include self-reports of how the products made the reviewers feel, how the products affected their lives, how the products have changed their own perception of themselves, etc. in the form of a forum or a blog. Second, shoppers would want to be informed and receive support regarding the context of their contributions to the supplying firms, to the economy, and to the planet. Consumers could post their experiences in being a test customer or a financier for a supplying firm. An independent auditing organization could post ratings, testaments, or certificates regarding the supplying firm's adherence to business, societal, and environmental norms. Third, shoppers would want to be informed and receive support regarding the mutual "contributions" between themselves and Amazon in the context of the transaction; in other words, the terms and conditions of the shopping purchase. Fourth, shoppers would want to be informed and receive support regarding the contributions which they could give and take with other shoppers in online communities regarding topics of mutual interest, organizing events, and sharing products. Businesses which repair and/or recycle products, as well as which provide supplementary services—e.g. cooking courses for the impassioned owners of kitchen knives—could participate in the community. The atmosphere in which products are treasured would raise the level of consuming interest, and, therefore, on the whole, raise the level of sales.

The after-selection customer experience would gain deeper meaning by being concerned with mutual contributions in multiple contexts. The Dexterity offer of coordinated standards would continue, and indeed may make up the majority of interactions between Amazon customers and the firm. Nevertheless, supplementing this core offer with the potential to gain insights into further contributions gives this offer Deep-Connect value.

In the prospective future offers of Amazon, the offer of Deep-Connect value in the three pillars would bind the pillars more closely together and integrate them more tightly than is the case today. For example, the particulars of what a supplying firm has agreed with Amazon regarding the supply chain would be part of the benefits to be communicated on the website, and an aspect of the contributions about which shoppers would want to gain insights. And the details of the customer exchange about the contributions would be closely observed by the customer service personnel and fed back to the supply chain personnel, who would adjust the supply chain operations accordingly.

To illustrate the features, benefits, and contributions of a future Deep-Connect offer to shoppers, the example of Amazon replacing a local farmer's market is presented here. The Best for Mankind value is summarized in Figure 10-4 and outlined in the following.

The current supply chain would be augmented with logistics operations which would be new to Amazon. Amazon would collect products from each farm—a service it already performs for some third-party sellers—and the products would be packed by the farmers in a wider variety of containers and packaging than currently in Amazon's portfolio. A significant share of the products would be for "subscribers," i.e. customers who receive a given amount of certain products on a regular basis. The deliveries for such subscribers could possibly be made by Amazon directly from the farm, with the products potentially packaged in re-usable containers owned and washed by the subscribers—good for the environment—and the "fulfillment centers" would be much smaller than the current fulfillment centers operated by Amazon and specially equipped to handle agricultural products. The "transport technologies" and "management practices" for this kind of local collection and delivery have been widely practiced for decades, e.g. farmers making the rounds with their pick-ups. The challenge for Amazon would be to integrate this kind of very localized logistics operation into the rest of its supply chain in a manner approximating its overall value offer of low costs and high level of service.

Element	Primary Degree	Primary Deed	Primary Dexterity
Area	Societal setting: Offline	Shopping Customer Activities: Online	Online Retail Market: After-Sale Customer Experience
Deep-Connect Value	Party-Determined Supply Chain: Best in Accommodating	Showcased Products and Firms: Selecting Own / Shared Benefits	Orchestrated After-Selection Customer Experience: Insights into Contributions
Aug-mented Offers	Collecting from each farm Farmers pack in individual containers Subscriptions Direct, customized deliveries	Showcasing of the farms, their practices and personnel Special offers from farms: tours, recipes, cooking courses and tips	Resolve problems with local delivery, payment terms, quality, etc. Sharing experiences and comments on food and farms Ratings of the products and the farms Audits and certificates of the farms Information corresponding to a local food / shopping consultant
Integra-tion Challenge	Into operations with low costs and high level of service	Into website with search and recommendations	Into customer call center service and customer reviews of products

Figure 10-4: Prospective Future Amazon Offer to Replace Farmers' Market

The Amazon website would showcase the products, delivery options, and farms, as well as present special offers: "subscriptions," visits to the farm, cooking tips and courses involving the farm's products, the telephone number of the farmer, and so forth. The challenge for Amazon would be to integrate all this information into its website in line with the advantages of its online features.

Amazon would orchestrate the after-selection customer experience by providing information, support, and problem-solving, as well as benefits and contributions when purchasing from local farms. Amazon customers would want the same kind of customer service as is currently offered for answering questions and resolving problems regarding delivery, payment terms, product quality, etc., in relation to the local farmers. Amazon customers would also want to share with other customers their experiences and comments on the food and the farms by posting videos and texts; learn about audits, customer ratings, and certificates for farms' products and practices; and receive the kinds of tips and insights which a food consultant who is specialized in the local area would be able to give. The challenge for Amazon would be to integrate these local aspects into its standardized processes in the customer call center service and customer reviews of products.

These three areas of the overall offer would be closely integrated, e.g. the reasoning which led to an individual agreement between a farmer and Amazon regarding the delivery service would need to appear on the website and would need to be explained by customer service personnel.

The overall offer would constitute value which is Best for Mankind for a number of reasons. The supply chain operations would bring a greater quantity of customers—households and restaurants and other businesses—qualitatively closer to the farmers, thereby benefiting both. Farmers would have more time to farm and greater potential to grow their business and/or to specialize. On the website, there would be the chance for a much more meaningful interaction between customers and farmers, where farmers would have the scope to further develop themselves in cooking services, customer events on the farms, and so on. Furthermore, both customers and farmers would have the basis to make choices based on value generated in relation to multiple contexts: self, local area, nation, humankind, and the environment. In the after-selection customer experience, there would be the basis for communities to be formed where the community members, whether private persons, restaurant personnel, farmers, or others, would enrich their lives and attain greater meaning through community interaction.

In sum, in the prospective future for Amazon presented here, Amazon would offer primary value in the Degree, Dexterity, Deed, and Deep-Connect dimensions. The Deep-Connect value dimension would both supplement the value offers in the other dimensions, as well as bind them more closely together into one, integrated offer.

Captivating Total Value Offer including Deep-Connect to Shopping Customers

Amazon has the potential to integrate primary Deep-Connect value into all its offers in the long-term future. A presentation of how Amazon could potentially integrate Deep-Connect managerial practices into its operations in all five Managerial Do-Well's is available for download at www.dimensions-of-value.com. If it were to to do so, Amazon's total value offer to Shopping Customers would be supplemented by the rightmost column in Figure 10-5. Customers would see themselves as being set in the context of Amazon's connecting offers: the offers connect to one another and connect the customers to their own contexts. The shopping process would offer shopping customers the context of meaningful contribution to the communities in which they take part. Their inner self would be absorbed, leading shopping customers to be captivated by Amazon's shopping process.

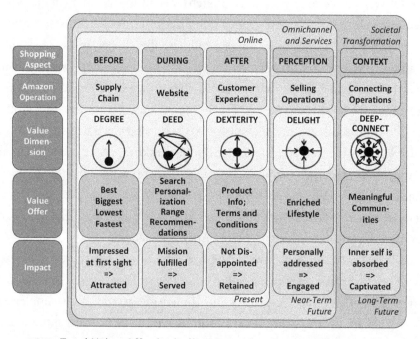

Figure 10-5: Total Value Offer including Deep-Connect to Shopping Customers

Taking stock: the history and prospective future of value management at Amazon

Amazon began with a vague combined offer of Dexterity and Delight: the all-around benefits of purchasing books online should, in some way, usher in a better life for all involved persons. Over the years, the firm came to understand what its parties wanted and to offer the corresponding value; for example, logistics was initially outsourced because it was thought to be merely an unimportant necessity in actually delivering the books ordered, whereas Amazon later learned how important delivery is to the overall value offer. Amazon was always ahead of its rivals in innovating the relations to parties and thereby discovering the features and benefits which they truly sought. The firm built market-leading Degree in the supply chain, Deed in the online ecosystem, and Dexterity in the after-selection customer experience. The value offers and management practices were intensively thought through before launch, tested via in-depth experimentation and tracking of market reactions, and finely honed to repeatedly represent cutting-edge innovation in online retail, when not in the business world. Amazon has realized the drive to make its mark on the world, from which hundreds of millions of parties around the globe benefit.

Amazon has come to dominate online retail, as scarcely any other firm dominates its industry, by exploring and, in many ways, forming party preferences in a new industry without precedent or established behaviors. Amazon consistently led the online retail industry in innovations across the value chain and in the relations with all parties. There is hardly a significant feature or benefit of value offers in the whole of online retail today which did not originate at, or be developed to market maturity by, Amazon. In this manner, Amazon has shown the way forward for all market participants in online retail—its own parties, its rivals, and their parties. In this sense, the mark it has left on the world extends beyond its own activities to impact the value gained by virtually all parties who participate in one way or another in the online retail industry.

The firm's scope has expanded well beyond online retail to become the most exciting and innovative player today in retail as a whole. More than that, together with its streaming services and AWS business, Amazon has become a leading player in the technology sector. Within a few years, it has spread its tentacles into other businesses with the same gusto with which it pushed forward the bounds of online retail such that a startling, robust proportion of revenues are generated outside of online retail: one-third at last count—and rising.

In pushing determinedly into new businesses, Amazon remains true to the objective which has driven it from the start: to leave its mark on the world. For this reason, in this book, it is foreseen that Amazon remains centered on retail, the industry which perhaps more than any other reflects and stimulates changes in how we live, think, act, and feel. The self-image and business logic of Amazon will keep it directed to the industry with the highest profile for the mass of people. It may be that it is this very characteristic of retail—at the throbbing center of our lives—making it the industry which, more than any other, has seen new stars rise and old names fall. This is the context in which Amazon wants to center its business activities and make its mark.

The view that Amazon will undertake what is needed to continue to make its mark suggests that it will continue to develop its organization to meet whatever the market is calling for. If indeed the market is calling in the ongoing present for omnichannel retail and the sale of services online, then Amazon will develop itself accordingly, including integrating Delight. The analogous speculative perspective can be suggested for the prospective long-term future of Amazon in a context of disruption in retail and transformation in society. If indeed such trends reflect the emerging prominence of value which gives meaning, then Amazon will adopt Deep-Connect value in order to stay on top of the market—and to leave its mark on the globalized world of meaning.

AFTERWORD

Applying the 5-D Value Managerial Framework

The managerial practices for value management illustrated in this book can, in fact, be applied to virtually any industry. Of course, the specific characteristics of the value exchange will vary according to the nature of the industry; i.e. the concrete features of a value offer exhibiting e.g. Delight value in another industry will differ from that in the online retail market, and the specific attributes of the inputs will differ as well. Furthermore, the relations to different types of parties, in particular, business partners, in any given industry will vary to some extent. Nevertheless, the underlying benefits of the offers and qualities of the inputs will fit to the five dimensions of value. And the managerial framework as such—the principles of the Markets Value Factors, the Managerial Do-Well's, the inherent weaknesses, and so forth—applies to all industries.

Thus, I encourage you to apply the 5-D Value managerial framework to an industry in which you are active or otherwise familiar. The approach would need to be the same as the one in this book: identifying the characteristics of the offers and inputs in terms of the value dimensions, categorizing the firms in the industry according to their primary and secondary D's, applying the Markets Value Factors, and, then, based on as much "inside" information about the firms as is available, applying the Managerial Do-Well's.

To support such an undertaking, templates to help structure the investigation are available for free download on www.dimensions-of-value.

com, along with additional information about the 5-D Value managerial framework.

About the Author

Benjamin Wall, M.Sc., was born in the US and studied at Yale University and the London School of Economics. He has spent his professional life in the Zurich area, where he now lives. He is active in management consulting with KPMG and as an independent consultant and also as a professor on business studies programs, with experience at the University of St. Gallen, Business School Lausanne, and the University of Applied Sciences in Business Administration in Zurich.

REFERENCES

The references for the book are divided between those used throughout the book—immediately below—and those supporting specific chapters.

Amazon Letters to Shareholders and Annual Reports 2012-2017, Proxy Statements 2012-2018 and www.amazon.com.

Richard L. Brandt, *one click: Jeff Bezos and the rise of amazon.com* (New York: Penguin, 2012).

Greg Jameson, *Amazon's Dirty Little Secrets* (New York: Morgan James, 2015).

Jodi Kantor & David Streitfeld, "Inside Amazon: Wrestling Big Ideas in a Bruising Workplace", *New York Times*, August 15, 2015. http://www. nytimes. com/2015/08/16/technology/inside-amazon-wrestling-big-ideas-in-a- bruising-workplace.html.

Carsten Knop, *amazon kennt dich schon: Vom Einkaufsparadies zum Datenverwerter* (Frankfurt: Frankfurter Societäts-Medien, 2013).

Philipp Puttkammer, *Amazon – die Millionärsfabrik* (Schortens, Germany: Puttkammer Vertriebs GmbH, 2014).

Brad Stone, *the everything store: Jeff Bezos and the Age of Amazon* (London: Random House, 2013).

Introduction

Michael Corkery, "Toys 'R' Us Files for Bankruptcy, Crippled by Competition and Debt", *New York Times*, 19 September 2017, accessed April 23, 2018, https://www.nytimes.com/2017/09/19/business/dealbook/toys-r-us-bankruptcy.html.

Gartner, "Gartner Says Worldwide IaaS Public Cloud Services Market Grew

29.5 Percent in 2017", accessed on August 1, 2018 https://www.gartner.com/newsroom/id/3884500.

Christiane Henkel, "Amazon wird wie Google und Facebook zur Werbeplattform", *Neue Zürcher Zeitung*, September 19, 2018.

Devin Leonard, "Will Amazon Kill FedEx?", *Bloomberg Businessweek*, August 31, 2016. https://www.bloomberg.com/features/2016-amazon-delivery/.

MarketLine, *Global Cloud Computing Industry Profile*, accessed on July 9, 2018 www.marketline.com.

Caroline O'Donovan (2015), "Amazon Rewards Employees Who Stay — But Turnover Is Still High", *BuzzFeed*, August 21, 2015. https://www.buzzfeed.com/carolineodonovan/amazon-rewards-employees-who-staybut-turnover-is-still-high?utm_term=.sjM8dprMO#.idzDzPGMR.

PWC.com, "Global Top 100 Companies by market capitalization", accessed July 12, 2017 www.pwc.com/top100.

Colin Robinson, "The Trouble with Amazon", *The Nation*, August 2/9, 2010: 29 – 32. https://www.thenation.com/article/trouble-amazon/.

Sara Salinas, "Amazon reaches $1 trillion market cap for the first time", *CNBC.com*, September 4, 2018. https://www.cnbc.com/2018/09/04/amazon-hits-1-trillion-in-market-value.html

Synergy Research Group, "The Leading Cloud Providers Increase Their Market Share Again in the Third Quarter" RENO, NV, October 25, 2018. https://www.srgresearch.com/articles/leading-cloud-providers-increase-their-market-share-again-third-quarter.

Lauren Thomas, "This chart shows how quickly Amazon is 'eating the retail world'", *CNBC*, July 7, 2017. https://www.cnbc.com/2017/07/07/amazon-is-eating-the-retail-world.html.

Phil Wahba, "Amazon Will Make Up 50% of All U.S. E-Commerce by 2021", *Fortune*, April 10, 2017. http://fortune.com/2017/04/10/amazon-retail/.

Arthur Zaczkiewicz, "Amazon, Walmart and Apple Top List of Biggest E-commerce Retailers", WWD 7.4.2017; http://wwd.com/business-news/business-features/amazon-Walmart-apple-biggest-e-commerce-retailers-10862796/.

Stefany Zaroban, "Online sales accounted for more than a third of total retail sales growth in 2015", *Digital Commerce 360*, 17.2.16; https://www.digitalcommerce360.com/2016/02/17/us-e-commerce-grows-146-2015/.

Stefany Zaroban, "US e-commerce sales grow 15.6% in 2016", *Digital Commerce 360*, 17.2.17; https://www.digitalcommerce360.com/2017/02/17/us-e-commerce-sales-grow-156-2016/.

Stefany Zaroban, "U.S. e-commerce sales grow 16.0% in 2017", *Digital Commerce 360*, 16.2.18; https://www.digitalcommerce360.com/article/us-ecommerce-sales/.

Chapter 1

Abigail Abrams, "Amazon Is Increasing the Price of Amazon Prime Memberships, Including Renewals", *time.com*, April 27, 2018. http://time.com/money/5256866/amazon-prime-membership-price-increase/.

Yvon Chouinard and Vincent Stanley, *the responsible company: What We've Learned from Patagonia's First 40 Years* (Ventura, California: Patagonia Books, 2nd edition, 2016).

GeekWire, "Change in Amazon's Ratings Algorithm", July 20, 2015, https://geekwire.com/amazon.

Daniel Leisegang, *amazon: Das Buch als Beute* (Stuttgart, Germany: Schmetterling Verlag, 2014).

John Mackey and Rajendra S. Sisodia, *Conscious Capitalism: Liberating the Heroic Spirit of Business* (Boston: Harvard Business Review Press, 2013).

Bryan Roberts and Natalie Berg, *Walmart: Key Insights and Practical Lessons from the World's Largest Retailer* (London: Kogan Page, 2012).

Noah Robischon, "Why Amazon is the World's Most Innovative Company of 2017", *Fast Company*, February 13, 2017. https://www.fastcompany.

com/3067455/why-amazon-is-the-worlds-most-innovative-company-of-2017.

Whole Foods Market Annual Reports 2010-2016

www.apple.com

www.costco.com

www.macys.com

www.patagonia.com

www.qvc.com

www.walmart.com

www.wholefoodsmarket.com

Chapter 2

Patti Domm. "Amazon's victims: These stocks have lost $70 billion so far this year", CNBC, July 11, 2017. https://www.cnbc.com/2017/07/11/stocks-amazon-killling-prime-day.html.

Marcia Layton Turner, *Kmart's Ten Deadly Sins: How Incompetence Tainted an American Icon* (Hoboken, New Jersey: Wiley, 2003).

Daniel Leisegang, *amazon: Das Buch als Beute* (Stuttgart, Germany: Schmetterling Verlag, 2014).

Parmy Olson, "How Toys 'R' Us Neglected the Web", *Forbes*, September 19, 2017. https://www.forbes.com/sites/parmyolson/2017/09/19/toys-r-us-chapter-11-amazon/#2a87d6bb2c50.

Don Reisinger, "Amazon is Planning to Hire 100,000 Full-Time Employees", *Fortune*, January 12, 2017. http://fortune.com/2017/01/12/amazon-full-time-employees/.

Lauren Thomas, "This chart shows how quickly Amazon is 'eating the retail world'", *CNBC*, July 7, 2017. https://www.cnbc.com/2017/07/07/amazon-is-eating-the-retail-world.html.

v12data, "25 Amazoing Omnichannel Statistics Every Marketer Should Know", accessed November 5, 2018 https://www.v12data.com/blog/25-amazing-omnichannel-statistics-every-marketer-should-know/.

Arthur Zaczkiewicz, "Amazon, Walmart and Apple Top List of Biggest E-commerce Retailers", WWD 7.4.2017; http://wwd.com/business-news/business-features/amazon-Walmart-apple-biggest-e-commerce-retailers-10862796/.

Chapter 3

Zoe Bernard, "Jeff Bezos Tells New Amazon Employees There Isn't a Work-Life Balance. Here's What He Says Instead", *Business Insider*, November 15, 2018. http://time.com/money/5456184/jeff-bezos-work-life-balance/

Grant Blank and Bianca C. Reisdorf, "The Participatory Web", *Information, Communication & Society*, 15 no. 4 (2012): 537 – 554.

Judith A. Chevalier and Dina Mayzlin, "The Effect of Word of Mouth on Sales: Online Book Reviews", *Journal of Marketing Research*, 4 no. 3 (2006): 345-354.

James F. Engel, Roger D. Blackwell and Paul W. Miniard, *Consumer Behavior* (Fort Worth: Dryden Press, 8th edition, 1993).

Fintechnews Switzerland, ""Bank of Amazon" is Disrupting the Financial Landscape", September 6, 2018. http://fintechnews.ch/fintech/bank-of-amazon-is-disrupting-the-financial-landscape/21954/.

GeekWire, "Change in Amazon's Ratings Algorithm", July 20, 2015, https://geekwire.com/amazon.

Sam Goldfarb, "Amazon Undertakes Rare Debt Offering", *Wall Street Journal*, August 16, 2017.

Christiane Henkel, "Der Online Händler Amazon startet mit der Einführung eines Mindestlohns für seine Lagermitarbeit eine Charmeoffensive", *Neue Zürcher Zeitung*, February 10, 2018.

Thorsten Henning-Thurau, Kevin P. Gwinner, Gianfranco Walsh and Dwayne D. Gremler, "Electronic Word-of-Mouth via Consumer-Opinion Platforms: What Motivates Consumers to Articulate Themselves on the Internet?", *Journal of Interactive Marketing*, 18 no. 1 (2004): 38 – 52.

Philip Kotler and Kevin Lane Keller, *Marketing Management* (Upper Saddle River, New Jersey: Prentice Hall, 2005).

Nanda Kumar and Izak Benbasat, "Research Note: The Influence of Recommendations and Consumer Reviews on Evaluations of Websites", *Information Systems Research*, 17 no. 4 (2006): 425-439.

Devin Leonard, "Will Amazon Kill FedEx?", *Bloomberg Businessweek*, August 31, 2016. https://www.bloomberg.com/features/2016-amazon-delivery/.

Susan M. Mudambi and David Schuff, "What Makes a Helpful Online Review? A Study of Online Customer Reviews on Amazon.com", *MIS Quarterly*, 34 no. 1 (2010): 185-200.

Noah Robischon, "Why Amazon is the World's Most Innovative Company of 2017", *Fast Company*, February 13, 2017. https://www.fastcompany.com/3067455/why-amazon-is-the-worlds-most-innovative-company-of-2017.

Wenqi Shen, Yu Jeffrey Hu and Jackie Rees, "Competing for attention: An empirical study of online reviewers' strategic behaviors", in *Proceedings of the 14th Conference on Information Systems & Technology (CIST)*, San Diego, CA, 2009. Retrieved from https://www.krannert.purdue.edu/academics/ MIS/workshop/papers/WS_02032012.pdf.

Sebastian Sohn (2012), *Kundenrezension auf Amazon.de – Eine Fallstudie* (Norderstedt, Germany: Grin Verlag, 2012).

Jeff Sommer, "The Mind-Boggling Ascent of Amazon and Jeff Bezos", *New York Times*, 28 July 2017.

D. S. Sundaram, Kaushik Mitra and Cynthia Webster, "Word- of-Mouth Communications: A Motivational Analysis", *Advances in Consumer Research*, no. 25 (1998): 527 – 531.

John Tarasoff and John McCormack, "How to Create Value without Earnings: The Case of Amazon", *Journal of Applied Corporate Finance*, 25 no. 3 (2013): 39-43.

www.glassdoor.com

Chapter 4

Nicholas Carr, "Amazon's Next Big Move: Take Over the Mall", *MIT Technology Review*, 120 no. 1 (2017): 97-99.

Christiane Henkel, "Amazon wird wie Google und Facebook zur Werbeplattform", *Neue Zürcher Zeitung*, September 19, 2018.

Daniel Leisegang, *amazon: Das Buch als Beute* (Stuttgart, Germany: Schmetterling Verlag, 2014).

Devin Leonard, "Will Amazon Kill FedEx?", *Bloomberg Businessweek*, August 31, 2016. https://www.bloomberg.com/features/2016-amazon-delivery/.

Noah Robischon, "Why Amazon is the World's Most Innovative Company of 2017", *Fast Company*, February 13, 2017. https://www.fastcompany.com/3067455/why-amazon-is-the-worlds-most-innovative-company-of-2017.

Chapter 5

Justin Fox, "A Job at Amazon Isn't for Everybody", Bloomberg View, August 17, 2015, https://www.bloomberg.com/view/articles/2015-08-17/a-job-at-amazon-isn-t-for-everybody.

Daniel Leisegang, *amazon: Das Buch als Beute* (Stuttgart, Germany: Schmetterling Verlag, 2014).

Bryan Roberts and Natalie Berg, *Walmart: Key Insights and Practical Lessons from the World's Largest Retailer* (London: Kogan Page, 2012).

Philipp Staab, "Neue Arbeit, alte Konfliktfelder", *OrganisationsEntwicklung* no. 2 (2017): 42-46, https://www.wiso-net.de/document/LMZ__20170413401825%7CLMZA__20170413401825.

www.glassdoor.com

www.quora.com

Chapter 8

Caroline O'Donovan (2015), "Amazon Rewards Employees Who Stay — But Turnover Is Still High", *BuzzFeed*, August 21, 2015. https://www.buzzfeed.com/carolineodonovan/amazon-rewards-employees-who-staybut-turnover-is-still-high?utm_term=.sjM8dprMO#.idzDzPGMR.

Chapter 9

Erika Chayes Wida, "Amazon Prime benefits are now available at Whole Foods in 12 states", *Today.com*, May 30, 2018. https://www.today.com/food/amazon-prime-benefits-are-now-available-whole-foods-t130005.

Michael Ferber, "Amazon soll Bankkonto-Angebot planen", *Neue Zürcher Zeitung*, March 6, 2018.

Lauren Gensler, "Toys 'R' Us Files for Bankruptcy, But Will Keep Stores Open", *Forbes*, September 19, 2017. https://www.forbes.com/sites/laurengensler/2017/09/19/toys-r-us-bankruptcy/#43275bcd574a.

Craig Giammona, "Whole Foods' 365 Offshoot Moving Ahead Under Amazon Ownership", *Bloomberg*, February 1, 2018. https://www.bloomberg.com/news/articles/2018-02-01/whole-foods-365-offshoot-moving-ahead-under-amazon-ownership.

Nikki Gilliland, "Is the Calvin Klein & Amazon deal a step-change for multichannel fashion retail?", *econsultancy.com*, December 4, 2017. https://econsultancy.com/is-the-calvin-klein-amazon-deal-a-step-change-for-multichannel-fashion-retail/.

Great Speculations, "Why Did Amazon Quit the Online Travel Market?", *Forbes.com*, October 20, 2015. https://www.forbes.com/sites/greatspeculations/2015/10/20/why-did-amazon-quit-the-online-travel-market/#20513e587581

Dennis Green, "Amazon just unveiled an alternative to vending machines" *Business Insider*, August 15, 2017. http://uk.businessinsider.com/amazon-instant-pickup-ready-in-minutes-2017-8?r=US&IR=T.

Werner Grundlehner, "Amazon und Google in der Apotheke", *Neue Zürcher*

Zeitung, October 14, 2017.

Heather Haddon and Sarah Nassauer, "Getting Your Product on Shelves at Whole Foods Just Got Harder", *Wall Street Journal*, February 8, 2018. https://www.wsj.com/articles/getting-your-product-on-shelves-at-whole-foods-just-got-harder-1518085801.

Christiane Henkel, "Amazon gegen den Rest der Welt", *Neue Zürcher Zeitung*, June 28, 2018.

Lauren Hirsch, "A year after Amazon announced its acquisition of Whole Foods, here's where we stand", *CNBC.com*, June 15, 2018. https://www.cnbc.com/2018/06/15/a-year-after-amazon-announced-whole-foods-deal-heres-where-we-stand.html

Christian Hetrick, "A year after Amazon takeover, Whole Foods still hasn't shed its whole paycheck status", *The Spokesman-Review*, August 26, 2018. http://www.spokesman.com/stories/2018/aug/26/a-year-after-amazon-takeover-whole-foods-still-has/.

Krystal Hu, "Amazon bought Whole Foods a year ago. Here's what has changed", *Yahoo*, August 20, 2018. https://finance.yahoo.com/news/amazon-bought-whole-foods-year-ago-heres-changed-191428325.html

Arjun Kharpal, "Amazon now lets you pick up Whole Foods orders from a store in 30 minutes without leaving your car", *CNBC.com*, August 8, 2018. https://www.cnbc.com/2018/08/08/amazon-launch-whole-foods-store-pickups.html.

Eugene Kim, "The head of Amazon's Prime program is turning his attention to Whole Foods", *CNBC*, February 8, 2018. https://www.cnbc.com/2018/02/08/amazon-prime-boss-greg-greeley-turns-attention-to-whole-foods.html.

Tae Kim, "Amazon could disrupt online travel industry next, Morgan Stanley says", *CNBC.com*, March 9, 2018. https://www.cnbc.com/2018/03/09/amazon-could-disrupt-online-travel-industry-next-morgan-stanley-says.html.

Marie-Astrid Langer, "Amazon will in die reale Welt", Neue Zürcher Zeitung, September 21, 2018.

Alice LaPlante, "Omnichannel: Why There's Hope for Retailers After Amazon", *Century Link Bright Ideas*, August 23, 2018. http://www.centurylinkbrightideas.com/omnichannel-why-theres-hope-retailers/

Adam Levy, "Amazon.Com Is Giving Prime Members Some Big Incentives to Shop at Whole Foods", *The Motley Fool*, February 22, 2018. https://www.fool.com/investing/2018/02/22/amazoncom-is-giving-prime-members-some-big-incenti.aspx.

Birgitt Loderhose, "Amazon zögert bei Fresh", *Lebensmittel Zeitung*, April 13, 2017. https://www.wiso-net.de/document/LMZ__20170413401825%7CLMZA__20170413401825.

Emily Monaco, "Amazon's Changes to Whole Foods Include Abandoning Local Connections", *Organic Authority*, September 22 2017. http://www.organicauthority.com/amazon-continues-to-implement-changes-at-whole-foods-market-including-abandoning-the-stores-local-connections/.

Emily Monaco, "Amazon to Open More Whole Foods Markets and Expand to New Store Formats", *Organic Authority*, 1 November 1, 2017. http://www.organicauthority.com/amazon-to-open-more-whole-foods-market-stores-and-expand-to-new-store-formats/.

Neue Zürcher Zeitung 28 March 2017, 20 April 2017, 24 April 2017, 31 July 2017.

Carla Palm, "Amazon und Whole Foods: Alles bio, alles gut?", *Handelszeitung*, October 25, 2017.

https://www.handelszeitung.ch/invest/aktien-amazon-und-whole-foods-alles-bio-alles-gut.

Harald Reil, "Frischeoffensive – Amazon Fresh will den Lebensmittelmarkt aufrollen", *Genios WirtschaftsWissen*, April 10, 2017. https://www.genios.de/info/wirtschaftswissen.

Kate Taylor, "Here are all the changes Amazon is making to Whole Foods", *Business Insider*, November 15, 2017. http://uk.businessinsider.com/amazon-changes-whole-foods-2017-9?r=US&IR=T/#whole-foods-immediately-slashed-prices-and-announced-another-round-of-price-cuts-in-november-1.

Lauren Thomas, "Kohl's opens its doors to Amazon's returns", *CNBC*, September 19, 2017. https://www.cnbc.com/2017/09/19/kohls-opens-its-doors-to-amazons-returns-at-82-stores.html

Howard Tiersky, "Amazon hasn't cracked omnichannel retailing (yet)", CIO.com, January 16, 2018. https://www.cio.com/article/3248590/retail/amazon-hasnt-cracked-omnichannel-retailing-yet.html

Brad Tuttle, "Amazon Is Giving $10 to Prime Members Just For Shopping at Whole Foods This Week", *time.com*, July 11, 2018. http://time.com/money/5334633/amazon-prime-day-2018-free-deals-whole-foods/

Jordan Valinsky (2018), "Amazon's latest Prime perk: 5% cash back at Whole Foods", *CNN Money*, February 20, 2018. https://money.cnn.com/2018/02/20/news/companies/amazon-whole-foods-rewards/index.html.

Herb Weisbaum, "Hey Alexa, where are all the lower prices at Whole Foods?", *NBC News*, December 6, 2017. https://www.nbcnews.com/business/consumer/whole-foods-where-are-all-lower-prices-n827046.

Elizabeth Weise, "Amazon Prime customers to get discounts at Whole Foods in bid to lure online shoppers to stores", *USA Today*, May 16, 2018. https://eu.usatoday.com/story/tech/2018/05/15/amazon-extend-prime-discounts-whole-foods-customers/612231002/

Chapter 10

John Mackey and Rajendra S. Sisodia, *Conscious Capitalism: Liberating the Heroic Spirit of Business* (Boston: Harvard Business Review Press, 2013).

CPSIA information can be obtained
at www.ICGtesting.com
Printed in the USA
BVHW070035240819
556701BV00003B/12/P